"I hear America singing,
the varied carols I hear"
Walt Whitman

"And the uttering of song
was like to the giving of light"
Sidney Lanier, *Psalm of the West*

A HISTORY
OF AMERICAN
CLASSICAL MUSIC

by

Barrymore Laurence Scherer

SOURCEBOOKS, INC.®
NAPERVILLE, ILLINOIS

FOR MICHELLE
For being beside me every step of the way
in this project and in life.

Published by Sourcebooks MediaFusion, an imprint of Sourcebooks, Inc.
P.O. Box 4410, Naperville, Illinois 60567-4410
(630) 961-3900
Fax: (630) 961-2168
www.sourcebooks.com

Originally published in the UK by Naxos Books.

Library of Congress Cataloging-in-Publication Data

Scherer, Barrymore Laurence.
   A history of American classical music / by Barrymore Laurence Scherer.
      p. cm.
   Includes bibliographical references and index.
   ISBN 978-1-4022-1067-9 (hardcover)
   1. Music--United States--History and criticism. I. Title.

ML200.S34 2007
781.6'80973--dc22

                                                        2007020380

Printed and bound in the United States of America.
         LB 10 9 8 7 6 5 4 3 2 1

Contents

CD Track List

Scott Joplin (1868–1917)

8 Maple Leaf Rag   3:12

Alexander Peskanov; piano   8.559114

George Gershwin (1898–1937)

9 An American in Paris (excerpt)   5:59

New Zealand Symphony Orchestra; James Judd   8.559107

(Hear the full 18:49 piece on the website)

Henry Cowell (1897–1965)

Irish Suite for string piano and small orchestra

10 Movement 1. The Banshee   4:28

Cheryl Seltzer, piano; Continuum; Joel Sachs   8.559192

Virgil Thomson (1896–1989)

11 Synthetic Waltzes   5:01

Cheryl Seltzer, piano; Joel Sachs, piano   8.559198

Ruth Crawford Seeger (1901–1953)

Three Songs

12 No. 1. Rat Riddles   3:15

Nan Hughes, mezzo-soprano; Marsha Heller, oboe;

Erik Charlston, percussion; Cheryl Seltzer, piano   8.559197

Samuel Barber (1910–1981)

Vanessa

13 Intermezzo   4:26

Royal Scottish National Orchestra; Marin Alsop   8.559135

John Cage (1912–1992)

14 Totem Ancestor   2:08

Boris Berman, piano   8.559070

Conlon Nancarrow (1912–1997)

15 Toccata for violin and player piano   1:39

Mia Wu, violin   8.559196

John Adams (b. 1947)
I Was Looking at the Ceiling and then I Saw the Sky
16 Act II, No. 23. Finale   4:57

Martina Mühlpointner, Consuelo; Kimako Xavier Trotman, Dewain;

Markus Alexander Neisser, Rick; Jeanette Friedrich, Leila;

Darius de Haas, David; Lilith Gardell, Tiffany; Jonas Holst, Mike;

Young Opera Company Freiburg; The Band of Holst-Sinfonietta;

Klaus Simon   8.669003–04

Leonard Bernstein (1918–1990)
Symphony No. 1, "Jeremiah"
17 II. Profanation   6:35

New Zealand Symphony Orchestra; James Judd   8.559100

Philip Glass (b. 1937)
Symphony No. 3
18 Movement 4   3:40

Bournemouth Symphony Orchestra; Marin Alsop   8.559202

TT: 78:06

www.naxos.com/naxosbooks/americanmusicusa

Visit the dedicated website for *A History of American Classical Music* and gain free access to the following:

Hours more music to listen to – over 150 tracks by 53 different composers

A concise timeline showing key developments in American music and concurrent historical and cultural events worldwide

To access this you will need:

ISBN: **9781402210679**
Password: **Gershwin**

Acknowledgments

This book represents a labor of love. Probably half the time I spent writing it I also spent listening to music – revisiting familiar works, discovering works I didn't already know, rediscovering works I had not heard in years. But for all the pleasure I experienced, writing and listening do form a pretty solitary occupation (albeit my solitude was relieved by the companionship of my little canine buddy Percy, who slept happily by my desk through even the most clangorous repertoire). Apart from Percy, I owe a debt of gratitude to a number of colleagues and friends.

First of all, my thanks to Klaus Heymann, head of Naxos, whose vision has made it such an adventuresome treasury of repertoire, American and otherwise. To Nicolas Soames and Genevieve Helsby, who have made Naxos Books such an educational powerhouse, for offering me this splendid project and for being such delightful, supportive colleagues during its arduous gestation period. To my editor at *The Wall Street Journal*, Eric Gibson, an insightful art critic and writer who helped me to clarify some points about late-twentieth-century art. To the excellent baritone and musician Elliot Levine, for answering several questions about eighteenth-century repertoire. To Richard Lynn, a magnificent poet and Shakespeare scholar, who was a cheerful sounding-board on matters of style. To Caroline Richmond in the UK, and Todd Green in the US, thorough professionals who proved that author and editors need not conduct business at lance-point. I am also profoundly grateful to several friends who took time from their own frenetic professional lives to read all or parts of the manuscript and offer their sage comments: George Jellinek, one of classical music broadcasting's greatest personalities and an opera authority whose knowledge and friendship I cherish; Alison Ames, formerly one of the most respected classical recording executives, now offering wise counsel in music promotion; her sister Katrine Ames, a canny music critic; Albert Imperato, an exceptionally inventive music professional – at times his enthusiasm for repertoire pales even mine; Stephen E.B. Acunto, gentleman, scholar, diplomat and generous patron of music and of emerging musicians. Between them, to paraphrase old Professor Jowett of Balliol, "if anything's known they know it, and what they don't know isn't knowledge."

My thanks to Gail Averill, who knows by heart the lyrics of *every* Broadway and Tin Pan Alley song, and who offered welcome feedback as an ideal member of the classical music audience. To Jere Herzenberg, my honorary "big sister" since graduate school and a profoundly knowledgeable source of American history and music – while meticulously editing the earlier essay version of this text she brought up a variety of historical points that I might easily have overlooked. To Larry Riederman, who knows opera and its professional world inside out and is always ready to offer me his calming wisdom and common sense in moments of perplexity. To my dear friend Didi Hunter, ever ready to lend a sympathetic ear and offer a rational answer. To Victoria Gould Pryor, whose quiet professional guidance has been invaluable. And to my wife, Michelle Jacobs, who has read and wisely commented on virtually every word I have written since I began writing anything worth reading.

Preface

The previous version of this survey, a Naxos boxed set called *The Story of American Classical Music*, contained a much shorter text accompanying representative selections of American music from the nineteenth century through the present day. In choosing those selections I was guided by the editorial mandate to include only complete works or at least complete movements, and by my desire to represent as many composers as possible on CD. Therefore many of the selections in that set are relatively brief. The present book offers a greatly expanded discussion of American classical music. For the accompanying CD, I have tried to offer a new selection of musical examples while still following the same mandate. Because of the length of certain works, I have been obliged to eliminate some composers from the line-up or to offer further examples on the Naxos website linked to this book.

Throughout, my intention has been to write a discussion of American music history for the educated layman rather than to frame a history textbook for trained musicians. Thus, there are many performance examples on the accompanying CD and the Naxos website but I have not included printed music excerpts, which tend to frustrate those who do not read scores. I have also tried mightily to keep my actual descriptions of music and of composers' techniques as free of complex theoretical and technical language as possible. Of course certain musical ideas need to be explained, especially when discussing twentieth-century music. I hope, therefore, that I have made those explanations easy to swallow, and easier to digest.

1   Introduction: The Dawn of American Classical Music

In 1780 the American Revolution was at a particularly low point, with American forces defeated at the battles of Camden and Long Island, and food and pay shortages driving many troops toward mutiny. To cap the year's misfortune, the brilliant American soldier and hero Benedict Arnold traitorously switched to the British side, partially reacting to his own financial insolvency.

During this dark spell, John Adams, the future American president, was in Paris struggling to gain French and Dutch support for the American cause. In frustration, he wrote to his wife, Abigail: "I must study politics and war, that my sons may have liberty to study mathematics and philosophy, geography, natural history and naval architecture, navigation, commerce, and agriculture, in order to give their children a right to study painting, poetry, music, architecture, statuary, tapestry and porcelain." Adams' wide-ranging list of pursuits over three generations neatly summarizes the equally long struggle that the newly founded America would face in order to achieve a distinctive musical voice.

Establishing a refined musical culture demands a stable environment and a steady economy. Early America was anything but secure. From the time that the English, French, Spanish and Dutch colonists founded the first permanent settlements along the Eastern seaboard and within the interior, the European newcomers were too preoccupied with staying alive and afloat to concentrate on developing their own indigenous musical style. Often, when

Illustration of the Battle of Bunker Hill during the American Revolution

engaged in song and dance, these transplanted Europeans, with some exceptions, still lingered over their own musical traditions. Eighteenth-century concert "subscription series" and benefit performances in urban centers, such as Charleston, New York, Philadelphia and later Boston, also reflected the colonists' propensity toward the performance of contemporary European composers such as Haydn and Handel.

Obviously North America had indigenous music before the Europeans began to settle along the coasts and across the interior of the country. From the Arctic Inuits to the Pueblos, Navahos and Apaches of the Southwest, the vast population of Native American peoples created a legacy of ceremonial chants, myth-telling songs and dances, preserved through the generations by oral tradition. But the development of this tradition in all the Americas lies outside the scope of the present discussion of "classical" music in the United States.

Classical American concert music, sacred music, opera and song all have their roots in European culture and settlement. As a consequence, the history of classical music in the United States, from its founding through the twentieth century, has essentially focused on the influence of European models, on the gradual independence gained from these models, and on the deliberate forging of a recognizably "American" idiom. In terms of the teaching of American music history during the mid-twentieth century, most music, from that of the earliest colonists through the work of our nineteenth-century American composers, was usually dismissed as derivative and unworthy of serious attention. Moreover, a great deal of early- and mid-twentieth-century work simply receded into the shadows with lamentable speed.

> The second half of the twentieth century has enjoyed an extraordinary explosion of new American music expressing a bewilderingly wide range of ideas and styles.

Late-twentieth-century scholarship, however, has helped reverse this opinion by reappraising earlier periods and reassessing such overshadowed figures as William Henry Fry, John Knowles Paine and Louis Moreau Gottschalk, not to mention early-twentieth-century luminaries, from Charles Tomlinson Griffes, Henry Kimball Hadley and Walter Piston, to others working alongside them. Moreover, the second half of the twentieth century has enjoyed an extraordinary explosion of new American music expressing a bewilderingly wide range of ideas and styles. Some composers, such as John Cage, Steve Reich, John Adams, Philip Glass and, of course, the long-lived Aaron Copland, have evolved into iconic figures whose names are familiar even to people who don't follow classical music in depth. But there are others worthy of equivalent attention (David Diamond, George Rochberg, Alan Hovhaness, Conlon Nancarrow, Morton Feldman) and contemporary writers whose work is still evolving (Joan Tower, Michael Torke, Tobias Picker, Paul Dresher, Aaron Jay Kernis, Ellen Taaffe Zwilich). The list is theoretically endless because new composers with new ideas are continually appearing on the scene.

Thus American classical music offers an extraordinarily stimulating repertoire, revealing influences that span three centuries of musical thought. Successively embracing the classical, Romantic, impressionist, modernist and post-modernist ideals, the work of America's composers provides an aural counterpart to American painting, sculpture, decorative arts and architecture. In short, the history of America's classical music gives voice to the history of the nation itself.

2   From Founding through Revolution

The legacy of American art music has traditionally focused on its European roots, beginning with the founding and exploration of the territories that would become the United States. Yet even within these strict structural confines, some limited indigenous music did begin to appear in very early colonial settlements of North America. Christopher Columbus's discovery of the new world in 1492 effectively heralded the "Golden Age of Spanish Culture," which was to last until the final quarter of the sixteenth century. Spain was reveling in its Catholic independence after overthrowing eight centuries of Muslim rule by the Moors and, in Columbus's wake, Spain sent exploration parties westward to stake their national claim and bring home gold, silver and other riches.

Among these conquistadores was Ponce de León, who in 1513 landed on a large peninsula which he thought to be an island, and which he named Florida, presumably because he had landed during Easter (called *Pascua Florida*, 'Flowery Easter' in Spanish). Soon the entire southeastern region of the future United States was claimed for the Spanish crown, though the settlement of St Augustine, known as the oldest city in the US, was not actually founded until 1565. Meanwhile Spain was making even greater inroads in Mexico, where conquistadores such as Francisco de Córdoba and Hernan Cortés systematically conquered lands of the Toltec, Maya, Mixtec, Zapotec and, most notably, Aztec civilizations. Allied with native forces who resented their Aztec overlords, Cortés overthrew the despotic Aztec Emperor Montezuma in 1520. After destroying Montezuma's capital,

Tenochtitlán, the following year the Spanish invaders used the ruins as the foundation of a new capital, Mexico City.

Zealously spreading Christianity wherever they ruled, the conquerors made a great effort to supplant the ancient and complicated Aztec traditions with Catholic rites. This included the musical element. By 1524 a Franciscan missionary, Pieter van Gent (1479–1572), known as Pedro de Gante, had established a school of music in Texcoco, formerly the second most important city-state of the Aztec empire. Father Pedro had been trained at the University of Louvain, in what was then Spanish Flanders. Assisted by fellow missionaries, he would teach his native students first to copy music from Spanish plainsong sources in his possession and after a year of this to read and perform plainsong; eventually he would teach them to play and even to make European musical instruments. The aim was to build a corps of native musicians to assist at church services.

In 1539 the first printing press arrived in Mexico City, and in 1556 it was used to print an Ordinary of the Mass, the first printed musical volume in North America. A dozen more volumes followed between 1560 and 1589, containing portions of the Mass as well as hymns, psalms and Passiontide music.

By the mid-sixteenth century other Spanish missionaries were building churches and monasteries throughout the territories that are now Florida, the Gulf states and California. Influenced by Pedro de Gante, they were teaching the local native Americans to sing the Roman Catholic Mass as well as non-liturgical music from those Mexico City publications. Later, European-born musicians who followed the missionaries were spurred on to compose their own settings of the Mass and of other portions of the liturgy for use in their parishes. In 1539, Canon Juan Xuárez was appointed the first *maestro de capilla* of Mexico City. He and his successor Hernando Franco were among the most important of these church musicians, the latter composing seven settings of the Magnificat in the great Spanish polyphonic tradition. Models were easily available to him as the cathedral in the capital of New Spain was well furnished with the works of Morales,

In 1539 the first printing press arrived in Mexico City, and in 1556 it was used to print an Ordinary of the Mass, the first printed musical volume in North America.

Guerrero and Victoria, copied from the cathedral archives in Seville and Toledo.

By this time French Huguenot emigrants were settling in Canadian Acadia and also along the Atlantic coast as far south as Florida, and the Protestant chorales they sang at worship probably constituted the earliest non-Hispanic body of song heard in North America. Somewhat later, beginning in 1585, the English arrived on North American soil. The initial settlement, at Roanoke, Virginia, didn't last. But in 1607 Captain John Smith and his party founded the first permanent English settlement, at Jamestown. Although music had always been a part of English domestic life, these early colonists made no mention of music in their diaries or journals. Nonetheless we can assume that this doughty company sang their customary psalms at worship and staved off homesickness by singing rounds and catches round the campfire.

> "We refreshed ourselves after tears, with singing of psalms, making joyful melody in our hearts, as well as with the voice..."

The earliest description of English song in North America comes from further up the coast, in the Massachusetts Bay colony: even before the Pilgrims set sail from England in 1620, they had gathered at their pastor's house in Southampton where, according to one of their number, Edward Winslow, who recorded this incident in his 1646 book *Hypocrisie Unmasked*, "we refreshed ourselves after tears, with singing of psalms, making joyful melody in our hearts, as well as with the voice ... and indeed it was the sweetest melody that ever mine ears heard." The Puritans of Massachusetts Bay brought along copies of Henry Ainsworth's *Book of Psalms*, compiled in 1612, which included thirty-nine psalm tunes of English, French and Dutch origin, and which they sang in their newly built churches. These *Mayflower* Pilgrims had been persecuted in England because they had literally separated themselves from the Anglican Church and its bishops. They were followed in 1630 by a second band of Pilgrims, who had remained faithful to the Church of England but were obliged to leave England because they wished to practice a simpler form of Anglicanism than that enforced by King Charles I. They too sang psalms in church, using a psalter known as "Sternhold and Hopkins," after its editors. Originally published in Geneva in 1556, and expanded thereafter, Sternhold and Hopkins contained psalm texts translated and adapted into metrical verse. It also contained anonymous tunes to which they could be sung. One of these, a French tune, is still sung today – the so-called Old Hundredth or Doxology, beginning with the line, "All people that on earth do dwell."

The jog-trotting metrical texts of Sternhold and Hopkins had been devised to simplify and popularize psalm singing, but an increasing number of Massachusetts Bay clergy began to feel that the translations strayed too far from the meanings of the original Hebrew psalms. So they appointed three English-trained scholars, Richard Mather, Thomas Welde and John Eliot, to make new and more faithful translations of the psalter. Their work resulted in *The Whole Booke of Psalmes Faithfully Translated into English Metre*, printed, without tunes, in 1640 by Stephen Day of Cambridge, Massachusetts. Day had received his small printing press from England in 1638, the gift of a group of Puritans still in Holland, and this new *Bay Psalm Book*, as it was soon widely known, was the first noteworthy book published in the English-speaking colonies. Indeed, such was the enduring demand for the *Bay Psalm Book* that it reached its twenty-seventh American edition by 1750, by which time numerous editions had also been published back in England and Scotland. Worshippers using the earlier editions of the *Bay Psalm Book* usually fitted the metrical texts to the tunes in Sternhold and Hopkins or Ainsworth, but when the ninth edition appeared in 1698, it contained thirteen tunes copied from several editions of John Playford's *Introduction to the Skill of Music*, first published in London in 1667. This volume was the first music book published in the English-speaking colonies.

Apart from singing at worship, some Puritans also made music for sheer pleasure. After all, it had been a happy Elizabethan tradition in many English households to be able to read and play music, to possess a small collection of string instruments, and to enjoy playing and singing songs and dances around a table after the evening meal. That this tradition traveled aboard the *Mayflower* is evinced by the variety of instruments mentioned in wills and bequests made as the first generation of settlers aged and died. In 1664 we read of a treble viol left by one Nathaniell [sic] Rogers, and in 1678 of a bass viol left by the Reverend Edmund Browne. Even at this rigorous time in American history, music was an issue of the eternal generation gap, and around 1660 a Harvard college student, requesting a fiddle from his uncle in London, received the following reprimand: "I suspect that you seek [music] both too soon and too much. ... if you be not excellent at it, it is worth nothing at all ... [excepting] for your sisters, for whom it is more proper. ... For them I say I had provided the instruments desired." One can only imagine what a verbal cudgeling this poor undergraduate would have received had he also asked for dance lessons.

Though secular music was hardly absent from the Puritan colonies, sacred music led the field. Nevertheless, a minority of Massachusetts Bay colonists maintained a dim view of music at worship, some extremists showing their dislike by conspicuously plugging their ears in church. Piety may not have been their only motivation, for, according to certain early commentaries, some congregational singing could be pretty hard on worshipful auriculars. Sometimes it wasn't just the congregation's lack of musicality that led to sour performance. Congregations were led in song by a precentor, who would choose a tune to fit a psalm, then sing each phrase for the congregation to repeat after him. This was fine if the precentor himself could hold a tune. But woe unto them whose precentor had a tin ear. And worse, some precentors, whether musical or not, liked to "help out" the tunes with embellishments of their own, which could lead the ensemble even further astray as it tried to repeat what it heard. Eventually travelers from one church to another could hear "Old Hundredth" sung a hundred different ways, none of them pretty. Thus we have George Hood writing in his pioneering *History of Music in New England* (1846) that, while "the number of tunes [sung to psalms before

1690] rarely exceeded five or six ... no two individuals sang them alike." Every melody was "tortured and twisted" as "every inskillful [sic] throat saw fit."

Melodies weren't all that got tangled. According to one of the tales that New Englanders loved to tell each other, a well-meaning but badly myopic precentor apologized to his congregation one Sunday for having difficulty reading out the first line of the hymn they were about to sing. "My eyes, indeed, are very blind," he announced contritely. The choir, chomping at the bit, took this for their first line and sang it to the chosen tune. The mortified deacon emphatically responded, "I cannot see at all," only to hear his choir sing this rhythmical comment too. Red-faced, he cried, "I really believe you are bewitched!" The choir sang it back to him, and concluded by singing back his final exclamation, "The mischief's in you all!" as the poor man slumped down in his chair, completely embarrassed.

In short, the hoary notion that the Puritans disliked music is false. In fact it was not they, but the older Quaker settlers, who forbade music in their society. And while the hardy New Englanders indulged in their public ululations, other settlers were bringing their music to different colonies along the Eastern seaboard. Sixteenth-century Spanish and French voyagers had created the first settlements in the Carolinas, superseded by the English, who claimed it in the name of Charles I as early as 1629. Following Louis XIV's revocation in 1685 of the Edict of Nantes, which ended tolerance of French Protestants (Huguenots) within Catholic France, many Huguenots fled to the Protestant Carolinas, bringing with them their own Calvinist hymns. They were joined there later by Hussites (Moravian followers of Jan Huss), who brought their own musical traditions to their settlements at Wachovia, Bethabara and Salem (now Winston-Salem). To the Delaware River valley, originally a part of Dutch New Netherlands, came settlers from Sweden and Finland. Dutch traders and planters lived in New York and parts of Connecticut, even after the English took over in 1664, while many Swedes, Germans and Bohemians

Added to this polyglot polyphony, as a result of the arrival of the first slave ships in Virginia around 1619, was an African musical heritage that would exert a deep and vivacious influence upon America's music in the centuries to come.

settled in the rolling hills of Pennsylvania. Added to this polyglot polyphony, as a result of the arrival of the first slave ships in Virginia around 1619, was an African musical heritage that would exert a deep and vivacious influence upon America's music in the centuries to come.

Despite the anti-musical stand of the older Philadelphia Quakers, music flourished particularly well in Pennsylvania thanks to the influx of German Pietists – or reformed Lutherans. Among the first of them to arrive in America during the seventeenth century was a musically inclined pastor, Justus Falckner, who was responsible for getting an organ shipped to his community from Germany. Falckner believed in music's power not only to attract native Americans to his flock, but also to help attract younger Quakers. When he became the first German to be ordained a minister in America, in 1703, the proceedings at his ceremony were accompanied not only by organ but by a small orchestra of strings, winds and timpani.

Moreover the Pietists, locally called the Wissahickon Hermits, were already so well known for their musical gifts that they had been engaged to supply choral and instrumental music for the consecration of Philadelphia's Old Swede's Church three years earlier. The broad religious tolerance in Pennsylvania also attracted groups of Moravians from Central Europe – Hussites, like their fellow Moravians in North Carolina. Music, for them, was an essential expression of their souls and, once they established such towns as Bethlehem, Nazareth and Emmaus, their churches rang with a fervent, particularly touching style of music. Yet, though the Moravians were highly esteemed by their neighbors, their insularity prevented their music from having any widespread influence outside their community.

> Virginia's elegant capital, Williamsburg, boasted the first playhouse in the colonies. There were balls and dances, with ensembles playing music imported from the homeland.

If the northern colonists dutifully sang hymns and psalms, the southern colonies delighted in entertainments. There, genteel Huguenot and Anglican plantation owners of Maryland, Virginia and the Carolinas – many of them descended from aristocratic European families – maintained their taste for the gracious country life they had left behind. By 1722, and possibly earlier, Virginia's elegant capital, Williamsburg, boasted the first playhouse in the colonies. There were balls and dances, with ensembles playing music imported from the homeland, and behind the welcoming porticos of southern manor houses the silvery timbre of the spinet delighted many a listener, especially when played by a comely young daughter of the house. In 1735 the genteel planters of Charleston, South Carolina, were regaled by the first opera to be performed in King George II's American colonies: *Flora, or Hob in the Well*, a farce revolving around the mishaps of a country bumpkin. Imported from London, it was an English ballad opera, in which dialogue, in this case written by the celebrated English actor-manager and Shakespeare bowdlerizer Colley Cibber, was interspersed with songs adapted from popular tunes of the day.

While there flourished in the Episcopalian South an increasingly cultivated musical life, efforts were made to raise the level at least of congregational singing in New England. The Reverend John Tufts of Boston started the ball rolling in 1721 by publishing *A Very Plain and Easy Introduction to the Art of Singing Psalm Tunes*. That same year saw the publication of America's first music theory text, Thomas Walter's *The Grounds and Rules of Musick Explained*.

Even as the century progressed, some clergymen and the more conservative church congregations still resisted any kind of musical training, fearing that refined musical performance was the devil's path to secularized worship. But, by the 1760s, singing schools and instruction books proliferated in urban and rural communities, while in cities such as Boston, Providence and Newport wealthy merchants with musical proclivities were having their own instruments shipped over from England.

Soon public concerts would also become a feature of musical life in Philadelphia and New York.

Newspapers of the period recorded a variety of musical activities. For instance, in December 1731 the *Boston Weekly News Letter* contained the announcement that "On Thursday the 30th ... there will be performed a Concert of Music on sundry Instruments at Mr. Pelham's great Room. ... Tickets ... at Five shillings each." Not only was this Boston's first public concert, it was also a telling social development in the colonies at a time when public concerts for paying audiences were only recently becoming customary in Europe. Soon public concerts would also become a feature of musical life in Philadelphia and New York. Indeed New York's first recorded concert, in 1736, featured the organist Charles Theodore Pachelbel (1690–1750), son of the German organist and composer Johann Pachelbel (famous for his Canon in D major). Pachelbel had previously served as organist of Newport's Trinity Church, and eventually settled in Charleston, South Carolina, where he was a leading musical figure until his death.

There was an increasing demand for skilled musicians: in December 1758 the Newport *Mercury*, printed by Benjamin Franklin's brother James, advertised that: "Any person who plays well on a VIOLIN, on application to the Printer hereof may be inform'd where he will meet with proper Encouragement." In June 1759 the same paper advertised a shipment of goods

> Imported from the last Ships from London and Bristol, and to be sold by Jacob Richardson, Wholesale and Retail, At his shop in Brenton's Row in Thames Street … Brass and Iron Jew's Harps … English Flutes, Violins, Bows, Bridges, best Roman Violin Strings …

A decade later Newport's musical life was continuing to gain in strength; and in September 1769 the same paper carried an advertisement for a colonial antecedent of modern Broadway's one-man show:

> This evening, at Mrs. Cowley's Assembly Room in Church Lane, will be read the Beggar's Opera by a person who has read and sung in most of the great towns in America. All the songs will be sung. He personates [sic] all the characters and enters into the various humors or passions of the Opera, as they change from one to another throughout the Opera. Tickets to be had at the printing office at half a dollar each.

John Gay's *The Beggar's Opera*, a pithy send-up of Italian opera and early Georgian morality, had been the great London sensation of 1728, and this performance in Newport reveals not only its lasting

Engraving by William Hogarth of a scene from The Beggar's Opera

popularity some forty years later but also the continuing strength of the musical ties between Britain and her colonies.

In 1770, less than a year after this Newport performance of Gay's ballad opera, an even more important American premiere took place in New York. Its leading musical figure, William Tuckey, a London-born organist, composer and choir director, led the first American performance of Handel's *Messiah* – or at least the overture and sixteen numbers from the score. Even Handel's native Germany had to wait two more years to hear it.

Nevertheless, by 1770 relations between Britain and her American plantations were growing increasingly strained on account of the levying of unwelcome taxes to pay for the heavy debt Britain had incurred in defending her colonists in the French and Indian wars. That year saw the publication of the first truly original American songbook: *The New-England Psalm-Singer, or, American Chorister*, by William Billings, a Boston tanner and self-taught composer and singer.

Instead of merely copying melodies from British tune books, Billings presented 127 of his own melodies for psalms, hymns, anthems and canons set for four unaccompanied voices. The plates for the musical portions of the volume were engraved by the silversmith and patriot Paul Revere. To give a truly American flavor to his work, Billings named many of his hymn tunes after local places and landmarks, such as "Amherst," "Dedham" and "Old Brick" (church). Billings, whose four-part canon "When Jesus Wept" boasts a truly beautiful melody, followed this work with a second collection, *The Singing Master's Assistant*, in 1778. America was bound up in the Revolutionary War by then, and the contents included several fiercely patriotic numbers. Billings' rugged tunefulness, his unpretentious attitude and his practical sensibility made him the dean of the "Yankee tunesmiths" who flourished in New England during the last quarter of the eighteenth century, writing and compiling music for the numerous music schools that had sprung up in this part of the country. The most popular of their pieces were usually the so-called fuging tunes, with their imitative entries for each voice. Many of these Yankee tunesmiths were part-time musicians, among them such figures as Samuel Holyoke, Jeremiah Ingalls and the aptly named tavern-keeper Supply Belcher, who moved northward from Stoughton, Massachusetts, to the woodlands where he became renowned as the "Handel of Maine." Yet, of all their productions, Billings' *New-England Psalm-Singer* remains a landmark of American choral song.

> 1770 saw the publication of the first truly original American songbook: *The New-England Psalm-Singer, or, American Chorister*, by William Billings.

Previously, in 1759, indigenous secular music had also begun to appear: Francis Hopkinson, a Philadelphia lawyer and future signatory of the Declaration of Independence, composed a genteel song for voice and keyboard, "My Days Have Been So Wondrous Free," for which he claimed to be "the first Native of the United States who has produced a Musical Composition." Hopkinson, a man of many talents, was not only a leading figure in Philadelphia musical society; later, as treasurer of the Continental loan office (1778–81), he designed several issues of Continental currency.

Moreover, as chairman of the Continental navy board (1776–8), he reputedly designed the first American flag, which, according to popular tradition, was sewn by Betsy Ross.

Hopkinson's Philadelphia had enjoyed its first two public concerts in 1757, and for the second one a young lieutenant colonel, George Washington, purchased 52/6 (52 shillings and 6 pence, or £2 12s 6d) worth of tickets in advance – a very hefty sum at that time, considering that, in 1787, Washington paid £7 10s (7 pounds 10 shillings) for a nine-piece orchestra to perform at a dinner in Philadelphia. Washington was particularly fond of music and of dancing, and several eyewitness descriptions of his ballroom gifts exist, including one by his step-grandson George Washington Parke Custis of a ball held a few weeks after the end of the American Revolution:

> The minuet was much in vogue at that period, and was peculiarly calculated for the display of the splendid figure of the chief, and his natural grace and elegance of air and manners … As the evening advanced, the commander-in-chief, yielding to the general gayety of the scene, went down some dozen couples in the contre dance with great spirit and satisfaction.

Philadelphia, which enjoyed conspicuous chamber-music activity in the homes of its more prosperous citizens, also witnessed the anonymous publication, in 1767, of the first opera by an American-born author/composer. It was not staged, and its title, *The Disappointment*, seemed to predict the uphill battle that many American composers would experience in the future.

The events of the American Revolution spurred a great many ballads commemorating victories or stirring the spirits of populace. Just as the songs in Gay's *The Beggar's Opera* had been parodies of popular ballads of their time, setting new words to familiar tunes, much of the balladry inspired by the revolution parodied existing folk songs. Often the verses came first, clapped together to celebrate an occurrence – the Boston Tea Party, the battle of Bunker Hill, the trouncing of British Colonel St Leger or General Burgoyne. It would be published as a crudely printed broadside (i.e., a single sheet of paper), and before long someone would either fit the words to an existing tune or invent a new one to suit. Military themes abounded, easily whistled, or sung brazenly around a steaming bowl of rum punch. America's future national anthem developed this way, from an old English drinking song, "To Anacreon in Heav'n, where he sat in full glee," which suggestively praised the pleasures of wine (Bacchus), women (Venus) and song (Anacreon). In 1798 it was fitted with a new patriotic text by one Thomas Paine (not the famous one): "Ye sons of Columbia, / Who bravely have fought, / For those rights, which unstained, / From your sires had descended." It was this tune that ran through Francis Scott Key's mind as he wrote his verses to "The Star-Spangled Banner" after the British bombardment of Fort McHenry in 1814. Hence the words fit perfectly. The song was sung as a popular patriotic number right into the twentieth century, but it wasn't until 1931 that it was officially declared the national anthem.

Certainly the most famous song of the Revolutionary War was "Yankee Doodle." The expression itself was apparently a British invention, "Yankee" having been a term of mockery for the clever, cocky, independent-minded colonials whose resolve to throw off Great Britain's traces had become increasingly apparent before 1770. "Doodle" was probably their term for an ineffectual fool – mid-Victorians used the word "noodle" to mean the same thing. The tune itself may well have been American, and it was used

George Washington was particularly fond of music and of dancing, and several eyewitness descriptions of his ballroom gifts exist.

in the aforementioned ill-fated opera *The Disappointment* to signify a rogue. Its first printed source was a Scottish volume (ca. 1775), in which it appeared with several other folk tunes from America. The British redcoats lustily sang "Yankee Doodle" everywhere in the colonies, even as they marched toward Lexington, Massachusetts, to apprehend rabble-rousing Samuel Adams and John Hancock. But, as they passed through Concord, they encountered a very determined band of colonial volunteers armed with muskets and ready to fight. The ensuing battle commenced with "the shot heard round the world," as Ralph Waldo Emerson later immortalized it. And, by the end, not only were the redcoats thrashed, but "Yankee Doodle" had changed hands, becoming the war-cry of the revolution. But even after this the English maintained their affection for the song, though they put a new spin on it: an English edition after 1780 emphasizes the former mother country's derision in the title and performance instructions: "Yankee Doodle, or (as now Christened by the Saints of New England) The Lexington March, The Words to be Sung thro' the Nose & in the West Country drawl & dialect." But no matter how it was performed, "Yankee Doodle" remained the archetypal American tune to generations of musical visitors in the century ahead.

Though the British were ultimately defeated by their former colonists, British influence hardly vanished from the newly established United States. Indeed, the increase in musical activity resulting from the gradual stabilization of society in the aftermath of the Revolutionary War was advanced in part by the continued arrival of professional British musicians who emigrated to the major cities. Four English expatriates were especially prominent: Raynor Taylor, Alexander Reinagle, Benjamin Carr and James Hewitt.

> No matter how it was performed, "Yankee Doodle" remained the archetypal American tune to generations of musical visitors in the century ahead.

Taylor (1747–1825) had taught Reinagle in London, and had been music director of the Sadler's Wells Theatre before emigrating to the United States in 1792. After brief stints as organist in Baltimore and Annapolis, he established himself permanently in Philadelphia, where he became a leading musical force. With Reinagle he composed a "Monody on the Death of Washington" (1799) and produced a ballad opera with a strikingly New World plot, *Pizarro, or the Spaniards in Peru* (1800).

Reinagle (1756[?]–1809), born in England but of Austrian parentage, traveled in Europe and apparently became a close friend of C.P. E. Bach. He sailed to New York in 1786, settling soon thereafter in Philadelphia. There he enjoyed a busy career as composer, conductor, singer and impresario, his activities frequently taking him to New York and Baltimore. Among his works were four piano sonatas (ca. 1790), which were the first American pieces written expressly for the piano, string quartets, a *Concerto on the Improved Pianoforte with Additional Keys* (1794), vocal and dramatic music, including the very popular song "America, Commerce and Freedom," and a

Masonic Overture (1800). Reinagle gave keyboard lessons to George Washington's step-daughter Nellie Custis (during the period when Philadelphia was the nation's capital), and his *Chorus Sung before Gen. Washington*, for the inauguration in 1789, claims the distinction of being the first musical work composed for a United States president, thus starting a tradition that would continue for two centuries, whether the honorees liked it or not.

Carr (1768–1831) was already known as a composer in London when he arrived with his father and brother in Philadelphia in 1793. There they opened Carr's Musical Repository, among the pre-eminent music retailers and publishers in federalist America, with branches in New York and Baltimore. Benjamin Carr himself was celebrated as a singer, pianist and organist, and enjoyed success with his new compositions. The published score of his *Federal Overture* (1794) represents the first American printing of "Yankee Doodle," which he incorporates as a theme. His tuneful ballad opera, *The Archers, or Mountaineers of Switzerland* (1796) was a musical treatment of the William Tell story that predated Rossini's grand opera by more than thirty years; its medieval tale of Swiss liberty heroically wrested from an Austrian tyrant perfectly suited America's post-revolutionary *Zeitgeist*. Carr's *Dead March for Washington* in 1799 was one of many outpourings of musical grief for the deified father of his country that year.

> *Chorus Sung before Gen. Washington*, for the inauguration in 1789, claims the distinction of being the first musical work composed for a United States president, thus starting a tradition that would continue for two centuries.

James Hewitt (1770–1827) arrived in New York in 1792 having garnered considerable experience in London, where he had been a publisher as well as a performer; he claimed to have played in a concert under Haydn's direction during the veteran composer's London visit, which began in 1791. Hewitt soon became conductor of New York's important Park Street Theatre, and composed and arranged a great deal of music for ballad operas, pantomimes and other productions there. This included his most notable work, the ballad opera *Tammany, or the Indian Chief* (1794). In 1805 Hewitt also began to involve himself in Boston's musical life. In 1811 he moved

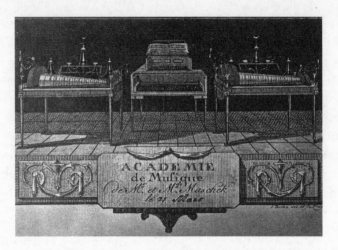

Two glass harmonicas flanking a keyboard glockenspiel
in an early-nineteenth-century Bohemian advertisement

to the city and became conductor of the Federal Street Theatre and organist of Trinity Church. The composer of over 150 instrumental, vocal and dramatic works, Hewitt ran his own publishing house and music retail businesses in New York and Boston, publishing editions of music by popular British composers such as William Shield and Michael Kelly, as well as scores by Handel, Haydn and Mozart.

Among all these native and emigrant musicians we should also note two of the nation's finest amateurs of the time: Thomas Jefferson, who passed many a pleasant hour playing his violin and was a lifelong musical patron, and Benjamin Franklin, an adept guitarist and harpist, who invented the glass harmonica in 1763 after hearing a concert in London played on a series of "musical glasses" pitched with graded amounts of spring water. Franklin's invention consisted of a nesting row of graduated glass bowls, fixed to a rod through their centers, which were half submerged in a trough of water. When the player turned the crank end of the rod with a treadle mechanism, the glasses were moistened so that, if the rims were touched lightly with a finger as they turned, they could be made to sound specific and sustained pitches. Mozart composed his Adagio in C major, K.356, for this instrument, and Donizetti specified it for the haunting obbligato in the Mad Scene of *Lucia di Lammermoor*, though he later substituted two flutes to make performances more practicable.

3   The Awakening

One of America's greatest allies during the Revolutionary War
had been France, whence the Marquis de Lafayette sailed to lend
his military expertise and support to General Washington. After
the establishment of the new nation, those French connections
remained strong – it was America's revolution, after all, that
inspired the French to revolt against the Bourbon crown in
1789. Benjamin Franklin, for instance, urged the French sculptor
François Houdon to travel to America and sculpt in marble
what proved to be one of the most celebrated portraits of George
Washington. And with the decision to establish the nation's capital
at the newly created District of Columbia came the French urban
architect Pierre Charles L'Enfant to design the distinctive layout
of its streets. In fact, L'Enfant had come over in 1776 as a French
soldier, eventually attaining the rank of Major of Engineers in the
Continental Army.

America's victory over Great Britain did not end the uneasy
relationship with the former mother country, and this uneasiness
grew increasingly acute during the early years of the nineteenth
century, when England was struggling to check the territorial
advances of France's Emperor Napoleon. In 1803 President Thomas
Jefferson agreed to pay cash-strapped Napoleon $15 million for
the Louisiana Territory, 828,000 square miles of land, from the
Mississippi River to the Rocky Mountains and from the Gulf of
Mexico almost to the Canadian border. It was an astounding sum at
the time, especially for a young nation to find, but the price proved

relatively cheap in the long term, for the land purchase effectively doubled the territory of the United States.

Disquieted by America's relationship with its mortal enemy, Great Britain increasingly antagonized the United States by using its Royal Navy to interfere with America's trade with French ports and by blockading American ports. Moreover, British warships began to raid American merchant vessels, specifically to remove American seamen and forcibly impress them into the British navy. War with Britain erupted in 1812. American forces burnt Toronto in 1813, and a large British force marched into Washington in 1814, burning both the Executive Mansion and the Capitol. Further battles ensued on land and sea, the most famous being the last, in January 1815, in which American troops under General Andrew Jackson foiled the British attempt to capture New Orleans. A month later news finally arrived that the Peace of Ghent, ending the Anglo-American War, had already been signed in December 1814.

The poorly defined boundaries established by the Louisiana Purchase caused further conflicts over the years, especially with Mexico, whose relations with the United States deteriorated during the 1830s and 1840s. America's annexation of Texas in 1845 led to the Mexican War (1846–8), which ended with Mexico's renunciation of its claims to Texas. And, in return for another $15 million, Mexico ceded the disputed territories of New Mexico and California to the United States. This latter agreement came not a moment too soon, for in January 1848, gold was discovered in California, precipitating the Gold Rush, which brought thousands of hopeful "Forty-niners" to the territory seeking their fortune. When California, with its exploding population and need for civil government, applied for statehood in 1849, the great debate in Congress was over whether the new state should enter as a slave-holding one or not. Indeed, slavery was the overriding issue that divided America during the first half of the nineteenth century. Apart from the fundamental moral and racial questions, the issue was fueled by the multi-layered rivalry between the slave-owning agricultural South and its non-slave-holding industrial North. The Civil War (1861–4) that resulted from this rivalry was to represent the watershed in American history for the next fifty years.

In the midst of this foment of nation-building, America's music was gradually finding its way. Between 1800 and the mid-nineteenth century, professional music organizations were formed in major cities. Most notable were the Boston Handel and Haydn Society (1815), which concentrated on full-scale performances of choral music with orchestra, and the New York Philharmonic Symphony Society (1842), which focused on the symphonic repertoire. Both are still flourishing.

At the same time, theatres in cities such as New York and Philadelphia, as part of their standard repertoire, held evenings of European opera, with performances by troupes who sailed across the Atlantic on commercial packet lines. Through the auspices of wealthy merchants engaged in European trade, Americans could now hear the latest operas by composers such as Rossini performed by well-known European singers, including the flamboyant tenor Manuel García and his daughter, the future diva Maria Malibran.

> Between 1800 and the mid-nineteenth century, professional music organizations were formed in major cities, including the New York Philharmonic Symphony Society in 1842.

Mozart's librettist Lorenzo Da Ponte (1749–1838) also set sail for New York, in 1805, pursued by an army of French, English and Italian creditors. First he set up as a city grocer and merchant, eventually moving his business to Philadelphia and augmenting his income by dealing in Italian books and teaching privately. In 1819 he moved back to New York, bent on introducing Italian culture to his new homeland through further teaching and bookselling. His activities were rewarded in 1825 by his appointment as Professor of Italian at Columbia College (later Columbia University), a chair that unfortunately carried more prestige than financial compensation. Da Ponte was in the audience when the García troupe gave the American premiere of Rossini's *The Barber of Seville* at the Park Theatre in 1825. (Among other celebrities in attendance that night were author James Fenimore Cooper and Napoleon's elder brother Joseph Bonaparte, former king of Spain, then living quietly in New Jersey.) It was the first American performance of an Italian opera in the Italian language, and the experience apparently led Da Ponte to persuade García subsequently to give the first Italian-language performance of Mozart's *Don Giovanni*, for which Da Ponte had written the libretto (in 1817 New Yorkers had seen the opera in an English-language version, with the score arranged and altered by the English composer Sir Henry Bishop).

Da Ponte continued to encourage the performance of classical music and the study of Italian literature and art, both as a vehicle for entertainment and as a stepping-stone toward social prestige. A few decades later a García pupil, Jenny Lind, mesmerized American audiences at her own concerts sponsored by the well-known showman Phineas Taylor Barnum. The ensuing Lind craze, sparked by her tour of the United States and Cuba in 1850–1, was the first major commercial exploitation of a celebrity figure, something commonplace today. Apart from idealized portraits of "the Swedish Nightingale," American manufacturers flooded the market with an extraordinary amount of commemorative paraphernalia, transfer-printed, cast, carved or otherwise emblazoned with her image. There were "Jenny Lind" teapots, teaspoons, vases, bonnets, cast-iron trivets – even "Jenny Lind" beds, distinguished by the particular spool turnings of their four posts.

> Jenny Lind mesmerized American audiences at her own concerts sponsored by the well-known showman Phineas Taylor Barnum.

Another Scandinavian star was the fascinating and gifted Norwegian violinist-composer Ole Bull (1810–1880), who toured America several times beginning in 1843. Considered second only to Paganini as a virtuoso, Bull was the inspiration for the Musician in Longfellow's *Tales of a Wayside Inn*, and he charmed connoisseurs with his performances of Mozart as well as his own brilliant works. Most of these were inspired by Norwegian folk music – he was a precursor of Edvard Grieg, and was instrumental in having Grieg sent to study in Leipzig as a boy. But Bull's wide-ranging intellect and keen sense of showmanship yielded a number of compositions with distinctly American themes, among them *Niagara*, *The Solitude of the Prairies* and *In Memory of Washington* (all composed 1844–5). At the age of sixty, and widowed, he married the twenty-year-old Sara Thorp, whose father was a Wisconsin senator and whose brother was Longfellow's son-in-law. Bull spent his last ten years shuttling between the United States and Norway, and following his death, in the 1890s, his widow became a major figure in the dissemination of Hindu culture and meditation in Boston.

Other Europeans toured the United States, especially pianists such as the Swiss-born Sigismond Thalberg (called "Old Arpeggio" for his keyboard effects), the German-born Leopold de Meyer (called the "Lion Pianist" for his mane of hair and keyboard ferocity) and Henri Herz (transplanted from Vienna to Paris). They thrilled audiences with their flashy operatic potpourris and pieces based on "Yankee Doodle" or other patriotic tunes. Non-musical celebrities also made lucrative tours, one of the most famous being Charles Dickens, who made two visits, in 1842 and 1867, the latter netting him a handsome $25,000.

Given all this flow of European talent, and the awe with which Europeans were regarded by Americans, it is easy to understand why during the first half of the century European music dominated the repertoire, even when performed by the emerging home-grown organizations. For example, the New York Philharmonic did not program an American work, George Frederick Bristow's Concert Overture, Op. 3, until its fifth season (1846–7), and during the remainder of the nineteenth century American works were featured only very rarely. Hence we find Bristow's elder colleague, the critic and composer William Henry Fry, deploring the situation in the *New York Tribune* in 1863: "To see ... seventy or eighty musical gentlemen [of the Philharmonic] content to advertise year in and year out, a piece of foreign production ... is a sorry sight ... no other country is so wanting in artistic pride."

> European music dominated the American repetoire during the first half of the nineteenth century.

From the Philharmonic's viewpoint, the avoidance was a deliberate part of its original mandate to bring only the finest classics to its audiences – especially as orchestral recordings were undreamt of then, and that audiences had no other way to hear orchestral music. Writing in celebration of the Philharmonic's fiftieth anniversary, in 1892, the critic Henry Edward Krehbiel summed up this thinking:

> [The Philharmonic's] concerts challenge more thoughtful attention
> than the doings of any musical institution in the land. ... Their
> purpose is more earnestly, more consistently, and more singly
> artistic. ... [The Philharmonic] has conceived its duty primarily
> to the conservation of musical compositions which the judgment
> and taste of the cultured would have admitted to the first rank.
> Only secondarily has it made propaganda for new and progressive
> composers who have widened the boundaries of the art. ... The
> Society is therefore relieved to a great extent of the necessity
> of casting about for novelties. It is also enjoined to exercise the
> greatest care in the admission of new compositions to its lists.

Such scant encouragement, not to mention minimal payment to
local musicians, offered little incentive for Americans actually to
compose music. Nonetheless, some persevered, as the country's
policy of territorial expansion encouraged a chauvinistic, American
spirit. Among the new composers was the Bohemian-born Anthony
Philip Heinrich (1781–1861), who took up music at the age of
thirty-six, playing violin in a Philadelphia theatre pit before moving
to a solitary log cabin near Bardstown, Kentucky. There he taught
himself to compose, and in 1820 he produced a volume of songs
and pieces for piano and violin, resoundingly entitled *The Dawning
of Music in Kentucky*, Op. 1. Heinrich brought out further collections
of his compositions, whose complexity prompted one critic to dub
him "the Beethoven of America."

Having settled in New York after 1840, Heinrich continued
to write large-scale descriptive instrumental scores, such as *The
Ornithological Combat of Kings, or The Condor of the Andes and the
Eagle of the Cordilleras* and *Scintillations of "Yankee Doodle," forming
a Grand National Heroic Fantasia scored for a Powerful Orchestra in 44
Parts*. Writing in the style of Haydn and Weber, Heinrich was the
first American composer to quote genuine Native American themes.
His music attempted to parallel in sound the majesty of nature then
being painted by such artists as Thomas Cole and other members
of the growing Hudson River school. Despite his aspirations, and
his great personal popularity as a musical figure, Heinrich died in
poverty at the outbreak of the Civil War.

Heinrich's elaborate and elaborately titled compositions represented pioneering efforts to create an American concert repertoire. Meanwhile a few composers achieved a good measure of pre-eminence operating on a more modest plane. The long-lived Henry Russell (1812–1900) was the prototype of today's singer-songwriter, performing and playing his own ballads at concerts up and down the Eastern seaboard. English-born, he arrived in Canada in 1833 after studying in Europe, where he got to know such figures as Donizetti, Bellini and Meyerbeer. His song "A Life on the Ocean Wave" has a genuine salt tang, and was adopted as the official march of Britain's Royal Marines in 1889.

"Woodman, Spare that Tree" was possibly his greatest success, prompting, on one occasion, an elderly gentleman to rise and ask Russell plaintively if the tree had indeed been spared. "It was, sir," Russell declared. "Thank God! Thank God!" cried the proto-environmentalist, "I can breathe again." Russell had two sons: the elder, Henry Russell, Jr., was an opera impresario in Boston, while the second adopted the name Landon Ronald and became a well-known British composer, pianist and conductor, eventually making recordings and receiving a knighthood.

> Writing in the style of Haydn and Weber, Heinrich was the first American composer to quote genuine Native American themes.

Four children of the composer James Hewitt also became prominent musicians during this period: Sophia Henrietta Hewitt (1799–1845) was one of America's first women concert pianists; James Lang Hewitt (1803–1853) set himself up as a music publisher; George Washington Hewitt (1811–1893) worked as a teacher and composer; and the most prominent of them, John Hill Hewitt (1801–1890), was a prolific song composer who achieved a measure of immortality with his powerful Civil War ballad "All Quiet Along the Potomac Tonight" (1863). Charles Horn (1786–1849) was another transplanted Englishman who made important contributions to the balladry and theatrical music of the pre-Civil War era, while singing families such as the Hutchinsons of New Hampshire toured round a vast circuit of town halls, churches, and even barns – wherever they could muster a paying crowd. Opening and closing their concerts with their theme song, "The Old Granite State," the Hutchinsons, comprising four singers, aimed to please the grassroots with a predominantly homemade repertoire of ballads and vocal quartets. They also sang many songs with a political edge, such as the abolitionist "Get off the Track! A Song for Emancipation" (1844), thus foreshadowing the protest singers of the Vietnam era. Other Hutchinson pieces addressed two more of their favorite causes, temperance and revivalism.

Nevertheless, of the musicians, entertainers, vocal ensembles, brass-band leaders and song composers active before the Civil War, the most famous today is Stephen Collins Foster. Born on July 4, 1826, the fiftieth anniversary of the Declaration of Independence (and coincidentally the day on which two primary signatories, John Adams and Thomas Jefferson, died), Foster came to embody an important aspect of the antebellum American character. He came from a prosperous Pennsylvania family that regarded music as a hobby only. Though he published his first song, "Open thy Lattice, Love," when he was only eighteen, his parents ordered him to pursue a business career, and he reluctantly joined his brother's Cincinnati firm as an accountant.

> Of the musicians, entertainers, vocal ensembles, brass-band leaders and song composers active before the Civil War, the most famous today is Stephen Collins Foster, born on July 4, 1826.

Musty ledgers could not stifle Foster's muse. Songs, mostly to his own lyrics, flowed from his pen – refined drawing-room ballads such as "Jeanie with the Light Brown Hair" (1854) and "Sweetly She Sleeps, My Alice Fair" (1851) and jaunty comic songs such as "De Camptown Races" (1850) and "Oh, Susanna" (written in 1848 and adopted as the veritable anthem of the California Gold Rush in 1849) – as did dance and instrumental pieces, which he published in the 1854 collection *Foster's Social Orchestra*. Adapted from the balcony scene in Shakespeare's *Romeo and Juliet*, Foster's duet "Wilt Thou Be Gone, Love?" (1851) approaches the poise of Italian opera, while the vocal quartet, "**Come where my love lies dreaming**" (1855) has the soaring melodic dignity associated with German Romanticism.

Foster laid particular store by such "Ethiopian" songs as "My Old Kentucky Home" and "Massa's in de Cold Ground," which were inspired by the life and music of African-American slaves who worked the cotton plantations of the South. He wrote many of these songs for Christy's Minstrels, the leading blackface troupe of the day.

Website
track 1
www.naxosbooks.com

Illustration and lyrics to Foster's song "Oh, Susanna"

Ironically, E.P. Christy paid Foster a nominal sum for the rights to one of the greatest of these songs, "Old Folks at Home" (also known as "Swanee River"), including the right – when the first edition was published in 1851 – to claim credit for composing it. Foster received posthumous credit only after the first copyright expired in 1879.

Foster was nonetheless the first person in the US to live exclusively off the earnings from his published works. He achieved fame and even financial success during his lifetime, accruing a not inconsiderable $15,000 in royalties between 1849 and 1860.

But unscrupulous publishers and the absence of performing or reproduction rights compromised his earnings. Marriage problems, separation, depression and drink also took their toll. Impoverished, Foster was living alone in a dreary New York hotel when he died at Bellevue Hospital on January 13, 1864.

Two years earlier, Foster had written one of his best songs, **"Beautiful Dreamer**," which was engraved but not brought out by his publisher. No sooner was he laid to rest than it was published with the headline "The Last Song Ever Written by Stephen C. Foster. Composed but a Few Days Previous to His Death." Regardless of the spurious claim, the song's lilting, arching melody became an immediate favorite of singers as well as wind-band arrangers who supplied repertoire for military and village bands throughout the nineteenth century.

It doesn't diminish the simple loveliness of Foster's melodic gift to observe that, like many American songwriters of that time, he tailored his piano accompaniments to the abilities of amateur players; hence they often sound remarkably bare in their original form. Early-twentieth-century arrangers, adapting his songs for radio broadcasts, tended to enrich the piano parts with inner voices and countermelodies. Pop arrangements abounded, but even the art-song arrangements, widely published in household Foster albums and song anthologies, project a Schubertian sophistication quite beyond Foster's own ideas.

William Henry Fry fervently believed that Americans could write operatic and symphonic music as interesting as that of Europeans, and he himself was ready to prove it.

By the time Foster arrived in New York for the first time in 1853, the New York Philharmonic Symphony Society was eleven years old. Among its founders was the music critic William Henry Fry (1813–1864). Fry fervently believed that Americans could write operatic and symphonic music as interesting as that of Europeans, and he himself was ready to prove it.

Ironically, while Fry campaigned for American operas on American subjects, especially as critic of the *New York Tribune*, his own operas, *Aurelia the Vestal* (1841), *Leonora* (1845) and *Notre Dame de Paris* (1864), take place in settings far from the precincts of Battery Park. *Leonora* was Fry's first staged opera and the work that kept his name alive, at

William Henry Fry

least in history books. His brother Joseph wrote the libretto, adapting
it from Sir Edward Bulwer-Lytton's romantic comedy *The Lady of
Lyons*, and transferring the action from *Directoire* France to colonial
South America to give it at least a whiff of New World atmosphere.
Premiered in Philadelphia in 1845, and revived several times through
1858, it was the first grand opera (i.e., entirely sung, without

spoken dialogue) by an American, and in a modern performance in New York during the 1980s it proved as melodious as the music of Bellini, with ensembles as skillfully developed as Donizetti's.

Like Heinrich, Fry composed a number of descriptive symphonies and tone poems. Among them are the concert overture *Macbeth*; *Santa Claus, a Christmas Symphony*; and the one-movement **Niagara** symphony (performed in New York in 1854). This last opens with a thundering roll of massed timpani to evoke the awesome power of the mighty cataract, and, quite strikingly for its time, it ends with a harmonically unstable diminished-seventh chord.

Often reveling in an almost childlike deployment of Lisztian bombast alternating with sentimental passages calculated to draw tears even from men, Fry's music is indeed European in style – he was not intending to strike out on an original path but to prove that he could follow the best European models, just as sophisticated American furniture designers and architects were doing at the time. Composed in 1864 but apparently never performed until 1999 (when it was recorded) *Macbeth* is a truly dramatic, richly Romantic score that reveals Fry's melodic gifts as well as his solid abilities as an orchestrator. From the opening declamation for trombone and tuba that rhythmically mimics the Witches' lines "Double, double, toil and trouble, / Fire burn, and cauldron bubble" to the martial conclusion describing Malcolm's victory, the idiom recalls that of early Wagner – especially the forceful brass writing in *Rienzi*, which the erudite Fry would have known well. Still, the uphill battle faced by American composers at the time can be deduced from a comment directed at Fry while he was working in Paris as a foreign correspondent in the 1840s. His offer to pay all the expenses of mounting *Leonora* at the Paris Opéra was waved away with the response: "In Europe we look to America as an industrial country – excellent for railroads but not for art."

America's first true concert star was Louis Moreau Gottschalk, a native of New Orleans, the first American concert pianist to be taken seriously in Europe.

Often linked with Heinrich and Fry as a pioneering figure working to establish a distinctive American voice in concert music, George Frederick Bristow (1825–1898) had joined the New York Philharmonic as a violinist in 1843, having studied that instrument with Ole Bull.

Louis Moreau Gottschalk

He also did occasional stints as a concert pianist and church organist. Like Fry, Bristow strove to write music just as good as its European models. Though his works often have American titles or themes, the style of such works as the Concert Overture (1845), the Symphony in F sharp minor (1858), the overture *Columbus* (1861) and even the late *Niagara Symphony* (1893) bespeak the healthy influence of Beethoven and Mendelssohn. Bristow's best-known work, *Rip Van Winkle*, produced in New York in 1855 and with music elegantly drawn along Donizettian and early Verdian lines, was the first American opera on an American subject. But even more pioneering than these works were his String Quartets in F major and G minor and his Violin Sonata in G, all three written around 1849, at a time when chamber music was rarely essayed by American composers.

If Fry and Bristow had to battle for the success of their appealing music, America's first true concert star was Louis Moreau Gottschalk (1829–1869), a native of New Orleans, seat of the country's French culture, and the first American concert pianist to be taken seriously in Europe.

Gottschalk's solo music combines a French-oriented sensibility with a pioneering use of indigenous Spanish melodies and rhythms which he gathered on his early concert tours of Spain and Europe.

In 1853 Gottschalk returned to America to seek his fortune on home turf. Unfortunately, his father's sudden death left him responsible for supporting his extravagant family, all of whom had moved to Paris to enjoy the city's prodigal delights. Forced to increase the number of concerts he played and the corresponding distances traveled, Gottschalk rode 15,000 miles by rail and gave eighty-five recitals during one four-and-a-half-month period. He was obliged to keep up this grueling pace for much of the remainder of his life, which ended prematurely when he was forty, in Rio de Janeiro in 1869.

Gottschalk wrote a vast amount of piano and orchestral music. There were his immensely popular, sentimental salon pieces, such as *The Dying Poet* and *The Last Hope*. There were dazzling virtuoso works such as *Tremolo, grande étude de concert*, Op. 58, and *La jota aragonesa, caprice espagnol*, Op. 14, the latter based on the same Iberian dance melody that also inspired orchestral and piano treatments by Mikhail Glinka and Franz Liszt. There were his patriotic potpourris such as ***L'Union, paraphrase de concert sur les airs nationaux "Star-Spangled Banner," "Yankee Doodle," and "Hail Columbia***," Op. 48, which drapes each theme in scintillating passagework before climaxing with all three national songs presented in counterpoint. He also wrote several orchestral works, most notably the delightful two-movement symphony *La Nuit des tropiques*. The slow first movement is straightforward Romantic music, with a plaintive solo trumpet theme leading to a series of contrasting heroic and sentimental episodes – Gottschalk and Fry drank at the same font of inspiration. The dazzlingly Caribbean-inspired second movement, however, is an eye-opener, a samba replete with an Afro-Cuban percussion section. Indeed, of all Gottschalk's oeuvre, what stand out principally to modern listeners are his numerous works incorporating Caribbean and Afro-Hispanic tunes and rhythms, which he collected on his concert tours of the US, the Caribbean and South America. When we hear the infectious rhythms and syncopations of *La Nuit des tropiques*, or piano works such as the *Souvenir de Porto Rico (Marche des Gibaros)*, Op. 31, and the irresistible ***La gallina*** ("The Hen"), Op. 53, the marvel is not just that Gottschalk anticipates such iconic twentieth-century music as Scott Joplin's rags, Copland's *El salón México* or Bernstein's *West Side Story*, but that this sultry, hip-swinging music was performed when Mary Todd Lincoln was wearing hoop skirts in the White House.

4   Transplanting Romantic European Traditions

The Civil War, in which thousands of victims were slaughtered on both sides, raged from 1861 to 1865 and resulted in a social upheaval in the former slave-holding states. During the war, poet Walt Whitman served compassionately as an army nurse in the Union field hospitals, recording his harrowing experiences in a poem entitled *The Wound-Dresser*. At the war's conclusion he worked as a clerk in the US Department of the Interior. His tenure was brief, cut short by James Harlan, President Lincoln's Secretary of the Interior, who in 1865 discovered that Whitman had written and published a rather unconventional book of poetry called *Leaves of Grass*. He fired Whitman immediately. As the essayist H.L. Mencken later wrote, "Let us remember ... that one day in 1865 brought together the greatest poet that America has ever produced and the damnedest ass."

In terms of music, the war was more of a watershed than an immediate influence, although the migrations resulting from the abolition of slavery would help spread African-American melody, harmony and rhythm around the country. Possibly the most lasting piece of music to emerge directly from the war was "The Battle Hymn of the Republic," its verses written by Julia Ward Howe in 1861 in response to a friend's challenge to fit uplifting words to the popular tune "John Brown's Body." But there were other war songs as well. George Frederick Root (1820–1895) contributed several that remained great household favorites well into the early twentieth century, especially two rousing ones, "Battle Cry of Freedom" ("For we'll rally 'round the flag, boys") (1862) and "Tramp, Tramp, Tramp, the Boys are Marching," subtitled "The Prisoner's Hope" (1864). He also wrote softer ballads such as "Just Before the Battle, Mother" (1862) and "The Vacant Chair" ("We shall meet, but we shall miss him") (1861), the latter recorded with particular beauty by John McCormack in 1914, after the outbreak of World War I made its sentiments current again.

Henry Clay Work (1832–1884), perhaps best known for the tick-tock refrain of "Grandfather's Clock" (1876), also achieved a measure of immortality with his wartime inspirations "Kingdom Coming" (1862) and "Marching through Georgia" (1865), which celebrated General Sherman's fiery march from Atlanta to the sea. And even if they no longer remember these, audiences still know "When Johnny Comes Marching Home" (1863), one of the few flag-waving numbers of the time written in a minor key. It was composed by one Louis Lambert, actually a pseudonym of the bandmaster Patrick Gilmore (1829–1892). It is frequently heard today in a bracing symphonic arrangement by Morton Gould. The Confederacy had its own songs, though the two most famous of them, "I Wish I Was in Dixie's Land" (1859) and "All Quiet Along the Potomac Tonight" (1863), were ironically written by two Northerners, Daniel Decatur Emmett (1815–1904) and John Hill Hewitt, respectively.

Apart from war songs, parlor songs were a household staple. Melodious, often sentimental, and gratifying to sing and play, these descendants of Foster's ballads found a ready market, and innumerable American composers wrote them. Many songs by the aforementioned Root and Work fell into this category, as did such post-Civil War classics as "Silver Threads among the Gold" (1872) by H.P. Danks (1834–1903), who lived to regret selling the song outright to a publisher, and "Carry Me Back to Old Virginny" (1878) by New York-born James A. Bland, who, for a while, enjoyed a tremendous acclaim in England as the "Prince of Negro songwriters."

In terms of concert music, however, if the period between the Revolutionary and Civil Wars saw Americans determined to prove that they could actually compose music, the postwar third of the nineteenth century saw the first attempt by composers to establish a genuine American school to stand as a musical counterpart to the work of American painters such as Albert Bierstadt, Frederic Edwin Church, Eastman Johnson, Winslow Homer and John Singer Sargent.

Expansionism was in the air, symbolized by the completion of the nation's first transcontinental railroad in 1869. Now that the earlier doctrine of "Manifest Destiny" lay unencumbered by the demands of Civil War, the nation was free to claim and settle all the territory previously gained from coast to coast, from North to South. Commerce and enterprise produced unprecedented wealth. Mark Twain dubbed this era "the Gilded Age," not just for its wealth, but for its ostentation, especially the ostentation of "self-made" men such as John W. Mackay, who rose from poor Irish immigrant to part-owner of the "Big Bonanza" silver mine of Nevada's Comstock Lode. In 1874 Mackay, known as "the Silver King," commissioned Tiffany & Co. to fashion an elaborate, 1,250-piece table service for his wife, using half a ton of silver sent directly from his mine.

> In 1877 Edison invented the phonograph, though its impact on music developed only after 1900.

Commerce and industry were aided by a host of new inventions, among them Edison's development of electric lighting and motor power during the 1870s and 1880s; Edison's ticker-tape machine, which revolutionized the stock market; and Bell's telephone (1876), which revolutionized communication. In 1877 Edison also invented the phonograph, though its impact on music developed only after 1900. Before then music boxes provided mechanical music for households that could afford them.

Music boxes operate on a principle used to work mechanical church carillons and musical clocks since the Middle Ages: the notes to be played are arranged as pins on a revolving cylinder and, as the cylinder revolves, the pins pluck the teeth of a tuned steel comb. Simple key-wound mechanical music boxes, with small cylinders containing a tune or two, are still found in children's toys. However, Victorian music boxes were elaborate affairs, with large spring-wound clockwork motors and cylinders often containing up to a dozen excerpts from popular songs, operas and symphonic works. The tinkling melodies are usually embellished with runs and arpeggios that evoke the realm of sugar-plum fairies even when the tune is by Wagner or Beethoven. Related to these domestic machines were their public counterparts: barrel organs, fairground organs, orchestrions and steam calliopes, which offered tooting, strumming, rum-tum-tumming musical entertainments on street corners, in saloons and dance halls, at county fairs, on carousels and in circus big tops. Player pianos and organs, their pneumatic mechanisms directed by a roll of perforated paper, also came into vogue around 1890 and remained so until around 1930.

Other than this, if nineteenth-century householders wanted to hear music at home, they had to make it themselves. In rural areas the banjo and guitar were popular, as was the violin, and this rural instrumental tradition of dance and song accompaniment has been perpetuated as an element of today's country and western music. But the two most prevalent instruments in middle-class parlors after the Civil War were pianos and harmoniums made by such firms as Steinway of New York, Chickering of Boston and Estey of Brattleboro, Vermont. The harmonium, or parlor organ, was developed to provide a reasonable, small-scale facsimile of the pipe organ. Foot-pedaled bellows drew air through tuned sets of brass reeds activated by the keyboard. The best harmoniums offered ranks of stops imitating those of a pipe organ, which allowed different color combinations to be played, together with knee-operated swell levers to provide a range of dynamics from soft to loud.

The two most prevalent instruments in middle-class parlors after the Civil War were pianos and harmoniums.

The year 1876 was especially important as the nation's centenary, and, in keeping with the international custom established with London's Great Exhibition of 1851, the United States celebrated its first century with a great Centennial Exhibition held in Philadelphia's Fairmount Park. In a vast array of international exhibits the arts and sciences, industry, commerce and agriculture were represented in this congratulatory fair, allowing America to show the world the material accomplishments of a century's growth. Everything from corn starch to gemstones was on display – Italian olive oil and leather goods, a temple of terracotta tiles by Doulton of England, silk embroideries from China, Liberian coffee goods, Japanese bronzes, elaborate silverware by Tiffany, Gorham and Reed & Barton, a mammoth grape vine from California and a model of the Liberty Bell fashioned of Kansas wheat, millet and broom corn. In Machinery Hall, all the motive power running the various drills, grinding wheels, furnace stokers, pumps, presses and woodworking machines on display was supplied by several miles of belts and drive shafts run by the immense double-acting duplex vertical steam engine – 40 feet high – built by George Corliss of Providence, Rhode Island. And, in the midst of this wealth of activity, music played its part, though not an entirely successful one.

The German-born conductor Theodore Thomas was in charge of the music for the exhibition. His crusade to raise the general musical taste in America had already led him to found the Cincinnati May Festival in 1873 (the nation's oldest choral festival, still going strong today) and would eventually lead to the formation of the Chicago Symphony Orchestra. Thomas commissioned three pieces to be performed at the opening ceremonies, two of them from Americans. In fact the music historian Louis Elson, writing around 1925, observed that, in 1876 "there were only two prominent native composers to whom the nation could turn for a lofty opening hymn, [John Knowles] Paine and Dudley Buck." Thus Paine, whom Harvard University had recently appointed to the nation's first professorship of music, composed the *Centennial Hymn*, to a text by John Greenleaf Whittier, who had been a major voice of the abolition movement. Buck, the era's leading composer of choral and organ music, composed the *Centennial Cantata*, to a text by the poet and musician Sidney Lanier. Lanier, normally a poet of smoothly flowing verses, had written a text whose ungainly rhythms almost defied musical setting, despite his detailed marginal notes concerning the style and mood of the music he envisioned for each contrasting section. Whether or not Buck found the marginalia helpful, the *Centennial Meditation of Columbia* (to give the cantata's full title), sung and played by a chorus of a thousand and an orchestra of 150,

> German-born conductor Theodore Thomas's crusade to raise the general musical taste in America would eventually lead to the formation of the Chicago Symphony Orchestra.

was greeted with loud cheering – indeed the bass solo, "Long as thine Art shall love true love, Long as thy Science truth shall know," was "enthusiastically encored," according to contemporary accounts. Only the third of these three commissions survives as a curiosity today, Richard Wagner's *Centennial March*. Wagner, plagued by continual financial problems that dogged the impending opening of his Festspielhaus at Bayreuth that summer, pocketed the hefty $5,000 fee and dashed off a textbook example of empty bombast.

Though Thomas and his orchestra later offered symphonic concerts, the Centennial Exhibition's greatest musical attraction was the visiting French composer Jacques Offenbach. Audiences flocked to Offenbach's concerts, not only to hear his irresistible music but to get a glimpse at the man himself, for America was continuing its love affair with European stars.

Europeans toured America in droves – pianists such as the Russian Anton Rubinstein and the German Hans von Bülow, violinists such as the Belgian Henri Vieuxtemps. Both Rubinstein and Vieuxtemps were, in addition, celebrated composers, and foreign composers continued to be prestigious audience draws: when Carnegie Hall opened in 1891 the program featured the American premiere of Tchaikovsky's B-flat minor Piano Concerto, played by the German virtuoso Adele aus der Ohe, with the composer himself in attendance. Probably the zenith of this kind of promotional device took place in 1904, when Richard Strauss conducted his new *Symphonia domestica* in the auditorium of Wanamaker's department store in New York (several days after giving the world premiere at Carnegie Hall).

Opera was a tremendous draw, as European singers and entire opera companies toured the country, drawn by blandishments of high fees and private railway carriages plushly fitted out by the Pullman company. In cities such as New York, Philadelphia and New Orleans the grand opera season was an essential feature of life in high society, while German and Italian immigrants packed the gallery to hear the likes of Etelka Gerster, Ilma di Murska and Adelina Patti star in popular operas of Verdi, Donizetti, Gounod and Meyerbeer. It was in this climate that, in 1883, New York's "new money," unable to secure boxes at the Academy of Music on 14th Street (the bastion of "old money"), established the Metropolitan Opera, way uptown at West 39th Street.

Despite all these developments in concert and domestic music, however, by and large the musical sophistication of the American public could be characterized by President Ulysses S. Grant's comment, "I know only two tunes. One of them is 'Yankee Doodle,' and the other isn't."

Nevertheless, forward-looking citizens were determined to raise the cultural level of the nation, and the 1880s and 1890s witnessed the successive establishments of important American symphony orchestras in St Louis (1880), Boston (1881), Detroit (1887), Chicago (1891), Cincinnati (1894), Pittsburgh (1895) and Philadelphia (1900). And the three musicians who had been connected with the Centennial Exhibition continued to be leading forces in American music of the time, especially Theodore Thomas (1835–1905). Having played the violin since he was two, he emigrated to the United States with his family when he was ten. After several years serving in theatre and concert orchestras in New York, in 1854 he joined the first violin section of the New York Philharmonic and the following year he joined forces with the pianist and composer William Mason for a series of chamber concerts. Their first program included the world premiere of Brahms' Piano Trio, Op. 8, and the Mason and Thomas Chamber Music Soirées continued thereafter for fourteen years, going a long way to spread the knowledge of the string quartet repertoire as well as other chamber music.

Thomas began conducting opera at New York's Academy of Music in 1859, giving his first orchestral concert in 1862. By offering mixed programs of serious and lighter fare, Theodore Thomas, arrived at a modus operandi with which he could attract and please audiences while educating them at the same time, introducing them, for example, to such then-daring novelties as the overture to Wagner's *The Flying Dutchman* in its American premiere. While serving as conductor of the Brooklyn Philharmonic Society from 1862 to 1891 he developed the Theodore Thomas Orchestra, which toured the US and Canada annually and helped to prompt cities such as Boston and Chicago to start their own orchestras. From 1877 to 1891 Thomas was conductor of the New York Philharmonic, but he remained frustrated that the orchestra was not a full-time organization. Then, after various setbacks, he was approached by a consortium of wealthy Chicago businessmen who offered to finance a permanent orchestra there under his baton. Heading the new Chicago Symphony Orchestra was not without its crises, or its frustrations, especially the lack of a satisfactory concert hall. Ironically, Thomas had only a few weeks to live after conducting the opening program at Orchestra Hall

By offering mixed programs of serious and lighter fare, Theodore Thomas arrived at a modus operandi with which he could attract and please audiences while educating them at the same time.

in December 1904, but the hall remains the Chicago Symphony's permanent home, while Thomas's legacy was the broad popularization of symphonic music throughout North America.

Education, both in schools and out, had a good deal to do with raising the public awareness of fine music. In the former arena Thomas's chamber music collaborator, the pianist William Mason (1829–1908), was a key figure. The son of Bostonian Lowell Mason (1792–1872), a celebrated hymn composer and pioneering musical missionary, and brother of Daniel Gregory Mason (1820–1869), an important music publisher and partner in the Mason and Hamlin piano manufacturing company, William Mason had studied with several European virtuosi, including Franz Liszt, before returning to America as a touring pianist and composer in 1854. Though he finally succumbed to audiences' demands for flashy stunts such as playing "Yankee Doodle" with one hand and "Old Hundredth" with the other, Mason always tried to program the best European music of the time. Eventually he gave up touring for teaching: he published several influential piano instruction books and composed four-hand piano works intended to be played jointly by teacher and student. Mason's earlier concert works reflect the influence of Liszt and his rivals. For example, his signature piece, **Silver Spring**, Op. 6, presents a gentle melody in the middle voice surrounded by a shower of scintillating arpeggio figures up and down the keyboard. This three-handed effect was the stock-in-trade of one of Liszt's chief competitors, Sigismond Thalberg. Starting around 1890, Mason's later piano compositions, such as the **Improvisation**, Op. 51, reveal a far greater intellectual

subtlety in his affinity for the rich, ambiguous harmonic language, intricate counterpoint and lyrical poise of Schumann, Brahms and Gabriel Fauré.

Music criticism was also an important vehicle toward educating American palates and refining their taste. Bostonian John Sullivan Dwight (1813–1893), trained as a minister, was widely regarded as the father of American music criticism. He established his *Journal of Music* in 1852 and, though it had a limited circulation, its reviews of music and performances proved highly influential in guiding musical opinion of the day. Starting out to introduce the wider public to the riches of Handel, Bach, Mozart and Beethoven, Dwight remained essentially conservative, denouncing the radical compositions of Berlioz and Wagner as musical blasphemy, until by the end of his long career he was regarded as too reactionary.

The next generation of music critics included several noteworthy figures whose writings are still worth reading, among them Henry T. Finck (1854–1926), a Harvard graduate and ardent Wagnerite who wrote for *The Nation*; Henry Edward Krehbiel (1854–1923), critic of the *New York Tribune*; William James Henderson (1855–1937), critic of *The New York Times*; James Gibbons Huneker (1860–1921), critic of *The New York Sun*; and Louis C. Elson (1848–1920), successively music editor of the *Boston Courier* and the *Boston Advertiser*. Admittedly these men fearlessly embraced conservative taste and flung witty barbs at post-Wagnerian developments: Krehbiel dismissed Schoenberg's music as "excrement," while Elson derided Debussy's *La Mer* as "Le Mal de Mer" (seasickness) and declared that the faun of *Prélude à l'après-midi d'un faune* needed the attention of a veterinarian.

Meanwhile, American composers continued to work industriously toward recognition. For example, Dudley Buck (1839–1909), of Hartford, Connecticut, trained in Leipzig and Paris and subsequently became a pre-eminent church organist in Chicago, Boston and Brooklyn. His Chicago episode ended with the Great Fire of 1871, when his house burnt, including his personal library, all his earlier manuscripts and the small organ recital hall he had built next door. After relocating to Boston, Buck began to write large-scale works for chorus, soloists and orchestra, such as the Mendelssohnian *Forty-Sixth Psalm* (1872) and the secular cantata *The Legend of Don Munio* (taken from Washington Irving's *Tales from the Alhambra*), which was premiered by Boston's Handel and Haydn Society in 1874. In 1875 Buck was appointed assistant conductor of the Theodore Thomas Orchestra in New York, hence the obvious lead to his commission from Thomas to compose the *Centennial Cantata* the following year. Meanwhile, Buck settled in Brooklyn (then an independent city), where he became organist and choirmaster of Holy Trinity Church, a perfect testing ground for his continuing series of anthems and service music.

In common with Victorian England and nineteenth-century Germany, Victorian America doted on choral music for several reasons. First, at a time when many industrial towns offered few pastimes for its working-class residents beside taverns and blood sport, the founding of amateur choruses, with their regularly scheduled rehearsals, offered many working-class men and women an opportunity for respectable social interaction, combined with the educational aspect of learning and performing music. Second, the establishment of the Cincinnati May Festival sparked a wave of other choral festivals around the country, which in turn created a demand for new choral repertoire, both sacred and secular. Moreover, even in the many towns lacking a full orchestra, choral works could usually be performed with only an organ accompaniment. Therefore most American composers hoping to earn income and secure a reputation wrote choral music.

During the 1880s Buck was America's chief choral composer. Among his sacred works, the *Festival Te Deum*, Op. 63 No. 1, thanks to its melodic grace and pleasing chromaticism, became his most widely performed liturgical anthem, remaining a staple well into the twentieth century – it was even recorded by Victor around 1930. His dozen secular cantatas for male chorus and mixed chorus chalked up more performances than any other American choral music. The poetry of Longfellow and the tales of Washington Irving offered Buck frequent inspiration. Of the former's work he set *The Nun of Nidaros* (1879), *King Olaf's Christmas* (1881), *Paul Revere's Ride* (1898) and the large-scale *Scenes from The Golden Legend* (for Cincinnati, 1880). From Irving, Buck derived his own libretti for *The Legend of Don Munio*

(1874) and *The Voyage of Columbus* (after Irving's *Life of Columbus*, 1885). It is also significant of his standing at the time that his *The Light of Asia* (adapted from Sir Edwin Arnold's epic poem concerning the life of Buddha, 1885) was premiered in London, sponsored and published by England's leading choral publisher, Novello & Co.

Buck, whose Grand Sonata in E flat of 1866 was the first organ sonata composed by an American, achieved national fame and genuine popularity because he combined an attractive melodic gift with a genuinely refined technique, writing music that appealed to a wide audience without compromising his high standards of craftsmanship. Among his works revived in recent years, his *Festival Overture on the Star-Spangled Banner* proves vivacious as well as artistic. Buck casts the overture in a watertight sonata form, opening with an arresting theme of his own, and initially presenting the patriotic melody as the quieter second theme, for cellos. He deftly fragments the famous tune and inventively works up motifs of both themes in the development section before building up to a final choral presentation of the patriotic song with cymbals crashing.

Buck had briefly taught at the New England Conservatory, but it was his Maine-born contemporary, John Knowles Paine, who became a lynchpin of higher music education when Harvard University appointed him to the country's first professorship in Music in 1875. Paine (1839–1906) had first studied rigorously with a German emigrant in Portland before going to Berlin in 1858 to complete his training in organ, orchestration and composition. While there he was greatly influenced by the ongoing revival of J.S. Bach's music, and during a three-year extension of his European stay he performed as a piano and organ recitalist in Germany and England, both meeting and playing for Clara Schumann. He returned to America

> John Knowles Paine became a lynchpin of higher music education when Harvard University appointed him to the country's first professorship in Music in 1875.

in 1861, deeply imbued with a taste for German music and fully equipped to capitalize on his gifts and his experience. Apart from presenting a series of organ recitals and lectures in Boston (which laid the groundwork for the Harvard appointment), Paine devoted himself to composing elegant chamber music, richly lyrical symphonies and striking choral works. His two symphonies (composed in 1871 and 1879 respectively) are profoundly influenced by the impassioned lyricism and romantic love of nature of Mendelssohn, Schumann and Joachim Raff, another major German figure of the time. The first is Mendelssohnian in its Romantic classicism. He entitled the second "In the Spring," its beautiful second movement featuring a soaring Schumannesque theme for violins, cellos and horn, its finale a veritable song of thanksgiving. It was received with almost hysterical acclaim and national pride at its premiere in Boston in 1879; the eminent critic John Dwight reportedly stood on his seat and opened and closed his umbrella as a sign of his approbation. At the time the chief debate did not concern whether this music sounded American, but whether Paine's obvious programmatic musical content veered too close for comfort to the descriptive tone poems of the radical Franz Liszt. The work was revived and recorded by Zubin Mehta and the New York Philharmonic in 1987.

Like Buck, Paine wrote numerous cantatas and other choral works for the ready market. His Mass in D, written during a second long visit to Germany and inspired by Beethoven's *Missa solemnis* in D, was premiered in Berlin in 1867 and performed frequently in America (it was revived at Harvard University in 2000). His vigorous oratorio *St Peter* received its premiere in Portland, Maine, in 1873, and was accorded a place of honor among the works programmed for the Handel and Haydn Society Triennial Festival in Boston the next year. Like many Austro-German choral works of the mid-nineteenth century, *St Peter* was modeled in mood, form and idiom upon Mendelssohn's *St Paul* and Bach's Passions. And after a long hiatus it was revived and recorded in

> Paine's symphony "In the Spring" was received with almost hysterical acclaim and national pride at its premiere in Boston in 1879

1989 by the indefatigable composer-conductor Gunther Schuller. A representation of Paine's excellent chamber and piano works has also been recorded – his sense of humor and love of Bach combine in his *Fuga giocosa*, for piano, built on the brief baseball tune "Over the Fence is Out, Boys." Paine suffered a major disappointment over the resistance to his sole grand opera, *Azara* (composed 1883–98), which never got beyond a concert performance in 1903.

At the start of his mature career Paine was dead set against the revolutionary ideas of Wagner and his circle and published some magazine articles criticizing what Wagner and Liszt heralded as "the Music of the Future." In time Paine modified this stance, incorporating more chromatic harmony in his own work, though he remained essentially conservative in his technique. At Harvard, Paine taught a generation of American composers, among them John Alden Carpenter, Arthur Foote, Frederick Shepherd Converse and Daniel Gregory Mason. His Harvard appointment led to the creation of similar professorships for two more important Americans, Horatio Parker, at Yale in 1894, and Edward MacDowell, at Columbia in 1896.

The mustachioed Parker (1863–1919), with his center-parted hair and starched appearance, could have stepped right out of the pages of Clarence Day's classic memoir *Life with Father*. Descended from an old Massachusetts Bay family, he was first taught piano and organ by his mother, who was a woman of some literary skill. In 1882, after composition studies in Boston, he was sent by his primary teacher there, George Whitefield Chadwick, to the Hochschule für Musik in Munich. There he undertook more advanced composition studies with Chadwick's teacher, Josef Rheinberger, a leading German organist whose other pupils included Ermanno Wolf-Ferrari, the future composer of the Italian comedy *The Secret of Susanna* and the verismo shocker *The Jewels of the Madonna*. When Parker returned to the US in 1885, he was thoroughly imbued with a taste for Germanic technique, especially in the direction of organ and choral music.

> Paine was dead set against the revolutionary ideas of Wagner and his circle.

Parker was a prolific composer, and though he wrote a fair amount of orchestral music his three great areas of concentration were sacred and secular choral music and solo song. In 1893 his cantata *The Dream-King and his Love* (setting an English translation of a German poem) won the National Conservatory Prize – the title alone suggests Parker's Romantic, Eurocentric literary predilections.

The year 1893 also saw the completion of the work for which Horatio Parker is best remembered today, the Latin oratorio *Hora novissima*. The text consists of excerpts from a lengthy Latin poem,

De contemptu mundi, by Bernard de Cluny (also known as Bernard de Morlass or Morlaix), a twelfth-century monk whose writings deplored the immorality of his time. *De contemptu* dwells upon the transitory nature of earthly life and on the supreme pleasure of life in heaven. Parker laid out his oratorio in eleven movements, alternating choruses with arias for the four soloists and solo quartets, and the music combines late Romantic spaciousness, instrumental weight and a contrapuntal richness akin to Brahms and Gounod. Parker's contrapuntal strength shines forth in such movements as "Pars mea" and the unaccompanied chorus "Urbs Syon unica," which offers a late-Victorian take on the style of Palestrina. Premiered in New York in 1893, *Hora novissima* was repeatedly performed by the Handel and Haydn Society, and in 1899, under Parker's own direction, at England's Three Choirs Festival at Worcester, marking the first American work to be given at a major British choral festival.

> The year 1893 saw the completion of the work for which Horatio Parker is best remembered today, the Latin oratorio *Hora novissima*.

At Yale, Parker taught two generations of composers, including Charles Ives and Roger Sessions; Ives, however, respected the man more than his music.

If Parker and Paine achieved deep admiration and respect, Edward MacDowell (1860–1908) achieved true star status as an American composer during his lifetime, his music esteemed abroad and genuinely revered at home.

A native New Yorker, MacDowell had studied piano with the fiery Venezuelan virtuoso Teresa Carreño, a towering figure who had once improvised for President Lincoln a set of variations on his favorite tune, "Listen to the Mocking-bird" (composed by the American Septimus Winner). From 1876 through 1884 MacDowell lived in Europe, studying successively at the conservatories in Paris and Frankfurt with some of the leading teachers of the day, most importantly the eminent German symphonist Joachim Raff (1822–1882).

> Edward MacDowell (1860–1908) achieved true star status as an American composer during his lifetime, his music esteemed abroad and genuinely revered at home.

MacDowell returned to the US in 1884 and settled in Boston. There, the new Boston Symphony Orchestra regularly programmed his works, among them his impassioned **Second Piano Concerto**, with the composer performing as soloist in 1889. A month earlier he had given the premiere of the concerto in New York, sharing the program with the American premiere of Tchaikovsky's Fifth Symphony. Though completely imbued with German late Romanticism, the score bespeaks MacDowell's adventurous grasp of concerto form. Instead of the conventional fast–slow–fast format, his first movement, *Larghetto calmato*, opens with a brief passage for high strings recalling Wagner's *Lohengrin*, followed by a commanding piano cadenza. Thematically, the movement itself anticipates the brooding language of Rachmaninov. The second movement, *Presto giocoso*, is pure fireworks, reflecting MacDowell's Paris days, with proto-jazzy syncopations that foreshadow the insouciance of Francis Poulenc, while the finale, *Largo – Molto allegro*, leads from another brooding episode to a scintillating concertante waltz.

MacDowell never accepted Dvořák's idea that the defining of an American symphonic language hinged on the use of folk material of Negro slaves.

In addition to his concertante pieces, MacDowell wrote a number of purely symphonic works – among them the tone poem *Hamlet and Ophelia*, Op. 22 (1885), and two orchestral Suites, Opp. 42 (1891) and 48 (1895). The first Suite – comprising movements entitled "In a Haunted Forest," "Summer Idyll," "In October," "The Shepherdess Song" and "Forest Spirits" – is obviously steeped in the Teutonic spirits of the Brothers Grimm.

MacDowell's Second Piano Concerto premiered in 1889, sharing the program with the American premiere of Tchaikovsky's Fifth Symphony.

MacDowell never accepted Dvořák's idea that the defining of an American symphonic language hinged on the use of folk material of Negro slaves. He was drawn more to American-Indian music, as he perceived it, and he responded to Dvořák's advocacy with a blunt rejoinder: "Masquerading in the so-called nationalism of Negro clothes cut in Bohemia will not help us. ... Why cover a beautiful thought with the badge of slavery rather than with the stern but at least manly and free rudeness of the North American Indian?" MacDowell carries this idea through in his **Suite No. 2**, called "Indian," each movement incorporating a theme based on Native American melodies, including an Iroquois women's dance, a war song, a love song of the Iowas and, the composer's personal favorite, a Kiowa dirge, which a critic of the day declared to be "the most profoundly affecting threnody since the *Götterdämmerung* Funeral March."

Given the central position of the piano in the composer's life, and certainly given the number of amateur pianists eager to play new repertoire in America and Europe, MacDowell wrote a large corpus of piano music. Of his major piano works, his four sonatas were greatly admired (the Third, "Norse," and the Fourth, "Keltic," dedicated to Grieg), as were his Six Idyls after Goethe and his First and Second "Modern Suites." His shorter piano works were bestsellers. Many bore picturesque titles, like the character pieces of Mendelssohn, Schumann and Grieg, which appealed to the thousands of amateur pianists across the land. *Sea Pieces*, Op. 55, *Fireside Tales*, Op. 61, and *New England Idyls*, Op. 62, were among his most popular; the most famous were *Woodland Sketches*, Op. 51, which remained part of the teaching repertoire of countless piano instructors even during the mid-twentieth century, when MacDowell's star had been eclipsed. The simple lyricism of "To a Wild Rose" explains why this particular piece was universally known at one time. In dramatic contrast are the swelling bass sonorities of "In Mid-Ocean," from *Sea Pieces*.

Between 1883 and 1902 MacDowell also composed a body of songs to German and English lyrics by authors including Goethe and William Dean Howells, as well as words by himself. The close emotional relationship between the musical settings and the texts, and the overall freshness of MacDowell's approach to what are essentially American lieder and his ability to convey through music the sense of nature in the open air, led the influential American critic Henry T. Finck to declare the composer in 1900, along with Edvard Grieg, one of "the two greatest living song writers." The statement sounds a bit windy nowadays, especially to ears familiar with contemporary song repertoire by composers as varied as Richard Strauss, Wolf, Debussy and Fauré. Nevertheless, MacDowell's output in this genre, which dates between 1883 and 1902, is marked by increasing musical simplicity. In an early song such as the 1883 setting of

Heinrich Heine's "**Mein Liebchen, wir saßen beisammen**" (My love and I sat closely together), from *Drei Lieder*, Op. 11, the vocal line rides upon a luxurious piano figuration of sparkling arpeggios further gilded with arpeggiated chords, rather like the style of young Richard Strauss. And there is a marked contrast between this and the restrained accompaniment of "**Tyrant Love**," from Three Songs,

Original manuscript of "Told at Sunset," No. 10
from MacDowell's Woodland Sketches

Op. 60, published in 1902. The verses are by MacDowell himself, supported by the merest underpinning of slightly melancholy chord progressions.

When Columbia University established its first music professorship in 1896, the chair was offered to MacDowell, "the greatest musical genius America has produced." He threw himself into the job, reserving his summers for composition. After taking a sabbatical to give concerts throughout the US and Canada (1902–3), he returned to Columbia only to find that the university's new president, Nicholas Murray Butler, had other ideas about organizing the fine arts curriculum. MacDowell expressed his dissatisfaction, but the university trustees regarded his candor as unbecoming, and he was obliged to resign in 1904.

The disappointment upset MacDowell's already unstable psychological state – medical examinations that year, following a traffic accident, disclosed brain disease. By 1905 he was totally incapacitated. For the remaining three years of his life his wife lovingly cared for him, while in 1906 a group of admirers, including Parker, Victor Herbert, J.P. Morgan, Andrew Carnegie and former President Grover Cleveland, launched a fundraising appeal for him. After his death, at the age of forty-seven, $50,000 was raised for the organization of the MacDowell Memorial Association; and the composer's summer home, at Peterborough, New Hampshire, became the MacDowell Colony, where American composers and writers now spend summers working undisturbed in separate cottages for a minimum fee. It is a distinctive legacy for the first American composer of genuinely international stature, whose music embodies real poetry, romantic beauty, freshness and charm.

5   Into the Twentieth Century: The Traditionalists

Americans greeted the twentieth century with extraordinary optimism. Not only were business and industry booming at home but, thanks to the victory in the Spanish–American War of 1898, the US had thrust itself into the imperialist arena. The former Spanish colonies of the Philippines, Guam and Puerto Rico were now American protectorates, with Cuba occupied by American forces pending the proclamation of an independent republic. The boundless confidence with which Americans saw the present and anticipated a divinely ordained future was summed up in a speech by President William McKinley in October 1899:

> From a little less than four millions in 1790 our population has grown to upward of sixty-two millions. … We have gone from thirteen States to forty-five. We have annexed every variety of territory from the … coconut groves of Key West to the icy regions of northern Alaska … and the Islands of the Pacific and the Caribbean Sea. … After 123 years the pyramid stands … firmer and gives greater promise of duration than when the fathers made it the symbol of their faith. May we not feel … certain that, if we do our duty, the Providence … that led us to our present place will not relax His grasp till we have reached the glorious goal He has fixed for us in the achievement of His end?

The nation's fine arts reflected this optimism with an opulent wave of creativity now known as the American Renaissance. Although some architects and designers such as Louis Sullivan and Frank Lloyd Wright were embracing new and modern forms, the visual language of the time overwhelmingly reflected America's identification as heir of Europe's great Renaissance tradition. Consecrating their aim with the gleaming palatial vistas of the "White City" designed to house the World's Columbian Exposition at Chicago in 1893, architects such as Charles McKim, Stanford White, Daniel Burnham and Cass Gilbert fostered the "City Beautiful" movement, designing government buildings, university campuses, churches, railway stations and even department stores and electric generating plants whose domes, arches, columns, stained-glass windows and mighty bronze doors allied the visual language of the Italian and French Renaissance to the latest architectural technology. Indeed, Gilbert's masterful Woolworth tower in New York City even adapted the soaring vernacular of medieval Gothic style to the most advanced of all building types, the commercial skyscraper. American artists transformed domestic and public interiors into places of visual wonderment as sculptors Daniel Chester French and Augustus Saint-Gaudens, painters John Singer Sargent, Elihu Vedder, William Merritt Chase and Edwin Austin Abbey, and designers Louis Comfort Tiffany, Ogden Codman and John La Farge supplied decorations from monumental bronze and stone figural groups to interior murals and exotic glass electric lamps that combined historical inspiration with cutting-edge experimentation of the time. Through this expansionist, bountiful era the voice of American music resounded with growing confidence, reflecting the same ideals of beauty and refinement that guided the visual arts.

> For every performance of an American concert work during the twentieth century probably a hundred other American works went unperformed.

The students of the first generation of university composers were understandably conservative, writing as they were taught, using traditional symphonic and chamber music forms in a highly attractive late-Romantic idiom. It was a direct and deliberate effort to compete with Europe. In many instances their work actually achieved audience recognition and repeat performances, though we have to acknowledge throughout this survey that for every performance of an American concert work during the twentieth century probably a hundred other American works went unperformed.

Arthur Foote (1853–1937) and George Whitefield Chadwick (1854–1931) represent the second generation of the "New England School," which evolved after Paine's appointment at Harvard.

Foote was the first notable American composer of this period who had *not* received European training. After studying composition with Paine at Harvard (where he conducted the Harvard Glee Club) he was awarded America's first master's degree in music in 1875. A successful Boston church organist and music teacher for fifty years, Foote composed orchestral and choral scores primarily in the earlier part of his career: his Serenade in E for strings was premiered by the Boston Symphony in 1886 and played again at the World's Columbian Exposition in Chicago in 1893 under Theodore Thomas, who also conducted Foote's Cello Concerto at a Chicago Symphony

> Arthur Foote composed around 100 songs, many of them sensitive settings of English poets that reveal his delightful melodic gift.

concert the following year. His Suite in E for strings (1910) was particularly popular during his lifetime, as was *A Night Piece* for flute and orchestra (a 1922 revision of his Nocturne and Scherzo for flute and string quartet of 1918). Similarly Foote turned four piano pieces from his Op. 41 into the orchestral *Four Character Pieces after the Rubáiyát of Omar Khayyám*, Op. 48 (premiered in 1912), giving full rein to his penchant for exquisite instrumental color. Among smaller works, Foote composed around 100 songs, many of them sensitive settings of English poets that reveal his delightful melodic gift.

Foote is best remembered for his exquisite chamber music, throughout which flows a deep current of German Romanticism – no surprise for a student of Paine who spent the summer of 1876 at the first Bayreuth Festival and who made seven more trips to Europe. If the music of Wagner and Brahms remained his lifelong ideals, one also must acknowledge that, to their overall harmonic language, Foote added his own spirit of introspection, a somewhat melancholy plaintiveness that is very moving in such works as his **Melody**, Op. 44 (1899), and Ballade, Op. 69 (1910), both for violin and piano.

George Whitefield Chadwick

Website
track 10–13
www.naxosbooks.com

Many of his finest works date from the period between 1881 and 1911: three string quartets, Opp. 4, 32 and 70, a **Piano Quartet in C**, Op. 23, and a Piano Quintet in A minor, Op. 38. The opening movement of the Piano Quartet (1890) establishes Foote's generous melodic flow, the arching theme in the strings interweaving with the bubbling textures of the piano. Foote himself played the piano part over forty times in concert, often in collaboration with the pioneering Kniesel Quartet. The work became so popular that it was also taken up by other quartets performing throughout the United States and Europe.

Chadwick, a Bostonian, had learned music theory from an older brother, and he was earning a small income as an organist by the age of fifteen. The income was necessary because his businessman father refused to countenance Chadwick's intention to be a professional musician. So apart from paying for his own lessons, the young man dropped out of high school to work in his father's insurance office while studying organ with Dudley Buck at the New England Conservatory, then primarily a keyboard training school for teachers. In 1877, feeling that he needed a more organized course of study, Chadwick went to Germany, unintentionally following in MacDowell's footsteps, and studied at the Leipzig Conservatory and with Rheinberger in Munich. While in Germany, Chadwick brought out his first major compositions, including two string quartets and the concert overture *Rip Van Winkle*. The last was not only judged the best composition at the annual conservatory concerts but given subsequent performances at Dresden and in Boston.

Like Foote, Chadwick returned to Boston as a church organist and taught at the New England Conservatory. In 1897 his appointment as director there, a post he would hold for thirty-three years, signaled a complete reorganization of the school into a fully modern musical college along European lines. By 1892 his prominence as a musical figure was such that he was commissioned, by the veteran Theodore Thomas, to compose the ode for the opening of the World's Columbian Exposition in Chicago. Against the backdrop of architect Daniel Burnham's great White City beside sparkling Lake Michigan, Chadwick's three-movement ode for chorus, orchestra and three brass bands was given under Thomas's baton in 1893.

> For all the Romantic dignity of his symphonic music, Chadwick frequently gave free rein to his genuine musical sense of humor.

Thereafter Chadwick was one of America's pre-eminent composers. He was particularly successful in orchestral music, exploiting a deeply Romantic vein of Wagnerian harmony, which he clothed in notably rich and colorful instrumentation. Unlike MacDowell, Chadwick embraced Dvořák's belief in Negro melodies and rhythms as a key to shaping an American musical idiom. African-American thematic ideas, such as the pentatonic melody in the scherzo of his **Symphony No. 2**, snapping rhythms that echo North American speech patterns, Caribbean syncopations, and turns of phrase reminiscent of New England psalmody lend a recognizably American flavor to such works as his imaginative String Quartet No. 4 (1896) and the *Symphonic Sketches* (1895–1904). The third movement of the quartet suggests a genteel barn dance, while the beautiful second theme of the "Jubilee" movement of the *Symphonic Sketches* breathes the same fresh, outdoor air as Dvořák's "New World" Symphony.

Website
track 154
www.naxosbooks.com

For all the Romantic dignity of his symphonic music, Chadwick frequently gave free rein to his genuine musical sense of humor. It brightens the scherzo movements of his three symphonies, while the *Suite Symphonique* (1905–9) features a cakewalk in 5/4 meter, a humorous touch as insouciant as anything by Eric Satie.

In addition to straightforward symphonic writing, Chadwick had an affinity for programmatic tone poems, many of them inspired by Classical subjects, for instance *Thalia* (1882), *Euterpe* (1903) and *Cleopatra* (1904). Since he was an art collector, sculpture was another source of inspiration. For example, **Aphrodite** (1910–11), one of Chadwick's most sensuous scores, was his musical response to a marble head of the goddess in the Boston Museum of Fine Arts. The symphonic ballad *Tam O'Shanter* (1914–15), based on Robert Burns' eponymous poem, is probably George Chadwick's hardiest score, and it continued to find its way on to occasional orchestral programs and recordings long after his other music receded into the shadows – a particular tragedy in the case of the Second Symphony and the *Symphonic Sketches*, which should be a part of today's standard concert repertoire.

Administrative duties at the New England Conservatory seriously cut into Chadwick's composing time, while ill health sapped his creative energies later in life. *Angel of Death* (1918) is a relatively late score, and his last programmatic one. Inspired by Daniel Chester French's bas-relief for the tomb of sculptor Martin Milmore, it interprets one of French's most poignant images, a lithe young sculptor at work, his hand arrested by a hovering

The symphonic ballad *Tam O'Shanter*, based on Robert Burns' eponymous poem, is probably George Chadwick's hardiest score.

angel. In Chadwick's majestic score, the sculptor dies envisioning his finished work, and a brass chorale rises to pay final tribute. Walter Damrosch and the New York Symphony Society gave the premiere in 1919 in memory of the recently deceased Theodore Roosevelt.

New Yorker George Templeton Strong (1856–1948), son of the noted diarist and New York socialite of the same name, stands somewhat apart from the other composers in this chapter, because in addition to training in Germany he eventually settled in Switzerland, an expatriate figure who vociferously deplored the lack of recognition accorded to American composers at home. Between 1897 and 1912 he abandoned composition for watercolor painting, and even after resuming composition he continued to paint. The cosmopolitan refinement of Strong's music also reflects a late-Romantic sensibility,

Website
track 14
www.naxosbooks.com

and the French and German titles of such works as *Die Nacht* (1913) and *Le Roi Arthur* (1916) and the Symphony No. 2 "Sintram" are partly inspired by F.H.K. de la Motte Fouqué's romance and by Dürer's celebrated engraving *Knight, Death and Devil*. They might also justify the question of "when is an American no longer an American?" Despite this conundrum, the appeal of Strong's music is undeniable and is abundantly evident in his Renaissance-inspired **Chorale on a Theme by Hans Leo Hassler** (1929), a haunting contrapuntal piece for strings and violin solo, written at the time of the stock market crash and the start of the Great Depression.

Website
track 15
www.naxosbooks.com

Trained first at Harvard, then in Boston under Chadwick, and finally under the indefatigable Rheinberger in Munich, Frederick Shepherd Converse (1871–1940) wrote the first American opera staged by the Metropolitan Opera, *The Pipe of Desire*, performed there in 1910. Converse, who taught composition at Harvard and was later Dean of the New England Conservatory,

In 1933 the *Musical Courier* declared Henry Kimball Hadley "probably the most important composer in the contemporary American musical scene."

wrote concert music in every form. Tone poems, however, were his favorite medium, his most famous compositions being **The Mystic Trumpeter** (1904), a lushly scored, vivid interpretation of Walt Whitman, and *Endymion's Narrative* (1901), one of two scores he based on Keats' poem. His distinct musical idiom, with its gleaming strings and exquisite wind writing, gilded with touches of triangle, celesta and other percussion, evokes the seductive style of César Franck. In *Flivver Ten Million* (1926), celebrating the production of the ten-millionth Ford motor car, Converse adopted a relatively modernist voice, inspired by Arthur Honegger's steam locomotive in *Pacific 231* and partly by Converse's own buoyant sense of humor.

Website
track 16
www.naxosbooks.com

In 1933 the *Musical Courier* declared that Henry Kimball Hadley (1871–1937) was "probably the most important composer in the contemporary American musical scene." At the time he was also renowned as a popular symphonic conductor, having held the chief posts at the Seattle Symphony Orchestra (1909–11) and San Francisco Symphony Orchestra (1911–15) and the associate conductor's seat at the New York Philharmonic (1920–7). He was the first American not only to conduct the Berlin Philharmonic and the Amsterdam

Concertgebouw Orchestra, as well as other leading orchestras in Europe, but also to conduct at the Metropolitan Opera. In addition he was a founder of the Berkshire (now Tanglewood) Music Festival at Stockbridge.

The son of a Boston Symphony Orchestra cellist, Hadley was another student of Chadwick's at the New England Conservatory, and he later went to Vienna to study counterpoint with Brahms' close friend and colleague Eusebius Mandyczewski, a pre-eminent scholar and editor of the complete works of Schubert, Beethoven, Haydn and Brahms.

As a composer Hadley was prolific in every form – symphonic, band, choral, opera, song and chamber works. His oratorio *Resurgam*, completed in 1922, was another triumph at its premiere, at the Cincinnati May Festival in 1923. Of Hadley's numerous operas, operettas and other stage pieces, his two-act *Cleopatra's Night*, based on a story by Théophile Gautier, was staged by the Metropolitan Opera in the season 1919–20.

Hadley had a particular affinity for program music, and his work in this area includes tone poems, such as *Herod*, Op. 31 (1901), *Salome*, Op. 55 (1905–6) and *The Ocean*, Op. 99 (1920–1). Among the most famous of these in its time was the delightful rhapsody ***The Culprit Fay***, Op. 62 (1908), inspired by the eponymous Hudson River poem by Joseph Rodman Drake. It had garnered a $1,000 prize offered by the National Federation of Music Clubs, and received a hysterical ovation at its premiere in Grand Rapids in 1909, thereafter being played by orchestras throughout North America and Europe.

Hadley also wrote five programmatic symphonies. Each movement of the **Fourth Symphony** in D minor, Op. 64 (1911), treats a point of the compass, and the lively third movement, "South" (*Allegretto giocoso*), offers a vivid example of the composer's ingratiating style, with its ragtime snap and sparkling orchestration. While his harmony in this movement is diatonic, Hadley adopted an increasingly impressionist harmonic palette, though he always avoided the unresolved dissonance of the more rugged modernists.

Amy (Mrs H.H.A.) Beach (1867–1944) is an example of the indomitable female spirit overcoming the barriers imposed by a man's world. She had made her debut as a pianist when she was

Amy Beach with four other American songwriters in April 1924.
From top left to bottom right: Harriet Ware, Gena Branscombe,
Mary Turner Salter, Ethel Glenn Hier, Amy Beach

sixteen, to great acclaim, but marriage two years later, to a physician twenty-five years older, changed her career. Dr Beach insisted that his wife limit her concert appearances to one yearly recital, and declared that instead of performance she would channel her musical energy into composing. As he would not allow his attractive young wife even to study with anyone, she taught herself composition and orchestration. And she did so brilliantly. Her first major work was a Grand Mass in E flat major, joyously extrovert and operatic, which was premiered by the Boston Handel and Haydn Society in 1892. Her vigorous **Symphony in E minor**, "Gaelic," premiered by the Boston Symphony Orchestra in 1896, was the first symphonic score by an American woman. Inspired by Dvořák's advocacy of folk tunes as the basis of a distinctive American idiom, Beach looked to her Irish roots for thematic material.

Website
track 18–21
www.naxosbooks.com

Beach completed her **Piano Concerto** in C sharp minor in 1899 and was soloist at its premiere with the Boston Symphony Orchestra in 1900. From the first stormy entrance of the piano, this concerto carefully balances powerful statements with an ingratiating lyricism, the themes of the first three movements taken from several of her songs. The tragic third movement, *Largo*, is based on her song "Twilight," a setting of verses by Dr Beach concerning dusk yielding to darkness and life yielding to death. The piano writing, softly accompanied by the orchestra, shows how keenly Amy Beach had absorbed the same rich language of late Romanticism that was inspiring Sergei Rachmaninov in Russia, nearly 5,000 miles away.

Let us conclude this episode by observing that, thanks to the largely German-oriented training of most late-nineteenth-century Americans, German late Romanticism shone like a crimson sunset through a great deal of American concert music well into the first decades of the twentieth century. Moreover, from our own vantage point in the twenty-first century, it would be unfair to dismiss this wealth of music as lacking a distinctive American sound, because that was not the overriding aim of its composers. Instead their finest achievement lay in creating a body of genuinely appealing music in all forms, large and small. Today we can accept and enjoy that appeal on its own terms.

6 American Impressionists and Folklorists

For all the German influence apparent in American music around 1900, some Americans, whether trained at home or abroad, did explore non-Germanic paths. Charles Martin Loeffler (1861–1935) was possibly the most cosmopolitan of all these composers. Born in Alsace, Loeffler was the son of German parents who moved variously to Russia, Hungary and Switzerland. Loeffler's father, a writer, as a result of political difficulties with the German government, eventually died in prison, which turned Loeffler against Germany to the extent that he adopted a French sensibility in every respect. Having previously studied violin with Brahms' great friend Josef Joachim at the Berlin Hochschule für Musik, Loeffler went to Paris to study composition privately.

After several years as an orchestral violinist Loeffler sailed to America, where he received citizenship in 1887. By this time he had been second concertmaster of the Boston Symphony Orchestra for five years – a position he maintained until 1903. He was also composing chamber and symphonic music, the often dark, enigmatic harmonies and programmatic leanings of which were regarded as decadent symbolism. Nonetheless his music was widely performed during his lifetime. The titles of many of his works reveal the influence of his distant travels and his wide reading – for example, *Les Veillées de l'Ukraine* (after Gogol; Loeffler's first orchestral score, premiered by the Boston Symphony Orchestra in 1891) and *La Mort de Tintagiles* (after Maeterlinck; premiered by the Boston Symphony

Orchestra in 1900). He was inspired by authors from Virgil and St Francis to Whitman, Poe, Yeats and Verlaine, while some of his compositions incorporated Gregorian chant, or Spanish, Russian or Irish folk tunes.

A close friend of painter John Singer Sargent, Loeffler admired many American composers. However, his own musical aesthetic was primarily French, and his evocative harmonic vocabulary and leanings toward archaic forms (as in *A Pagan Poem*, inspired by Verlaine's *La Bonne Chanson*) are strongly allied to French impressionism. The haunting second movement of his **Music for Four Stringed Instruments** (1919) vividly exemplifies this. Written in memory of Victor Chapman, the first American pilot killed in World War I, all three movements are unified by Loeffler's use of the Introit from the Latin Easter Mass, while in the second movement, entitled "Le Saint Jour de Pâques" (Easter Sunday), he also quotes the plainchant sequence "Victimae paschali laudes" (Praise to the Paschal victim).

Equally haunting for its subdued impressionist color is the piano music of Charles Tomlinson Griffes (1884–1920). Born in Elmira, New York, Griffes went to Germany to study with Engelbert Humperdinck, composer of the opera *Hänsel und Gretel*. After returning to the US in 1907, Griffes became music director of the prestigious Hackley School in Tarrytown, New York – a short rail journey from New York City, where the composer was a prominent member of the musical community. Within his brief lifetime, Griffes' personal style continually evolved. It began in the Wagnerian manner that he had absorbed from his teacher (whose richly contrapuntal overture to *Hänsel und Gretel* Griffes arranged for two pianos), progressed through a dreamy French style, for which he was accorded the title "the American Impressionist," and reached an even more enigmatic idiom in such final works as the **Three Preludes** (1919), of which No. 2 encapsulates his visionary power in less than a minute. Two of his most luxuriant works were originally written for piano and later orchestrated as tone poems – *The White Peacock* and *The Pleasure Dome of Kubla Khan*, an interpretation of Samuel Taylor Coleridge's unfinished oriental fantasy.

Trained in Pittsburgh, Charles Wakefield Cadman (1881–1946), another masterful composer of chamber, piano and vocal music, was one of several Americans fired by Dvořák's advocacy of American folk material as the basis of a distinctive American idiom. Indeed, though Cadman's 1914 **Piano Trio in D**, Op. 56, is a full-bodied late-Romantic work, the final movement represents one of the earliest uses of ragtime motifs in American chamber music.

Website
track 26–28
www.naxosbooks.com

Cadman was best known, however, for his interest in American-Indian music, which he began to study and adapt for his own use around 1907. His opera *Shanewis, or the Robin Woman*, written for the Metropolitan Opera, was staged there in 1918 and 1919. It was the first American opera both to incorporate authentic Indian melodies and to be staged for two consecutive seasons. Cadman's songs, among them the soaring "At Dawning" and "From the Land of the Sky-Blue Water," were extremely popular and frequently recorded. The latter was freely based on two tribal melodies of the Omaha Indians.

Unfortunately Cadman's reputation faded once America's interest in "Indianist" culture dwindled after 1930. His star was eclipsed by newer figures such as Aaron Copland and Walter Piston, whose Parisian training lent their music a sleek modern sophistication more in tune with the times.

7 New England Iconoclast: Charles Ives

While the New England School composers steeped themselves in European late Romanticism, one young New Englander in Danbury, Connecticut, was literally marching to his own drum. At the age of twelve Charles Ives (1874–1954) became a drummer in his father's band. George Ives, who had been a regimental bandmaster during the Civil War, also taught his son to play piano and cornet. Moreover, Ives senior had distinctive ideas about music: in order to broaden young Charlie's musical horizons, George would play familiar melodies in one key while harmonizing them in another. So even in the 1880s the future composer of the spiky "Concord" Sonata was completely at home with bitonality and with prolonged dissonances as tart as Yankee cider vinegar.

Charles, who had been every inch the child prodigy, was organist in a local church when he was thirteen, occasionally astounding the congregation by jokingly playing hymns in several keys at once. This early experimentation led him at seventeen to compose his polytonal *Variations on America* for organ. Protestant church music, band marches and popular songs flowed through Ives' veins, and he would make free and often deeply nostalgic use of them in his mature works.

Once he had entered Yale University in 1894, Ives literally discovered the standard classical repertoire. Here he gained access to symphonic scores for the first time. Horatio Parker gave him a thorough classical training, preparing him to join the ranks of the

Charles Ives

other New England School composers. Indeed, Ives' First Symphony, composed under Parker's supervision as his Yale graduation thesis in 1898, is astonishing, not just for the skill he shows in handling the large-scale form but for the faintly ironic tone, especially in the first movement, which foreshadows Prokofiev's "Classical" Symphony by almost two decades.

Although some of his early and more conventional songs had been published during his varsity years, Ives didn't pursue composition professionally upon leaving Yale in 1896: it would have been too risky. Instead he joined a New York insurance firm, keeping his virtuoso skills honed by playing the organ at Central Presbyterian Church. In 1907 Ives and a colleague formed their own insurance agency, which prospered sufficiently to provide him and his wife, Harmony, with a considerable income. Indeed, having helped devise the concept of "estate planning," Ives wrote a pamphlet, *The Amount to Carry*, which became standard industry reading. Meanwhile, he continued to compose on weekends and vacations: four violin sonatas, five more symphonies (including *New England Holidays*), the clangorous *Robert Browning Overture*, the philosophical *The Unanswered Question* for small orchestra, *Three Places in New England* (the first in a series of orchestral "sets," or suites), and a sheaf of chamber works, piano pieces and songs. He wrote in the white heat of inspiration, happily, provocatively, and he did so despite the fact that, even when he tried to arrange private performances, his eclectic, truly individual work found few sympathetic listeners, let alone performers willing and able to master its fearsome complexities. After all, Ives was writing before and during World War I, when American audiences and musicians overwhelmingly preferred the more traditional idiom of figures such as Chadwick, Hadley and Beach.

Then the turning point came: Ives suffered a serious heart attack in 1918, complicated by diabetes. So weakened that he could barely hold a pen, he had to cut back all activity. Moreover, a combination of factors – the election of nonentity Warren G. Harding to the presidency in 1920, the strain of working in two disparate fields, and the persistent rejection of his music – finally snuffed out his creative flame. In 1921 he produced a last wave of songs. Then, although he made numerous revisions of earlier works, he wrote almost nothing new until his death in 1954. Admittedly, recognition did come his way as composers such as Henry Cowell, Bernard Herrmann and Jerome Moross began to spread word about him after 1930. In 1939 pianist John Kirkpatrick gave the first complete performance of the "Concord" Sonata, in New York's Town Hall, prompting the conservative critic Lawrence Gilman to declare it "the greatest music composed by an American." In 1947 Charles Ives received a Pulitzer Prize for his Third Symphony (completed in 1911).

In 1947 Charles Ives received a Pulitzer Prize for his Third Symphony.

Between the residual effects of his illness and his own reclusive personality, Ives didn't mingle with those in America's musical mainstream. He attended no concerts and owned neither recordings nor even a radio. But thanks to his father and to Yale, Ives knew intimately a vast repertoire, from Beethoven and Brahms to the jewels of Tin Pan Alley. Hence one of the fundamental aspects of his own music is that, beneath his remarkable dissonance, there is a sheer delight in quoting and manipulating familiar tunes, in effect inviting the listener to engage with Ives in shared experiences. The **Second Symphony** (composed between 1900 and 1910 and repeatedly touched up until 1950), often regarded as the most "American" of all symphonies, is literally a web of patriotic tunes, hymns and Stephen Foster songs. And the generally diatonic idiom makes the

Website
track 29
www.naxosbooks.com

score one of the most inviting introductions to Ives' vast oeuvre. For example, the Brahmsian slow movement quotes the hymn "Beulah Land" (interwoven with "America the Beautiful") and "Columbia the Gem of the Ocean."

Ives was also extraordinary in his almost prescient gift for anticipating many of the technical developments that would become identified with twentieth-century music. For instance, in his *Robert Browning Overture*, he evokes what he called a "surge into the baffling unknown" in Browning's poetry by using atonality, polytonality and twelve-tone writing. The second movement of the "Concord" Sonata (each movement of which salutes, respectively, Emerson, Hawthorne, the Alcotts and Thoreau) calls for a strip of wood to be applied to the black and white piano keys to create an echo effect, thus creating the first "prepared piano" four decades before composer John Cage made it famous. Ives was also a pioneer in using tone-clusters (created by playing a piano with the fist), polyrhythms (two or more rhythms played simultaneously), polymeters (such as waltz time played against march time) and quarter-tones (in the space between, say, B natural and C natural on the piano).

The Unanswered Question, which Ives styles a "cosmic drama," is probably his most famous work, and shows how vividly he could translate philosophical ideas into music in a highly accessible atonal language. Out of a mystical string chorale, "The silence of the Druids," a solo trumpet plays an enigmatic theme, "The personal question of existence." And each time the question is posed, a wind quartet responds with "fighting answers" until they vanish in a primal scream. The last time the trumpet repeats the question, the response is silence.

But for all the seriousness, Ives is never far from having fun. His raucous **Country Band March** pays fond homage to the enthusiastic amateur bands of his boyhood in Danbury. "They didn't always play right & together," Ives wrote, "and it was as good either way." Here polyrhythms and polytonality emerge from a truly catchy jumble of ragtime and march tunes.

So, who's afraid of Charlie Ives now?

8   From Bandstand to Broadway: The 1890s to 1930s

The bandstand on the village green is a symbol of life in America's heartland. Painted white and trimmed with Victorian gingerbread, these little pavilions often come to life during the summer when a real volunteer band gives a concert or two. Back when Grover Cleveland was president, however, band concerts were a primary musical activity in the US. Big cities had their symphony orchestras, but in small-town America a band concert often provided the sole opportunity for people to hear music played by massed instruments.

Enterprising bandmasters, such as Irish-born Patrick Gilmore (composer of "When Johnny Comes Marching Home"), often became celebrities. In 1869, four years after the end of the Civil War, Gilmore organized a "Peace Jubilee" in Boston, a monster festival that featured an orchestra of 1,000 players and a chorus of 10,000. It was such a popular triumph that he staged a second one in 1872. This time he doubled his original forces, adding artillery for some of the music, and a band of fifty firemen hammering at as many anvils for Verdi's "Anvil" chorus.

Gilmore and his jubilees earned a special niche in American musical history, but only one bandmaster still holds a special place in American *hearts*: John Philip Sousa (1854–1932). Born in Washington, DC, Sousa grew up in a cosmopolitan musical family. His mother was Bavarian; his father, born in Spain of Portuguese descent, was a trombonist in the United States Marine Band and studied voice, violin, piano, flute and several brass instruments at a local conservatory.

John Philip Sousa, posing for a publicity photograph

At the age of eight Sousa played violin in a dancing academy; at eleven he organized a dance orchestra. Two years later his father got wind of the boy's plan to run off with a circus band, so he enlisted him, instead, as an apprentice musician in the US Marine Band.

In 1876 Sousa played first violin in the orchestra of the American Centennial Exhibition at Philadelphia, under Jacques Offenbach as guest conductor. Three years later he was music director of a Philadelphia troupe performing Gilbert and Sullivan's *HMS Pinafore*. Typically, as the US had no international copyright agreements at the time, the production was unauthorized, so Sousa made his own orchestration from the piano score.

> Annual tours and recordings for the Edison and Victor labels made Sousa's Band a byword of American music for the next four decades.

In 1880 Sousa, now twenty-six, returned to the US Marine Band, this time as its conductor, and during his twelve-year tenure made it the nation's greatest band. While upgrading the level of performance, he vastly augmented its repertoire with wind arrangements of symphonic and operatic pieces, not to mention new marches of his own, including *Semper Fidelis* (1888) and *The Thunderer* (1889). He would compose 135 marches by 1931.

At the same time Sousa began to establish himself as an operetta composer, with *The Smugglers* (1882). In this field he looked to Sullivan and Offenbach for basic models, with his ear also attuned to the piquant harmonic effects he found in the operas of Gounod and Wagner. But it is significant that Sousa's favorite composer was Mozart, whose scores he repeatedly read for sheer pleasure, according to his biographer, Paul Brierly.

In 1892 Sousa resigned his commission to form Sousa's Band, whose annual tours and recordings for the Edison and Victor labels made it a byword of American music for the next four decades. It was for this stellar ensemble that he wrote many of his concert works and many of his most famous marches, among them *The Liberty Bell* (1893), **Hands Across the Sea** (1899) and the definitive Sousa march, *The Stars and Stripes Forever* (1897).

Unlike most march composers, Sousa achieved his most memorable effect by avoiding the traditional *da capo* – i.e., a return

Scott Joplin

to the opening section after a middle-section trio. Instead, he would present his trio melody softly, then, after a dramatically harmonized bridge passage, emphatically repeat the trio with full band. In concert he would have his cornets, trumpets and trombones walk downstage to give that trio finale even greater "oomph," as in the aforementioned *Hands Across the Sea*.

Sousa and his band made annual tours, including four to Europe. However, it was his tour of 1900 that electrified European audiences by introducing them to American ragtime. If Sousa was the acknowledged "March King," the "King of Ragtime" was Scott Joplin (1868–1917).

Joplin did not invent ragtime. On the contrary, it had been developing since the mid-nineteenth century out of various African- and Caribbean-American influences, some of which had already cropped up in Gottschalk's piano works. At the risk of oversimplification, rag harmony is very straightforward – mainly tonic, dominant, subdominant and secondary dominant chords of major keys. For a slightly sentimental touch, rag harmony also exploits the secondary dominant chords often used at climactic phrases and resolving briefly to minor chords on the sixth (vi) or second (ii) degree of the scale – in C major, you achieve this effect with the progression from an E major seventh chord to A minor,

Ragtime was already gaining ground in dance halls before Joplin made his mark.

or with an A major seventh chord leading to D minor. But these harmonies, already quite commonplace in nineteenth-century music, are not at the heart of ragtime.

Rhythm is the heart. Although Joplin and others wrote ragtime waltzes, ragtime rhythm is usually in duple meter (4/4 or 2/4) steadily established by the deliberately percussive "ump-chink" accompaniment of the stride bass in the left hand. Meanwhile the right-hand melodies are syncopated, or "ragged," producing an infectious tension, with stresses off, or "across," the beat.

Ragtime was already gaining ground in dance halls before Joplin made his mark. In 1897, two years before Joplin's first published composition, the pianist Ben Harvey published a *Ragtime Instructor*, which popularized the style. But it was Joplin's exceptional melodic gift that placed him on the ragtime throne.

Born in northeast Texas, the son of a free-born black woman and a former slave, Scott Joplin had spent much of his youth in Texarkana, on the border of Texas and Arkansas, and although his formal schooling was rudimentary his mother was actively involved in his early education. Moreover, he was surrounded by music early on – not only did members of his family play different instruments, but Joplin made contact with an educated German immigrant, one Julius Weiss, who had been engaged by one of Texarkana's landowners as tutor to his children. Weiss, recognizing young Joplin's gifts, gave him lessons for free and opened him to the repertoire of European art music. As Joplin's biographer Edward I. Berlin observes, Weiss imparted "an appreciation of music as an art as well as an entertainment ... [and] helped shape Joplin's aspirations and ambitions toward high artistic goals." As a young professional, Joplin was an itinerant musician, working at a variety of jobs in different Missouri towns. One job in 1893 took him to Chicago, where he played cornet and led a band at the World's Columbian Exposition.

Between 1894 and 1901 Joplin lived in Sedalia, Missouri, where he played cornet with the African-American Queen City Cornet Band

and started his own dance band as well as the Texas Medley Quartet, a traveling vocal group. He was also composing, and his first two published pieces appeared in 1895: the songs "Please Say You Will" and "A Picture of Her Face." From 1898 Joplin began appearing as pianist at the Black 400 Club and the Maple Leaf Club in St Louis, and he also struck up a relationship with the publisher John Stark, who would eventually publish a significant portion of his music. *Original Rags*, Joplin's first piano rag, appeared under the Stark banner in 1899, having been sold outright, according to the custom of popular music at the time.

Wisely, Joplin sought legal counsel before his next publication, and forged a royalty agreement with Stark thereafter. It was a good move, for his next publication, the **Maple Leaf Rag**, not only immortalized the club where he played but, after a slow start, eventually totted up sales of half a million copies by 1909. Joplin's pre-eminence was thus established in the field. It was followed by a stream of ragtime masterpieces, among them *Peacherine Rag*, *Gladiolus Rag*, *Elite Syncopations*, *The Chrysanthemum* and *The Entertainer*.

Joplin's rhythmic ingenuity and melodic freshness strongly influenced generations of composers, including W.C. Handy, James P. Johnson, Duke Ellington, "Fats" Waller and Eubie Blake, not to mention non-African Americans such as Joseph F. Lamb (a great ragtime composer in his own right), Irving Berlin, George Gershwin and Leonard Bernstein. He also influenced women rag composers, for example May Frances Aufderheide of Indianapolis and Charlotte Blake of Detroit.

No matter how popular it became, especially during the years 1910–15, ragtime was still regarded with disdain by many people not just as "popular music," but as raffish popular music, never quite able to throw off the stigma of brothels and saloons. Nevertheless, Joplin was determined throughout his career to be regarded as a serious composer rather than a mere entertainer, and beyond their surface appeal his piano rags are distinguished by their refined craftsmanship – their careful voice leadings, strong bass lines and wonderfully satisfying harmonic progressions. At the height of his fame Joplin earned considerable money from his piano music.

His greatest ambition, however, was to write for the stage, and he would break his heart and his bankroll in the attempt. A ballet, *The Ragtime Dance*, was staged in Sedalia in 1899. Joplin wrote his first ragtime opera, *A Guest of Honor*, dramatizing educator Booker T. Washington's then-controversial dinner at Theodore Roosevelt's White House in 1902 (Roosevelt had gone out on a political limb by extending such an honor to a black man). The composer toured with the opera in 1903, but had to disband his troupe when the receipts were stolen. The score remained unpublished and was eventually lost. Joplin's move to New York in 1907 was motivated primarily by his hope of finding a publisher for his next opera, *Treemonisha*, which told the story of a black foundling raised by black plantation workers and educated by a sympathetic white woman: at the age of eighteen, Treemonisha, now fully trained as a teacher and leader, opens her neighbors' eyes to the emptiness of superstition and the importance of education.

Apart from its overture, which shows Joplin applying sparkling rag ideas to an extended composition, *Treemonisha* contains several magnificent ragtime numbers – "We're Goin' Around," "Aunt Dinah, Come Blow Your Horn" and the finale, "Marching Onward (A Real Slow Drag)" – woven into a texture of arias, ensembles, choruses and recitatives in an idiom derived from "gay nineties" balladry and gospel song rather than Verdi or Puccini. Yet because of this, *Treemonisha* does indeed sound American in a way that more technically accomplished American operas of the time do not.

Joplin's second ragtime opera, *Treemonisha*, was completed in 1910 but not publicly performed until 1972.

Joplin completed *Treemonisha* in 1910, but no publisher would touch it. So he published the vocal score from his own pocket in 1911, and garnered praise in a review published in the *American Musician and Art Journal*. Nevertheless, none of the intended productions of the opera came to pass. Instead Joplin footed the costs of a single reading with piano accompaniment, in 1911. Two years later the final number was staged in Bayonne, New Jersey, and in 1915 the "Frolic of the Bears" ballet from Act II was given an orchestral playing in New York. Less than two years later Joplin died in a mental hospital, a victim of syphilis. *Treemonisha* was not publicly performed complete until 1972, by the Atlanta Symphony Orchestra, prompted by the publication of Joplin's complete works the previous year. The first full staging was mounted in 1975 by the Houston Grand Opera, which led to Joplin's posthumous Pulitzer Prize in 1976.

Like Joplin, Sousa also sought acclaim as a stage composer. He achieved it to some degree with such works as the aforementioned *The Smugglers, Désirée* (1884) and *The American Maid* (1913), but especially with his operetta *El Capitan* (1896), containing the themes of the eponymous march. With its exotic Peruvian setting (reminiscent of Offenbach's *La Périchole*), its toe-tapping march tunes and sultry waltzes expressing the optimistic *Zeitgeist* of President McKinley's era, *El Capitan* ran for four years in America and six months in England. But while some of the operettas by Sousa enjoyed commercial success in their day, the dean of American operetta from the 1890s through World War I was Victor Herbert (1859–1924).

Dublin-born Herbert was the grandson of the Irish poet, novelist, painter and composer ("The Girl I Left Behind Me") Samuel Lover (1797–1868). After studying cello and composition in Stuttgart he was engaged by the court orchestra there, for which he wrote and performed his first major concert pieces. These included a Suite for Cello and Orchestra, Op. 3, and his First Cello Concerto, Op. 8. In 1886 Herbert arrived in New York as principal cellist in the Metropolitan Opera orchestra, and for several seasons he was a solo cellist with the New York Philharmonic, giving the premiere of his own Second Cello Concerto in 1894. By that time he had succeeded Patrick Gilmore as bandmaster of the 22nd Regiment Band, whose fame rivaled that of Sousa's Band, and for which Herbert wrote several excellent marches. He also served as conductor of the Pittsburgh Symphony Orchestra (from 1898 to 1904), writing several major commissions while there, including the tone poem *Hero and Leander*, the *Auditorium Festival March* and the four-movement **Columbus Suite**. Herbert had composed much of the last score as music for a grand illustrative spectacle dramatizing Columbus's voyage for the 1893 World's Columbian Exposition at Chicago. When the dramatic project folded owing to lack of funding, Herbert put the score in his drawer and later expanded it for its premiere during his final season at Pittsburgh in 1903. The contemplative third movement, "Murmurs of the Sea," is a gentle wash of instrumental color that, while hardly impressionistic in its harmony, shows a side of Herbert's muse far removed from his familiar exuberance.

Ironically, when Herbert had first cast about for an operetta libretto, which in 1894 resulted in *Prince Ananias*, his formidable reputation as a concert artist and composer raised doubts that he could make the jump into the popular vein. But by the undoubted success of his next operettas, *The Wizard of the Nile* (1895), *The Serenade* (1897) and *The Fortune Teller* (1898), he proved the skeptics wrong. From these years through World War I, Herbert reigned as Broadway's leading composer, with almost fifty operettas to his credit. In a field whose contributors were often mere tunesmiths, Herbert used his symphonic craftsmanship to produce solidly constructed ensembles and elaborate finales, with rhythmic charm, interesting counterpoint and expressive harmony. Whereas many Broadway composers used arrangers to orchestrate their work, Herbert did his own orchestrations – something of which he was justifiably proud. Occasionally he got carried away. The symphonic prelude to *Babes in Toyland* (1903) had to be cut before the premiere because, despite its abundance of splendid themes, it was considered too long for a theatre crowd.

As a dramatic composer, Herbert was primarily a melodist whose chief concern with words was that they should provide enough singable vowels. His exceptional melodic gift was at the heart of his success: numbers such as "Toyland" and the ubiquitous "March of the Toys" (*Babes in Toyland*, 1903), "Kiss Me Again" (*Mlle. Modiste*, 1905), "The Streets of New York" (*The Red Mill*, 1906) and "Ah! Sweet Mystery of Life" and "Italian Street Song" (*Naughty Marietta*, 1910) remained classics even after the original operettas were no longer staged. During the 1930s *Naughty Marietta* and *Sweethearts* (1913) were revived, with greatly altered books, as screen vehicles for the immensely popular Hollywood singing team of Jeanette MacDonald and Nelson Eddy, while *Babes in Toyland* was transformed into a memorable film for the comedy team of Laurel and Hardy (1934). Herbert, together with several assistants, also arranged orchestral selections from his operettas, which he frequently programmed on tours with his own Victor Herbert Orchestra. **Selections from "The Red Mill"** provides an engaging sampling of a major Herbert operetta, as well as an accurate idea of the catchy dance rhythms and soaring lyricism that prevailed along the Great White Way before World War I.

Website
track 32
www.naxosbooks.com

The years between 1890 and 1920 witnessed, in addition to operetta, a veritable stampede of popular American songwriters, among them Tin Pan Alley stars such as Charles K. Harris (1867–1930), whose "After the Ball" (1892) sold five million sheet music copies, and Ernest R. Ball (1878–1927), whose string of hits included "When Irish Eyes are Smiling" (1913) and "Will You Love Me in December as You Do in May?" (1905), to lyrics by a future mayor of New York, James J. Walker. There were also writers whose genteel songs were taken up by concert singers for two generations. Among the most popular of these was Carrie Jacobs Bond (1862–1946): an impoverished doctor's widow, Bond began publishing her own songs, including "I Love You Truly" (1906), in her Chicago home and made a fortune. German-trained Ethelbert Nevin (1862–1901) was enormously popular for songs such as "Mighty Lak' a Rose" (1901) and "The Rosary" (1897), not to mention his piano piece "Narcissus" (1891). Oley Speaks (1874–1948) is best remembered for two classic baritone songs, the romantic "Sylvia" (1914) and the jaunty "On the Road to Mandalay" (1907) to Rudyard Kipling's verses. Simpler in musical style than the full-fledged American lieder of MacDowell, Beach, Parker and their circle, these lyrical descendants of Stephen Foster balladry nonetheless offered singers and listeners vivid melodic charm – the waltz refrain of "After the Ball" so strongly evokes the "gay nineties" spirit that Jerome Kern interpolated it in the climactic "New Year's Ball" scene in his 1927 musical play *Show Boat*. Moreover, parlor song composers knew well the thrill of an operatic climax, which is why songs such as "The Rosary" and "On the Road to Mandalay" were sung as often by major concert artists as they were by families enjoying a musical evening around the piano.

Admittedly the heyday of American operetta, with its full-blown romance and operatic singing, also witnessed the rise of musical comedy, with its lighter musical textures, its greater emphasis on dance numbers and its less operatic vocal style. George M. Cohan (1878–1942) wrote some of the best of these. *Little Johnny Jones* (1904) contained such numbers as "Give My Regards to Broadway" and the flag-waving "Yankee Doodle Boy." *George Washington, Jr.* (1906) included "You're a Grand Old Flag," which Cohan sang while literally waving a large American flag. It was a characteristic gesture for the future composer of the morale-boosting song "Over There," which sold a million copies upon its publication in 1917 and won him the Congressional Medal of Honor in 1941.

Despite the competition from musical comedy, operetta held sway on Broadway, and Victor Herbert was gradually joined and then superseded there by two Central European composers who added their own recognizable style to American operetta, the Hungarian Sigmund Romberg (1887–1951) and the Czech Rudolf Friml (1879–1972). Romberg, who had arrived in New York in 1909, was engaged by the Broadway producer J.J. Shubert as staff composer in 1914. By 1917, the year the United States entered the world war against Germany and Austria-Hungary, he had written music for seventeen

> The heyday of American operetta, with its full-blown romance and operatic singing, also witnessed the rise of musical comedy, with its lighter musical textures, its greater emphasis on dance numbers and its less operatic vocal style.

Shubert productions. That year he scored his first box-office triumph with the Viennese-style operetta *Maytime*, which became famous for its waltz duet "Will You Remember" ("Sweetheart, Sweetheart, Sweetheart").

The war had profoundly dampened the public's enthusiasm for operetta, yet Romberg hit his stride during the 1920s with three more of them. *The Student Prince* (1924) relates a bittersweet tale of love and royal duty set in Heidelberg University, and its nostalgic male choruses and moving waltz duets revived the public taste for the Viennese style. *The Desert Song* (1926) was inspired by the political tensions in what was then French Morocco, not to mention the Araby craze set off by Rudolph Valentino's silent films *The Sheik* and *Son of the Sheik*. While the sultry title song – the central love duet – sent female hearts fluttering, Romberg struck a captivating exotic note with the Eastern modal refrain of its big tenor number "If One Flow'r Grows Alone in Your Garden." *The New Moon* (1928) revolves around French colonists in Louisiana

The morale-boosting song "Over There" sold a million copies upon its publication in 1917 and won George M. Cohan the Congressional Medal of Honor in 1941.

at the time of the French Revolution. Romberg's pleasant mixture of waltzes, rousing march numbers and swooning romantic climaxes – seasoned with appropriate local color – kept these three scores in revivals for decades, in Hollywood and especially in regional and even major opera companies.

Friml had some more modernist ideas than Romberg, especially in his use of a kind of chromatic harmony later exploited by Hollywood composers, in particular for science fiction thrillers such as *Frankenstein*. But Friml's track record was less consistent than Romberg's. A former student of Dvořák at the Prague Conservatory, he toured Europe and America as pianist for his classmate, violinist Jan Kubelík, for ten years before deciding to settle in New York in 1906 as a concert pianist and symphonic composer. A few years later he was mustered into service to compose the score of an operetta already slated for production when the Italian diva Emma Trentini had a falling out with the contracted composer of the piece, Victor Herbert. The resulting work, *The Firefly*, was an overwhelming hit at its premiere in 1912.

Friml continued to compose Broadway operettas through the war years, but only after 1920 did he truly rise to pre-eminence with two pieces that became classics of the genre, *Rose-Marie* (1924) and *The Vagabond King* (1925). The former had ranks of crimson-jacketed Mounties (Royal Canadian Mounted Police) singing against vast painted backdrops of the Canadian Rockies, as well as forty chorus girls costumed as totem poles for the rhythmic "Totem Tom-Tom" number. Its title song was a jaunty foxtrot, whose brief phrases were refreshingly American-sounding at the time, while its central love duet, "Indian Love Call" was charged with chromatic harmony suggestive of the great American outdoors. *Rose-Marie* became a hardy musical symbol of operetta make-believe, especially after singers MacDonald and Eddy starred in a Hollywood screen version in 1936. *The Vagabond King*, loosely based on the escapades of the medieval French beggar-poet François Villon, had a particularly throbbing score of high romance and a string of memorable numbers – "Someday," "Only a Rose," "Valse Huguette," "Love Me Tonight" and the stirring "Song of the Vagabonds." After 1930, by which time operetta's day had ended on Broadway, Friml went to Hollywood to write film scores and oversee screen versions of his earlier successes.

Owing to their sentimentality, to the frank silliness of most of their libretti (not one of the imitators of W.S. Gilbert ever came close to matching the linguistic dexterity or sense of humor that made Gilbert's topsy-turvydom work so masterfully) and to their quasi-Viennese emphasis on waltz, polka and march rhythms, the American operettas of Sousa, Herbert, Romberg, Friml and such lesser lights as Reginald de Koven (*Robin Hood*, 1890), Gustav Luders (*The Prince of Pilsen*, 1903) and Ivan Caryll (*The Pink Lady*, 1911) come off as period pieces to modern listeners. Nevertheless, they are period pieces of exceptional charm when performed with respect for their own aesthetics and listened to with an understanding of the world for which they were originally created.

Friml's "Indian Love Call" was charged with chromatic harmony suggestive of the great American outdoors.

An important stylistic difference between operetta and musical comedy is that the former calls for classically trained voices and emphasizes waltzes and other European rhythms, while the latter calls for a less operatic singing style and contains more modern dance rhythms. And where operetta mingled songs, ensembles and choruses, musical comedy tends to capitalize on song-and-dance numbers. Of the composers and songwriters who contributed to the continuing rise of the Broadway musical during the 1920s, one of the most distinctive was Vincent Youmans (1898–1946), with *Wildflower* (1923), *No, No, Nanette* (1925) and *Hit the Deck* (1927). However, the great transitional figure of this period was Jerome Kern (1885–1945), who had collaborated with the comic novelist P.G. Wodehouse on a series of witty, lightweight musical comedies such as *Very Good Eddie* (1915). Kern created history in 1927 with the production of *Show Boat*, based on Edna Ferber's novel. Apart from looking racism in the face (unprecedented on the musical stage), *Show Boat* departed from the usual Broadway practice in which a show's songs and dances often had little dramatic underpinning. In Kern's score, and Oscar Hammerstein II's libretto, every musical element sprang from the plot and characters. And the strength of those musical elements has remained undimmed by time. Neither an operetta nor a musical comedy, *Show Boat*, with its genuinely serious story line, effectively inaugurates the genre of the American *musical*.

> Neither an operetta nor a musical comedy, *Show Boat*, with its genuinely serious story line, effectively inaugurates the genre of the American *musical*.

Kern had a keen ear for interesting turns of phrase and novel harmony, which he used deftly in later works such as *The Cat and the Fiddle* (1931), *Music in the Air* (1932) and *Roberta* (1933), all of which boast numbers that entered the proverbial "American Song Book" as standards – "The Night Was Made for Love," "I've Told Ev'ry Little Star" and "The Song Is You" among them. But the qualities that make his Broadway shows of the 1930s so delectable to hear today often proved somewhat too cerebral for Depression-era audiences. Moreover, the Depression itself put a damper on Broadway that forced many fine shows to close after disappointing runs. So, when Hollywood beckoned, Kern found greater success writing scores and songs for such films as *Swing Time* (1936), with Fred Astaire and Ginger Rogers.

George Gershwin (1898–1937) and his lyricist brother Ira (1896–1983) also went to Hollywood when the atmosphere back east soured for them. But through the early 1930s Broadway was eager to savor their distinctive work, which mingled literary wit and a novel deployment of trendy jazz formulas. At the age of sixteen George Gershwin was plugging popular songs as a pianist in New York music shops. At nineteen he wrote his first major hit song, "Swanee" – which sold over a million sheet-music copies and 2.4 million phonograph records. Between 1920 and 1924 he contributed numbers to the annual *George White's Scandals* revues,

Jerome Kern at the piano with Oscar Hammerstein II

thereafter writing the complete scores to a raft of hit shows, among them *Lady, Be Good!* (1924), *Tip-toes* (1925), *Strike Up the Band* (1927), *Girl Crazy* (1930) and *Of Thee I Sing* (1931). The last, a political satire, was the first musical to win a Pulitzer Prize, albeit only for the book, by George S. Kaufman, Morrie Ryskind and Ira Gershwin – the Pulitzer committee didn't believe that music should be included in what was then strictly a literary award. At the same time Gershwin was writing concert music that incorporated jazz syncopations and "blue" harmonic

At the age of sixteen George Gershwin was plugging popular songs as a pianist in New York music shops. At nineteen he wrote his first major hit song, "Swanee."

progressions while assiduously attending concerts offering music from the Renaissance to his own time. His labor yielded a crop of scores that are standard concert repertoire today, notably the landmark *Rhapsody in Blue* (1924), the Piano Concerto in F (1925), **An American in Paris** (1928) and the rumba-based *Cuban Overture* (1932).

The genesis of Gershwin's *Rhapsody* illustrates the close circles that have always characterized New York's concert scene. In 1923, Paul Whiteman, then the leading jazz orchestra leader but formerly principal violist in the Victor Herbert Orchestra, planned a national tour called "Experiment in Modern Music," commencing with a concert at New York's Aeolian Hall. Whiteman invited a number of leading and promising figures to contribute works, among them Victor Herbert, Irving Berlin and Gershwin, who subsequently said that the rhapsody "began as a purpose, not a plan":

> At this stage of the piece I was summoned to Boston for the premiere of *Sweet Little Devil*. I had already done some work on the rhapsody. It was on that train, with its steely rhythms, its rattlety-bang that is so often stimulating to a composer … I suddenly heard – and even saw on paper – the complete construction of the rhapsody from beginning to end. No new themes came to me, but I worked on the thematic material already in my mind, and tried to conceive the composition as a whole. I heard it as a musical kaleidoscope of America, of our vast melting pot, of our national pep, of our blues, our metropolitan madness. By the time I reached Boston, I had a definite *plot* of the piece, as distinguished from its actual substance.

The first concert took place on the snowy afternoon of February 12, 1924, before an audience that included among the musical luminaries Fred and Adele Astaire, Jascha Heifetz, Fritz Kreisler, Rachmaninov, Sousa and Stravinsky, not to mention every major music critic. It was a long program, made physically uncomfortable for the audience by the failure of the hall's ventilation system. Over two hours later, perspiring listeners began to leave after Herbert's *Suite of Serenades* – music from a composer uncomfortable with jazz, notwithstanding

Gershwin entertains the Shall We Dance *team: left to right,*
Hermes Pan (dance director), Fred Astaire, Mark Sandrich (film director),
Ginger Rogers, George, Ira, Nathaniel Shilkret (RCA Victor music director)

the delicious sloe-eyed saxophone melody of its "Cuban" movement. Then, as dispirited applause rustled through the stuffy auditorium, Gershwin strode out to the piano and glanced at Whiteman, and a lone clarinet sounded a low trill, ascending like a rocket to a slurred climax that has become one of the most familiar concert openers in the orchestral repertoire. Stopped in their tracks, people at the exits hastened back to their seats, and by the final enigmatic chord *Rhapsody in Blue* had entered the American musical consciousness.

George Gershwin's iconic status today, however, doesn't reflect accurately his equivocal position in the closing years of his life, which, despite his outward wealth and celebrity, were beset by personal disappointment, exacerbated by increasingly pronounced symptoms of a fatal brain tumor. His biographer Joan Peyser observes that "Gershwin's career began to plunge in 1932. ... From this time on, George experienced nothing but failure as a composer ... During that period his creative work met with severe criticism: *Second Rhapsody* (1932), *Cuban Overture, Pardon My English* (1933), *Let 'Em Eat Cake* (1933), *Variations on I Got Rhythm* (1934)." Added to this was the harsh criticism accorded *Porgy and Bess* after its New York Premiere in 1935 (discussed in the next chapter).

In fact, because Hollywood's view at the time was that George Gershwin's winning days might well have been behind him, the offers he and Ira Gershwin received from the film studios were considerably less than what they had requested. But today, when the warm and satisfying E major saxophone theme in *Rhapsody in Blue* soars through a concert hall, or you hear the irresistible melody of a Gershwin song such as "Swanee" or "Love Walked In" or the flood of ideas in *An American in Paris*, the harsher realities of Gershwin's career only lend poignancy to the more immediate reality of his musical legacy.

9 The Earlier Struggles of American Opera

In nineteenth-century America, audiences with any musical sophistication were concentrated in a few major cities, and, with the exception of francophone New Orleans, where French opera ruled the boards, these audiences interpreted the term "opera" to mean *Italian* opera. The idea of American opera was, ironically, foreign to their thinking. But, as we have seen, stalwarts such as the critic-composer William Henry Fry strove to establish an American operatic school. Fry modeled his work on that of Bellini and Donizetti, founding his libretti on European literature and drama. He was followed on this path by such figures as the German-born Julius Eichberg (1824– 1893), whose opera buffa *The Doctor of Alcantara* (1862) actually enjoyed some success on the American circuit, and by a Chicago musician unpromisingly named Silas Gamaliel Pratt (1846–1916). The composer of a sprawling grand opera, *Zenobia, Queen of Palmyra* (1882), Pratt combined a taste for spectacle with so spectacular a sense of his own importance that, upon meeting the composer of *The Ring of the Nibelungen*, he declared, "Herr Wagner, you are the Silas G. Pratt of Germany."

From 1850 through roughly 1920, most leading American composers tried their hand at opera, resulting in a melancholy treasury of works that have rarely, if ever, come off the shelf since they were new: George Frederick Bristow's *Rip Van Winkle* (New York, 1855; the first noteworthy attempt at opera on an American subject); Harry Lawrence Freeman's *The Martyr* (Seattle, 1893; the first known performance of an opera by an African American); Walter Damrosch's *The Scarlet Letter* (Boston, 1896); Frederick Converse's *The Pipe of Desire* (Boston,1906; the first American opera performed at the Metropolitan Opera, in 1907); Victor Herbert's *Natoma* (Philadelphia, 1911); Horatio Parker's *Mona* (the first American opera to be premiered at the Metropolitan, 1912); Mary Carr Moore's *Narcissa* (Seattle, 1912); Herbert's one-act *Madeleine* (Metropolitan Opera, 1914); Reginald de Koven's *The Canterbury Pilgrims* (Metropolitan Opera, 1917; by all accounts a little Chaucer and water with music by an operetta composer well past his prime); Henry Hadley's *Azora, the Daughter of Montezuma* (Chicago, 1917); Charles Wakefield Cadman's *Shanewis, the Robin Woman* (Metropolitan Opera, 1918); Hadley's *Cleopatra's Night* (Metropolitan Opera, 1920). And there were others.

> From 1850 through 1920, most leading American composers tried their hand at opera, resulting in a melancholy treasury of works that have rarely, if ever, come off the shelf.

Conventional wisdom suggests that these operas failed because they were somehow flawed. Indeed, many of them were composed to impossibly poor libretti whose stilted "operatic" English was hard to sing and even harder to understand. Herbert's **Natoma** exemplifies this. Offered a tale of an American Indian princess's unrequited love for an American lieutenant in Spanish California (she conveniently becomes a nun at the end), Herbert approached the project, however naïvely, with utmost seriousness. He stated:

Website
track 33
www.naxosbooks.com

> I have composed all of *Natoma's* music, at least the greater part of it, out of fragments of Indian music, which I have collected and studied for some time past. ... I have fashioned melodies by using fragments of this and that Indian theme. ... Indian music is not harmonized, and the moment a musician harmonizes it he has made it into something different. ... In [one] instance, the "Dagger Dance," I have introduced an Indian tune almost verbatim, of course with my own harmonization.

Indeed, the tom-tom-driven "Dagger Dance," which Herbert incorporated in the climax of his orchestral suite from the opera, was quickly adopted by legions of silent-film pianists as vivid musical background to Indian scenes in countless Westerns. Nevertheless, between its racially patronizing melodramatic plot and risible, highfalutin language, Joseph Redding's libretto doomed *Natoma* to eventual oblivion. Another problem was that, however lovely Herbert's music, and however much it strives for the grand operatic gesture, it remains the music of an operetta composer adept at addressing the requirements of entertainment rather than the deeper musical, dramatic and psychological demands of opera in the era of Puccini, Debussy and Richard Strauss.

Yet even composers better equipped to write serious operas were faced at the time with a nation poorly prepared to receive them. The sprawling, egalitarian United States did not have Europe's well-established network of royal, princely and otherwise state-supported opera houses, which offered composers and their publishers a ready outlet for marketing and distribution of new operas. On the contrary, the so-called opera houses in American towns, from Ashtabula, Ohio, to Leadville, Colorado, rarely housed opera. The silver kings and mercantile princes who erected these civic ornaments chose to call them "opera houses" instead of the more accurate "meeting houses," which sounded churchy, or "theatres," which sounded downright immoral at a time when, to many folk, the acting profession still implied licentiousness.

In 1933 the Met produced two American operas that showed promise of staying power: Howard Hanson's *Merry Mount* and Louis Gruenberg's *The Emperor Jones*.

Moreover, American audiences and impresarios were unable to decide if they really wanted to support American opera or not. The disappointment suffered by the versatile George Whitefield Chadwick is a case in point. Having already composed an operetta, *Tabasco* (1893–4), a fluffy Oriental send-up, he resolved to write not just a serious opera but something divorced from the usual historical pageantry and completely up to date. Chadwick's *The Padrone* (1912) is a verismo opera concerning poor Italian immigrants oppressed by a Mafia bully. In preparation he had made a close study of Puccini and late Verdi scores, as well as those of Leoncavallo and Mascagni, and in order to ensure a sense of genuine contemporary realism he had intended that the Italian characters should sing in Italian while the Americans should sing in English. Ultimately the entire libretto was written in English – his first disappointment. Then the opera was rejected by the Metropolitan. Then Chadwick's hopes were completely dashed when a possible production in Chicago came to naught. *The Padrone* had to wait, in fact, until 1997 for a premiere, which was given by the New England Conservatory Opera Theatre. According to the American musicologist and biographer of Chadwick, Victor Fell Yellin, "Had it been produced [in its original time] it might well have pointed the way to a new manner of operatic composition in the USA, one making the most of Americans' traditional directness and realistic outlook."

During the 1920s and 1930s, the Metropolitan, under its dutiful general manager Giulio Gatti-Casazza, continued to mount operas by Americans. Critic, author and composer Deems Taylor provided *The King's Henchman* (1927), to Edna St Vincent Millay's Anglo-Irish treatment of the Tristan story, and *Peter Ibbetson* (1931), adapted from George du Maurier's proto-psychological novel. The latter, in which the character of the evil Colonel Ibbetson gave baritone Lawrence Tibbett plenty of scenery to chew, scored enough success for the Met to revive

> The most durable American opera to appear during the 1930s was *Porgy and Bess*, Gershwin's most ambitious stage work.

it in three successive seasons. In 1933 the Met produced two more American operas that showed promise of staying power: Howard Hanson's *Merry Mount*, based on Hawthorne, and Louis Gruenberg's *The Emperor Jones*, based on Eugene O'Neill's play about a murderous Pullman porter who crowns himself ruler of a Caribbean island. Again, both were vehicles for Tibbett, who played the title role of the latter in blackface and made commercial recordings of scenes from both.

The Metropolitan was the most prestigious operatic venue in the United States at that time, but it wasn't the only one, and the 1930s witnessed premieres of a number of American operas unconnected to the old "brown brick brewery on West 39th Street." Among them were Gian Carlo Menotti's early comedy *Amelia Goes to the Ball* (1937) and his opera for radio *The Old Maid and the Thief*

(1939), Douglas Moore's witty *The Devil and Daniel Webster* (1939) and Marc Blitzstein's strident *The Cradle Will Rock* (1938). Menotti's *Amelia* proved so successful when it took a bow at Philadelphia's Curtis Institute of Music that the Met produced it the following year on a double bill with Strauss's *Elektra*. After Blitzstein's anti-establishment piece was dropped by the government agency that had commissioned it, John Houseman and Orson Welles produced it in a tiny downtown New York theatre where, despite an injunction against performance, it played over 100 times.

Above all, the most durable American opera to appear during the 1930s was *Porgy and Bess*, Gershwin's most ambitious stage work. Adapted from the novel *Porgy* by Dubose Heyward, it was conceived for a cast of black singers at a time when segregation was still rampant in the US and white entertainers in blackface were still

The famed Blevins Davis-Robert Breen touring company of Gershwin's Porgy and Bess *on a world tour, in Dallas, Texas, June 1952. Leontyne Price as Bess (with money in her garter), Cab Calloway as Sportin' Life (in white shirt), and William Warfield as Porgy (behind the man in the striped shirt)*

acceptable on stage. But though Gershwin and his brother intended it to be performed by a major opera company, no major opera company of the time would touch it. So after tryouts in Boston, *Porgy and Bess* opened on Broadway in 1935, to a critical scourging. "[Gershwin] has not completely formed his style as an operatic composer," wrote Olin Downes of *The New York Times*. "The style is at one moment of opera and another of operetta or sheer Broadway entertainment." Other New York critics took an equally jaundiced view. However, no lash was more biting than that of Virgil Thomson, whose diatribe, published in *Modern Music*, stooped to outright anti-Semitism:

> Gershwin has not and never did have any power of sustained musical development … the material is … a piquant but highly unsavory stirring-up together of Israel, Africa and the Gaelic Isles. … It is clear, by now, that Gershwin hasn't learned the business of being a serious composer. … I do not like fake folklore, nor fidgety accompaniments, nor bittersweet harmony, nor six-part choruses, nor gefilte fish orchestration.

Despite the reviews, such songs as "Summertime," "I Got Plenty o' Nuttin'" and "It Ain't Necessarily So," and the glowing duet "Bess, You Is My Woman Now" became extraordinarily popular and kept the opera alive until later generations could accord it the respect it deserved.

10 Modernism Elbows its Way into the Concert Hall

In 1913 the New York Armory Show brought European avant-garde art to American eyes for the first time. Suddenly, the American Renaissance, the "City Beautiful" movement, the elegant paintings of Sargent, the heroic statuary of Daniel Chester French were all being derided as old fashioned. Then World War I rang the death knell of America's late-nineteenth-century culture. In its wake followed the "lost generation," disillusioned by the carnage of the battlefield and seeking a good time. Women's hemlines rose; men's high collars fell and lost their starch. Fast cars were on the roads, hot jazz in the air. Art deco was the rage, its streamlined geometric motifs applied to the new skyscrapers that defined the modern American cityscape. American artists, writers and musicians flocked to Paris, where they marveled at the exciting work of Europeans such as Pablo Picasso and Georges Braque. The art world continued in the state of flux in which it had been since the prewar decades – cubism gave way to the dada movement, abstraction grew in dominance, and in 1925 the first group exhibition of surrealist painting was organized in Paris. Society hungered for novelty, for anything that broke with the past, and a rising generation of American composers embraced modernism with all the energy of youth making its radical point.

Dadaism exerted a considerable influence on modernist music during the early 1920s. Its compelling negative energy had begun shaking up the fine arts around 1915. Starting in Zurich, then spreading quickly to Paris, New York and finally Berlin, dadaism was essentially an intellectual cry of anguish and cynicism over the devastation of World War I. The name "dada," French for "hobby-horse," was said to have been chosen at random from a dictionary that fell open at that word. Dadaism's progenitors, among them the artists Marcel Duchamp, Max Ernst, Hans Arp and Georg Grosz, the Romanian poet Tristan Tzara and the German writers Richard Hülsenbeck and Hugo Ball, deliberately embraced sarcastic notions of irrationality, inversion and anti-aestheticism, seeking to undermine the traditional values of artistic culture and social order. For example, Duchamp, already notorious for his 1914 abstract painting *Nude Descending a Staircase*, shocked viewers with his dada series of "ready-mades," in which commonplace, mass-produced objects were arbitrarily raised to the level of works of sculpture (such as his scandalous urinal, which he exhibited in New York in 1916 with the signature "Mutt"). In literature, dadaism asserted instinct over intelligent expression – a single word or a succession of words could mean anything the writer or reader wanted, or nothing at all. And, plunging into this cultural foment, radical composers gleefully turned American concert music on its ear. Remember, during this decade composers such as Chadwick and Converse were still active.

> Society hungered for novelty, for anything that broke with the past, and a rising generation of American composers embraced modernism with all the energy of youth making its radical point.

Among the leading musical radicals were Henry Cowell and the remarkably long-lived Leo Ornstein. Ornstein (1892/3–2002) literally shoved his way through the frontiers of what was regarded as acceptable listening around 1910. Born in Ukraine, the son of a Jewish cantor, he had studied at the St Petersburg Conservatory before emigrating with his parents to New York in 1907. After further studies at the Institute of Musical Art (the future Juilliard School) he made his New York debut as pianist in 1911, performing standard repertoire to great acclaim. Two years later he began playing modern music by composers then unfamiliar in America: Debussy, Ravel, Scriabin, Bartók, Schoenberg, Stravinsky. He also began programming his own modernist

> Radical composers gleefully turned American concert music on its ear.

Website
track 157
www.naxosbooks.com

Website
track 34
www.naxosbooks.com

compositions, *Dwarf Suite, Suicide in an Airplane* and *Wild Men's Dance (Danse sauvage)*. **Wild Men's Dance** (ca. 1913), with its infectious spinning dance rhythms, percussive effects and steely dissonance, raised eyebrows and tempers among conservative critics, while modernist sensibilities hailed Ornstein as an American counterpart of Schoenberg and Stravinsky. In the programmatic **Suicide in an Airplane** (ca. 1913) the sparks of dissonance flash up and down the keyboard, suggesting the troubled mind of the pilot, underpinned by a relentless bass trill evoking the drone of the airplane engine. Yet, instead of a final crash, the drone gradually fades to silence at the end, leaving us to wonder if the suicidal pilot has relented or if the doomed aircraft has simply passed out of earshot. Either way, a public familiar with Romantic opera's suicides by poison, stabbing and pistol would have found Ornstein's title, with its implication of a brave new machinery of death, deliberately startling.

Ornstein acquired considerable celebrity through a concert tour of Europe (1913–14), where he met modernist leaders such as the formidable pianist, composer and teacher Ferruccio Busoni, several of whose powerful Bach transcriptions Ornstein programmed at a London concert, together with some Schoenberg and several of his own works. After giving further concerts in New York, Ornstein achieved cult status for the next decade. He became famous for his trademark tone clusters, produced by striking groups of keys with the fist or forearm, which he introduced in his compositions around 1915. Such was his position in modern American music that at the early age of twenty-seven he became the subject of a major biography and analysis of his work, published in 1918. In 1922 Ornstein stopped making regular concert appearances (with such notable exceptions as his performance as soloist in the premiere of his Piano Concerto with the Philadelphia Orchestra). He redirected his energies to teaching, initially as head of the piano department at the Philadelphia Music Academy, and later at his own Ornstein School of Music. Moreover, like Richard Strauss, who retreated from modernism after his expressionist opera *Elektra* (1909), Ornstein began to move away from the hard-line avant-gardism of his earlier works. In an interview he once observed that "[my] Op. 31 [the Sonata for Violin and Piano of 1914] had brought music just to the very edge, and as I … have no suicidal tendencies at all, I simply drew back and said, 'beyond that lies complete chaos.'"

Two new strains of music began to take shape in Ornstein's oeuvre. The first movement of his **Fourth Piano Sonata** (1924) typifies his new work in a more Romantic or impressionist vein reminiscent of Rachmaninov or Scriabin, with richly sonorous chords, cascading passagework and a memorable lyricism. Similarly, his Piano Quintet (1927) is firmly tonal and deeply emotional.

Website
track 35
www.naxosbooks.com

With Ornstein's retirement from the concert platform, both he and his music faded from the scene until Vivian Perlis and several other scholars rediscovered him during the 1970s. His Third String Quartet (1976) and Seventh Piano Sonata (1988) exemplify the third strain in his musical output, which combines his later Romanticism with the dissonance of his earliest work. The Seventh Sonata, together with the Eighth (1990), contains exceptionally vigorous writing for any composer, let alone one well past ninety.

Slightly younger than Ornstein, Henry Cowell (1897–1965), an experimental composer, was himself the result of his parents' experimentation in non-traditional education. His individuality had been set from the start by his parents, both writers of a nonconformist bent who lived in a rural cottage in Menlo Park outside San Francisco and divorced when Cowell was six. As Cowell had revealed his musical talent in early childhood, his parents started him off learning the violin, intending that he should develop into a child prodigy. Instead he developed a tic from overwork, and his violin lessons were suspended. He and his mother eventually settled in Kansas, where she continued to teach him at home (he spent only a brief time in public school), though they returned to Menlo Park in 1910. Meanwhile, the adolescent Cowell earned money as, among other things, a collector of wildflowers. Between his mother's schooling and his jobs, Cowell developed a vast general knowledge, especially of botany. In 1912 he managed to scrape together $60 to buy a used upright piano and began experimenting with non-traditional methods of playing it.

Reviews for Cowell's debut as a composer-pianist in 1914 persuaded his father that he needed more formal training, and he was enrolled later that year in the University of California, Berkeley. There he encountered the composer and ethnomusicologist Charles Seeger (1886–1979), future husband of composer Ruth Crawford Seeger and father of the folksinger and songwriter Pete Seeger. The freshness and freedom of Seeger's ideas were a revelation to Cowell, while Seeger found in Cowell "the first brilliant talent of my teaching experience." Their intellectual relationship yielded, among other things, the first draft of Cowell's book, *New Musical Resources*, containing what he termed his "theory of musical relativity." Finally published in 1930, it became fundamental reading for several generations of avant-garde composers in America and Europe, among them John Cage, Lou Harrison, Conlon Nancarrow and Karlheinz Stockhausen. It was in this text that Cowell named and defined tone clusters as elements of musical composition:

> In order to distinguish groups built on seconds from groups built on thirds or fifths [i.e., chords], they will hereafter be called tone-clusters. Tone-clusters, then, are chords built from major and minor seconds, which in turn may be derived from the upper reaches of the overtone series and have, therefore, a sound foundation. In building up clusters from seconds, it will be seen that since both major and minor seconds are used, just as major and minor thirds are used in the familiar systems in thirds, there is an exact resemblance between the two systems, and the same amount of potential variety in each.
>
> ... A cluster, obviously, must be measured to show its size, and this may easily be done as intervals are measured, using the distance between the outside members of the clusters. Thus, a cluster of three consecutive chromatic tones may be called a cluster major second, a cluster of four consecutive tones may be called a cluster minor third, etc. The important tones, the ones that are most plainly heard, are those of the outer edges of a given cluster,

just as we hear best the soprano and bass line of a four-part chord. Given a series of clusters of the same interval, we can conveniently designate them by the names of their lowest tones.

Though Cowell is credited with inventing the term, he used the tone cluster in a different way than did Ornstein or Ives, or Bartók, who wrote Cowell in 1923 to ask permission to use clusters in his own work. For example, Cowell's piano piece **Deep Color** (1938), which was inspired by the purple tint of Irish vales, presents an essentially tonal, anthem-like melody in the treble above a sonorous chordal accompaniment in which he deploys deep-bass tone clusters to give a magisterial percussive effect. These echoing bass strokes, combined with the running contrapuntal line at the climax of the piece, suggest something midway between the finale of Mussorgsky's original piano version of *Pictures at an Exhibition* and the resounding bass-drum strokes in Copland's *Fanfare for the Common Man*. Cowell also used clusters in non-keyboard works, such as the Fifth String Quartet (1956) and his Fifth (1948) and Sixth (1952) Symphonies (of an eventual twenty – he was working on his twenty-first symphony on his deathbed). In his constant search for new colors, Cowell was also an early proponent of sounding the actual piano

Website
track 36
www.naxosbooks.com

Henry Cowell playing tone clusters on the piano; Berlin, 1923

strings by plucking them with the fingers or striking them with different objects. In the first movement, "The Banshee," of his **Irish Suite**, for string piano and small orchestra (first performed in 1929), Cowell directs the performer to stroke the length of the bass-register piano strings (hence the term "string piano"). Because these heavy strings are coiled in metal wire for strength, their surface is like a rat-tail file, and stroking them produces a truly hair-raising effect, in keeping with this suggestion of Irish domestic ghosts (banshees) that wail outside a house wherein someone is about to die.

Cowell launched himself in earnest as a champion of ultra-modernist music, playing his own compositions in concerts and making a series of five European tours between 1923 and 1932. Not surprisingly, his tone clusters and unorthodox use of the piano and of other instruments outraged mainstream audiences and conservative critics. "He assailed the innards of a grand piano," wrote a Boston critic in 1929, who concluded: "Many of the sounds which Mr. Cowell achieved last evening might be duplicated with a tack hammer and any convenient bit of unupholstered furniture." In Berlin, in 1932, one critic dismissed his *Synchrony* as "a huge musical paste" (*ein gewaltiger Tonkleister*), while another snidely asked why Cowell limited himself only to his fists and forearms to play his tone clusters, when "with one's behind one can cover many more notes!" But, while the mainstream jeered, Schoenberg and other leading European modernists welcomed Cowell into their midst with considerable enthusiasm.

While the mainstream jeered, Schoenberg and other leading European modernists welcomed Henry Cowell into their midst with considerable enthusiasm.

Cowell also dedicated himself to furthering the cause of other American composers, founding in 1925 the New Music Society of California and two years later the quarterly journal *New Music*.

His own continuing stream of new compositions eventually reached over 900 works embracing every mode of expression, and, to the observation that he was not developing a recognizable personal voice, his answer was that he deliberately rejected a consistent style. From the intense chromaticism of his First String Quartet (1916) he went on to make use of extremely complex rhythm in his *Quartet Romantic* (1917; two flutes, violin, viola) and simultaneous meters (polymeter or polytempo) in his *Quartet Euphometric* (1919; string quartet). A decade later his *Polyphonic*, for small orchestra (1930), explores intricate dissonant counterpoint. The increasing complexity of his musical thinking prompted him to experiment with novel ways of notating his thoughts and of arranging the actual structure of his works. For *A Composition* (1925) he uses graphic notation (literally written on a graph), while *Ensemble* (1924, revised 1956) incorporates a degree of improvisation. His experimental thinking was boundless, leading him to collaborate with the inventor-musician Leon Theremin on developing the Rhythmicon, an instrument that could play simultaneously sixteen different rhythms. He put it to very effective use with orchestra in the 1931 composition *Rhythmicana*. Cowell also developed a healthy interest in non-Western and folk music, from Appalachia to Tahiti. For instance, apart from his *Irish Suite*, this grandson of a dean of Kildare Cathedral in Ireland incorporated his reflections upon Irish folk music into *The Fairy Answer* (ca. 1929), alternating a hymn-like

Cartoon drawing of Henry Cowell

melody with echo-like responses produced by stroking the piano strings *glissando* with the backs of the fingers, which produces a

Even while he sought new means of expression, Cowell never lost his sense of humor.

soft, distant sound, akin to that of an autoharp or zither. Cowell had been well acquainted with Chinese, Japanese and other musics of the Pacific Rim since childhood, and his studies of Balinese gamelan music and Indian music theory during the early 1930s resulted in his article "Towards Neo-Primitivism" (published in 1933) as well as the String Quartet No. 4, "United" (1936), in which he incorporated ideas gleaned from world music in an effort to "build a new music particularly related to our own century."

Yet, even while he sought new means of expression, Cowell never lost his sense of humor, as attested in his *Three Anti-Modernist Songs* (1938), which he wrote during his four years in San Quentin Prison following a conviction on a morals charge in 1936. (A bisexual, he had a number of liaisons with men before his happy and intellectually fruitful marriage to the female ethnomusicologist Sidney Hawkins Robertson.) Yet even behind bars Cowell devoted considerable energy organizing a music education program for his fellow inmates.

An inspiring and devoted teacher, Cowell held positions variously at the New School for Social Research, Columbia University and the Peabody Conservatory, and accepted numerous guest lectureships, his students running the musical gamut from John Cage and Lou Harrison to Burt Bacharach.

George Antheil (1900–1959) was similarly an iconoclast, motivated by Oscar Wilde's youthful craving to be "famous, and if not famous, notorious." At the age of twenty-two he toured Europe as a pianist, outraging his listeners with ultra-modern works whose very titles (*Airplane Sonata*, *Sonata Sauvage*, etc.) were calculated to shock and to attract publicity. In 1923 he settled in Paris, quickly joining the circle of Cocteau, Joyce, Man Ray, Satie and other avant-garde leaders and creating a furor at his debut that October: "Rioting broke out," he wrote in his 1945 autobiography *The Bad Boy of Music*. "I remember Man Ray punching somebody in the nose in the front row. Marcel Duchamp was arguing loudly with

George Antheil climbing up the Shakespeare & Co. bookshop in Paris in the 1920s

somebody else in the second row. In a box nearby, Eric Satie was shouting, 'What precision! What precision!' and applauding ..." Antheil's first Parisian score was the **Symphony for Five Instruments** (1923), strongly influenced by Stravinsky's *Petrushka* and *Ragtime*. The cheeky gallop finale offers an amusing idea of his style at the time.

Website
track 158

www.naxosbooks.com

In 1926 Antheil unveiled his most famous work, *Ballet mécanique*, a rhythmically zesty suite adapted from his score for a film by the painter Fernand Léger. With its eight pianos, large battery of percussion, electric buzzers and droning airplane propellers, it sparked the fury he hoped for, and he was hailed again as music's *enfant terrible*. But when he embraced neoclassicism for his 1927 Piano Concerto, Paris abandoned him. Later that

George Antheil was an iconoclast motivated by Oscar Wilde's youthful craving to be "famous, and if not famous, notorious."

year the New York premiere of *Ballet mécanique* at Carnegie Hall backfired. Despite the uproar and notoriety, Antheil was rejected. In America his obscurity lasted until the 1940s, though the 1930 premiere of his jazz-flavored opera *Transatlantic* in Frankfurt attracted wide European attention.

A move to Hollywood in 1936 finally restored Antheil's musical health. Stimulated by his success as a film composer, he completed his Fourth Symphony in 1942, and its premiere by the NBC Symphony under Leopold Stokowski in 1944 put him back in a favorable light. By now his idiom combined elements of neoclassicism, Romanticism and impressionism with a bracing harmonic vocabulary. Meanwhile he pursued a number of non-musical projects, including the design of a torpedo device in collaboration with the film star Hedy Lamarr.

Antheil maintained his more expressive idiom in such later works as the Serenade for String Orchestra (1948), the Piano Sonata No. 4 (1948), the *Songs of Experience* (1948) and *Volpone* (1949) – the most well received of four operas he wrote through the early 1950s. During his final years he regularly composed film and television scores. Yet, however mellowed he had become in Hollywood, Antheil never quite relinquished his iconoclastic streak: in 1953 he revised his *Ballet mécanique*, reducing the instrumentation. This time the score was received as merely passé, though half a century later it

Photograph by Malcolm Crowthers

80th birthday portrait of Aaron Copland, 1980

stands as a modernist landmark.

While Antheil courted notoriety in Paris, Aaron Copland (1900–1990) was quietly perfecting his craft in the same city with the eminent teacher Nadia Boulanger. The youngest child of Russian-Jewish immigrants who had settled in Brooklyn, he had attended the Boys' High School there. Having learned piano since childhood, he began studying harmony and counterpoint in 1917 with Rubin Goldmark (nephew of Karl Goldmark, the Hungarian Romantic symphonist and opera composer). Within three years Copland had his first piece published, *The Cat and the Mouse*, a Debussy-influenced "Scherzo humoristique," as he styled it. France's siren song was already in his ears. Copland arrived in Paris in 1921 keenly interested in composers such as Scriabin and Ives. Boulanger encouraged him to explore the latest musical techniques while developing a personal style. Under her guidance Copland opened his mind to every stimulus, exploring jazz as well as the music of Stravinsky, Prokofiev, Milhaud and other composers.

In 1924 he returned to New York with a ballet (*Grohg*, in one act) as well as sketches for his *Symphonic Ode* and *Music for the Theatre*. In January 1925 Boulanger traveled to New York as organ soloist for the premiere of Copland's bitingly dissonant Symphony for Organ and Orchestra under the baton of Walter Damrosch. Afterward, the 62-year-old Damrosch commented: "If a young man at the age of 23 can write a symphony like that, in five years he will be ready to commit murder." Copland subsequently revised the score, eliminating the organ part and renaming the work his First Symphony. Later that year Serge Koussevitzky led the premiere of *Music for the Theatre* with the Boston Symphony Orchestra, and in 1927 he introduced Copland's Piano Concerto, with the composer as soloist. Audiences were hearing a striking new American voice, though not everyone was delighted with it. Characteristically, when not distressed by the Stravinskian dissonance of his style at this time, the more conservative Boston Symphony Orchestra subscribers looked down their patrician noses at the surprising jazz influence in Copland's concerto; but Koussevitzky ignored their protests and remained the composer's champion.

> Aaron Copland arrived in Paris in 1921 keenly interested in composers such as Scriabin and Ives.

Slightly older than Copland, Virgil Thomson (1896–1989) was a fellow student of Boulanger from 1921 to 1922, having already studied at Harvard. After a brief return to Boston he settled back in Paris in 1925, setting up home in an apartment on the Left Bank where he lived until 1940 (thereafter returning to the United States to become one of the nation's most trenchant music commentators as critic for the *New York Herald Tribune*). During his Parisian years, Thomson was embraced by influential musicians, writers and artists, among them Jean Cocteau, Christian Dior, F. Scott Fitzgerald, André

Symphony on a Hymn Tune (1928) and Symphony No. 2 in C major (1931–41), whose tunes and harmonies recall the homey music of his Missouri boyhood, Thomson, like Copland, achieved a genuine American musical voice, which he also applied to film scores such as *The Plow that Broke the Plains* (1936) and *Journey to America* – a "short" for the 1964 World's Fair, which he arranged for concert performances as *Pilgrims and Pioneers*. "There is no law against the common chord," Thomson told the *Baltimore Sun* in 1973, when he was seventy-seven. "It usually creates a scandal when music is supposed to be bumpy. The press is beginning to discover that I am a conservative composer because my music is quite often grammatical."

11 Europeans Abroad

Even before Americans made a beeline to Paris, French and European composers made a beeline the other way, among them Edgar (born Edgard) Varèse, Ernest Bloch and Dane Rudhyar (born Daniel Chennevière). Rudhyar (1895–1985), a painter and philosopher as well as a musician, interestingly had gone to Hollywood in 1920 to write scenic music for such mystical silent films as *The Pilgrimage Play* and *The Life of Christ*, and while he was there he also played the role of Christ in the prologue to Cecil B. De Mille's early silent epic *The Ten Commandments*. He had changed his birth name to one derived from old Sanskrit, reflecting his profound interest in Indian and East Asian culture, out of which he developed a spiritual theory of dissonance. Such works as his *Nine Tetragrams* (1920–67), *Pentagrams* (1924–6) and the orchestral tone poems *The Surge of Fire* (1921) and *Soul Fire* (1922) illustrate his belief in dissonance as the perfect expression of America's cultural diversity. Through dense chord structures Rudhyar builds toward what he called "cumulative resonances" that he intended to linger in the memory.

Ernest Bloch (1880–1959) went to America during World War I and joined the faculty of New York's Mannes School of Music in 1917. Seven years later, by which time he was director of the Cleveland Institute of Music, he took American citizenship. His own music, at the time inspired primarily by his Jewish background, began to attract attention, as soon as he arrived, including his most famous composition, the rhapsody *Schelomo*, for cello and orchestra (1915), and the symphony *Israel* (1916). In 1919 his Suite for viola and piano won the chamber music prize established by Elizabeth Sprague Coolidge. In 1926 Bloch was appointed director of the San Francisco Conservatory, and in that year his large-scale symphonic work *America* won a prize established by *Musical America* magazine. *America, an Epic Rhapsody in Three Parts* incorporated native American and old English themes, the hymn "Old Hundredth," American folk melodies, jazz syncopations and even automobile horns, and joyously shouted Bloch's heartfelt thanks to his adopted country. After its premiere, by the New York Philharmonic in 1928, it was taken up by other American orchestras for a number of years. Other works by Bloch proved longer lasting, among them the Concerto grosso for strings (1925), the *Sacred Service*, for synagogues (1930–3), the Violin Concerto (1938) and the suite *Baal shem*, for violin and piano (later orchestrated). Among his chamber works are five string quartets (composed between 1916 and 1956), a Piano Quintet (1923) in which he exploited quarter-tones, and the *Méditation hébraïque* (1925) and *From Jewish Life* (1925), both for cello and piano.

Ernest Bloch's music, at the time inspired primarily by his Jewish background, began to attract attention, including his most famous composition, the rhapsody *Schelomo*.

Bloch based himself in Switzerland during the 1930s, though he returned permanently to the US to teach at the University of California, Berkeley, from 1940 through his retirement in 1952. A compelling teacher, he enjoyed a large student following, among whom were George Antheil, Quincy Porter, Douglas Moore, Leon Kirchner, Randall Thompson and Roger Sessions.

Varèse (1883–1965) settled permanently in New York in 1915 and threw down the gauntlet with his first American composition, *Amériques*, which he completed in 1922. The score opens with a sultry flute melody, repeated several times, joined by other solo lines and increasingly forceful outbursts by the orchestra. The outbursts, contrasted with quieter passages, build in violence, and with it a palpable tension that is not relieved until the final crashing, pounding measures. Early on, one New York critic compared it to a depiction of "the progress of a terrible fire in one of our larger zoos."

America, an Epic Rhapsody in Three Parts joyously shouted Bloch's heartfelt thanks to his adopted country.

Edgar Varèse

Varèse followed *Amériques* with further iconoclastic scores such as *Offrandes* (1922), *Hyperprism* (1923), *Intégrales* (1925) and his most famous piece, the all-percussion *Ionisation* (1930–1). Like Antheil, indeed like numerous modernists, Varèse availed himself of an astounding variety of percussion instruments. Searching for the kind of sonorities that would only be available with the introduction of electronic music thirty years later (and which he would exploit in works such as ***Déserts*** of 1950–4 and *Poème électronique*, composed for Le Corbusier's Philips Electronics pavilion at the 1958 Brussels World's Fair), Varèse defined music as "organized sound," making no distinction between what was recognized by the mainstream as music and what was derided as mere noise. Hence, upon hearing Stokowski conduct the premiere of *Intégrales*, for wind and percussion, at New York's Aeolian Hall in 1925, the critic and scholar Ernest Newman wrote in the *New York Evening Post* that "It sounded a good deal like a combination of early morning in the Mott Haven freight yards, feeding time at the zoo and a Sixth Avenue trolley rounding a curve, with an intoxicated woodpecker thrown in for good measure." Critics knew how to enjoy themselves in those days.

Arcana, composed between 1925 and 1927, was one of the

Website
track 37–43
www.naxosbooks.com

Website
track 44
www.naxosbooks.com

most brazen compositions of the time, written for an orchestra of 120 musicians: eight percussionists playing forty percussion instruments, five of each woodwind, five trumpets, eight horns, three trombones, two tubas, two sarrusophones, heckelphone, contrabass clarinet, contrabass trombone, and seventy strings. Leopold Stokowski infuriated many subscribers by giving the premiere of *Arcana* with the Philadelphia Orchestra in 1927, and subsequent European performances inspired critics to the heights of invective: "an abortion of sounding madness ... so unendurable to many listeners, that they fled," wrote a Berlin critic of the work in 1932. "Endless and senseless tonal piggery," was the opinion of another. Listeners today, inured to the wide-ranging effects achieved by film music and the amplified levels of rock concerts, find it more stimulating than offensive.

Pure sound in all its awesome glory was at the center of Varèse's inspiration; his scores throb and pound with extraordinary combinations of sound, some passages raucous, others soft and sensuous. He is fond of using repeated notes and repeated motifs to drive the composition forward or to define its inner forms, and he writes high and low tones at the extremes of an instrument's compass. Vibrant dissonances clash or whisper in almost orgiastic discord as instrumental lines strike one another like bumper cars in an amusement park. The music pulses with energy and vitality. Yet even in the most discordant passages the instrumental texture and rich color glow with a lucid clarity long identified with the French school.

One of Varèse's greatest admirers was the extraordinarily inventive rock musician and composer Frank Zappa.

Varèse transcended the usual – and unusual – orchestral instruments, even employing sirens in several of his scores, beginning with *Amériques*. Early critics dismissed this as effrontery. But as the American music scholar H. Wiley Hitchcock has observed, the arching curves of the siren's sound "embodied and projected one of Varèse's most important concepts: that of music as a spatial art, as 'moving bodies of sound in space.'" Surprisingly, though Varèse identified with the undulating sound of a siren, he disliked the vibrato characteristic of string instruments – similarly undulating but with a quicker pulse. Only four of his published compositions contain string parts. For him only wind and percussion could provide the sonic intensity he sought.

First-time listeners to a work such as *Ionisation* will be astonished at the intensity and variety of timbres, textures and rhythms Varèse achieves with only percussion instruments – bass drums in three sizes, bongos, snare drums, guiros (the guiro is a dried Cuban gourd, its serrated side stroked with a stick), Chinese blocks (high, medium and low), slapsticks, high and low tam-tams, gong, cymbals, Cuban claves, triangle, Cuban maracas, castanets, tambourine, high- and low-pitched anvils, triangle, chimes, celesta and, of course, two sirens, one high-pitched, one low, whose quiet undulating tone, which sounds like a sort of muted slide trombone, lends the piece its solitary cantabile line. And as the work unfolds, over roughly six minutes, we can understand Varèse's concept of musical form as "crystallization ... the result of a process" rather than "filling a form."

Even in a work such as *Density 21.5*, for solo flute, Varèse creates new and beguiling soundscapes, exploring the instrument's tone color throughout its registers, and even inventing a new instrumental effect midway in the score by having the player create a counterpoint of percussive clicks by hitting the keys audibly with his fingers. The piece was composed in 1936 to inaugurate the new platinum flute of the flautist Georges Barrère, and is named for the chemical density of platinum.

Today, *Density 21.5* or a work such as *Amériques*, with its flutes, harp glissandi, seductive drum beats and flamboyant brass rhythms, sounds positively lush, in fact no more incomprehensible than Stravinsky's *Rite of Spring* or Strauss's *Elektra*. Indeed, listening with twenty-first-century ears to Varèse's music, and to music of other avant-garde composers of the earlier twentieth century, we acknowledge that the initial audiences and critics were hearing these new works with ears firmly attuned to Wagner and Brahms (not to mention Converse and Foote), just as early opponents of Wagner's music were approaching it with ears couched in Rossini, Meyerbeer and Verdi. Our perceptions all boil down to a matter of relativity in which the passage of time has a mellowing effect on all. And it might interest many readers to learn that one of Varèse's greatest admirers was the extraordinarily inventive rock musician and composer Frank Zappa (1940–1993), who wrote an article on "The Idol of My Youth" for *Stereo Review* in 1971. Zappa drew upon Varèse's sonic vocabulary (as well as that of Stravinsky and Ives) in such rock albums as *Burnt Weeny Sandwich* (1970), not to mention his serious concert albums with the London Symphony Orchestra (*LSO: Zappa*, 1983–7) and the Ensemble Intercontemporain (*The Perfect Stranger*, 1984).

12 Between the World Wars: Americans Struggle to be Heard

The conductor Artur Rodzinski once noted that "You should never criticize a new work until you have heard it at least ten times." Unfortunately, new music during the twentieth century rarely received such careful consideration, and after their premieres many new scores went begging even for a second hearing, let alone a tenth. It was a situation even more pronounced in America than in Europe. Hence, despite their imagination, their creative energy and the European attention they often received, American composers faced widespread indifference at home (the attention of conductors such as Serge Koussevitzky in Boston and Leopold Stokowski in Philadelphia notwithstanding). To support their work they had to seek financial grants from wealthy patrons and newly organized foundations. Aaron Copland, for instance, was the first composer to receive a Guggenheim Fellowship (which he held from 1925 to 1927). He was followed by Roy Harris, another pupil of Nadia Boulanger in Paris, who was able to extend his stay there thanks to successive Guggenheim Fellowship awards (1927, 1928).

American composers also banded together to promote their work. The International Composers' Guild, spearheaded by Edgar Varèse, was established in 1921 in New York and was followed in 1923 by the formation of the League of Composers, which sponsored the influential journal *Modern Music*. Three years later Copland and fellow composer Roger Sessions began "the Copland–Sessions Concerts," a New York concert series presenting new compositions that would not otherwise get performed. Copland's Two Pieces, for violin and piano (1926), and *Vitebsk: Study on a Jewish Theme*, for piano, violin and cello (1928), are examples of his work during this period.

In 1927 Henry Cowell, anonymously funded by Charles Ives (who often used the wealth he had earned in insurance to assist younger composers), founded his "quarterly of modern composition," *New Music*, to publish "noncommercial works of artistic value." The very first issue contained the score of Carl Ruggles' orchestral suite *Men and Mountains*, and over the years the periodical published actual scores by other emerging Americans, including Ruth Crawford and Wallingford Riegger, as well as Ives, Schoenberg, Varèse and the preeminent Mexican Carlos Chávez. Ives, in fact, was so taken with the strength of Ruggles' score that the two men became great friends, and when in 1932 *New Music* published Ives' own *Lincoln, the Great Commoner*, Ruggles, a painter as well as a composer, designed the issue's cover.

> Particularly self-critical, Carl Ruggles destroyed many of his youthful compositions, left other works unfinished, and tended to devote his creative energy to painting.

Carl Ruggles (1876–1971), descended from one of the oldest families in Massachusetts, spent his childhood on a coastal farm, and after studying shipbuilding in Boston took private lessons in composition from a faculty member of the Boston Conservatory. Having absorbed all he could, he was referred to John Knowles Paine at Harvard for further study, but he quickly decided that university life was not for him. Instead he headed westward with his new wife, settling in Winona, Minnesota, in 1909. There he founded an orchestra, which he conducted for the next decade, before moving back east. And he composed. Particularly self-critical, Ruggles destroyed many of his youthful compositions, left other works unfinished, and tended after the 1930s to devote his creative energy to painting (some of his canvases are in the collections of the Whitney, Detroit, Williamstown and Brooklyn museums). Of his mature oeuvre, only eight compositions were actually published, yet each attests to Ruggles' independent approach to modern techniques. Though familiar with the work of the Second Viennese

School, he deployed atonality in his own way. In a piece such as *Evocation No. 2* for piano (1941), the opening utilizes all twelve notes of the chromatic scale, but not in the manner of serialism.

Ruggedness and spaciousness often describe the composer's idiom. The craggy sonorities of *Men and Mountains* – its title taken from William Blake's line "Great things are done when men and mountains meet" – suggest the dour New England panorama of his boyhood, and in the brazen invocation of the "Men" movement, dominated by horns, we hear the heroic call to overcome adversity. The opening theme of *Sun Treader* (1926–31), with its wide and striving intervals, rises through the brass, woodwinds and strings over a relentless pounding of timpani, lonely, resolute, heroic. "Be glad of obstacles," Ruggles told his students at the University of Miami. "Stumbling blocks should be stepping-stones."

Ruggles took pleasure in size and space. In his Vermont home, his composing room was the 40-foot square interior of a former one-room schoolhouse, and when working out the climactic thirty-nine measure triple canon in *Sun Treader* he wrote on a 20-foot long sheet of paper, ruling his own oversize staves. As a composer he had a great love of English and American Romantic poets. The title of *Sun Treader* was inspired by Robert Browning's epithet for Percy Bysshe Shelley, while Browning's poetry and that of Walt Whitman inspired eloquent settings in *Vox clamans in deserto*, for soprano and small orchestra (1923). Ruggles inscribed another line of Whitman on the first page of *Portals* (for strings, 1925, and revised significantly in 1929, 1941 and 1953): "What are those of the known but to ascend and enter the Unknown?"

Wallingford Riegger (1885–1961) was another rugged member of the Cowell–Ives circle. Born in Georgia but raised in Indianapolis and New York, he was in the first graduating class of New York's Institute of Musical Art in 1907. For the next ten years he spent periods of time in Germany and America, studying and pursuing a career as an orchestral cellist and conductor before America's entry into World War I obliged him to return home for good in 1917. Here he found conducting engagements scarce because audiences still only wanted to hear big-name Europeans. Thus for several years Riegger supported himself and his family by accepting academic posts. He also began composing in earnest, winning the Paderewski Prize in 1922 for his Piano Trio and two years later becoming the first American to win the Elizabeth Coolidge Prize, for his setting, for voices and chamber ensemble, of Keats' gripping poem *La Belle Dame sans Merci*. In 1927, while still teaching at Ithaca College, Riegger broke decisively with tonality and produced his first mature score, *Study in Sonority*, for ten violins "or any multiple thereof." In this work each violin plays a separate part, and the music's biting dissonance elicited hooting when it was performed by the Philadelphia Orchestra under Leopold Stokowski in 1929. Henry Cowell, on the other hand, called it "the choiring of angels."

> As a composer Ruggles had a great love of English and American Romantic poets. The title of *Sun Treader* was inspired by Robert Browning's epithet for Percy Bysshe Shelley.

The world premiere of Riegger's *Dichotomy*, for chamber orchestra, in Berlin in 1932 prompted the critic of the influential *Allgemeine Musikzeitung* to observe that "it sounded as if a pack of rats were slowly being tormented to death." *Dichotomy* is essentially a complex working-out of a tone row, in which Riegger concentrates on producing an impressive kaleidoscope of instrumental color rather than exploring Schoenbergian twelve-tone techniques. The climax is a dazzling fugato.

During the 1930s Riegger was increasingly involved in modern dance, which was then being shaped by choreographers influenced by trends in abstract art: Martha Graham, Doris Humphrey and Hanya Holm. Among his dance scores were Graham's *Chronicle* (1936), Charles Weidman's *Candide* (1933) and Holm's *Trend* (1937), on which he collaborated with his friend Edgar Varèse. For Humphrey, he wrote a trilogy of provocative scores: *New Dance*, *Theatre Piece* and *With My Red Fires* (1935–6).

Once Riegger settled on the exploration of dissonance as his métier, he stuck with it to the end, composing some of his most enduring music after his terpsichorean sojourn: two string quartets, *Music for Brass Choir*, a Piano Quintet, a Woodwind Quintet and a Concerto for Piano and Woodwind Quintet. In the piano suite *New and Old* (1944) each of the twelve pieces explores a specific device particular to modernist music, among them polytonality, dissonance, complex counterpoint and tone clusters. The Third Symphony (1946–7) boosted Riegger's reputation considerably; apart from winning the 1948 New York Music Critics' Circle Award and later a Naumburg Foundation Recording Award, it was taken up by Stokowski, and was performed repeatedly in Europe by the conductor Hermann Scherchen.

Riegger deliberately wrote to jar the senses, with aggressive, almost brutal rhythmic force propelling his masses of strident harmony. Constantly striving to create sonorous edifices, he called for legions of extra instruments added to the usual orchestral palette, battling with instruments' limitations, always hoping to extend their top or bottom range by a pitch or two to encompass the exceptionally wide ranges of his themes. At the same time his work bespeaks a Bach-like affinity for contrapuntal devices – canon, fugue, passacaglia. Not only did these offer him a fundamental mode of expression, but their structures lent order to his explosive harmonic and thematic material. "When I undertook to create, it was in spite of my environment," he once observed tellingly. And to the end of his long life he remained true to his radical ideals.

The Third Symphony boosted Wallingford Riegger's reputation considerably; it was taken up by Stokowski, and was performed repeatedly in Europe.

In 1926 Henry Cowell named the young Chicago composer Ruth Crawford to the board of his New Music Society, and two years later she became a founding member of the Chicago chapter of the International Society for Contemporary Music, by which time she was at the center of America's musical avant-garde. Crawford (1901–1953) had initially come into contact with Cowell through her piano teacher, a disciple of the influential Russian modernist Alexander Scriabin. At the same time she got to know the poet Carl Sandburg, whose verses inspired her to write many songs, as well as her own poetry, and whose influence spurred her own interest as a major collector and editor of American folk song.

The young Chicago composer Ruth Crawford was at the center of America's musical avant-garde.

During the 1920s Crawford's music combined Scriabinesque post-Romantic harmony with highly atmospheric dissonance, a combination exemplified by the wonderfully dream-like opening movement of the **Violin Sonata** (1925–6). Other works from her "Chicago period" include *Kaleidoscopic Changes on an Original Theme, Ending with a Fugue*, for piano (1924), the series of nine Preludes for piano (1924–8), the Suite for Small Orchestra (1926) and the vivacious Suite for Five Wind Instruments and Piano (1927, revised 1929, but not publicly performed until 1975). Crawford moved to New York in 1929, and the following year Cowell persuaded his erstwhile teacher Charles Seeger to take her as a student. In 1930 she also received the first Guggenheim Fellowship in composition awarded to a woman. During her ensuing European travels she was embraced by such pre-eminent musical figures as Bartók, Honegger and Nadia Boulanger. And when she returned to New York, in 1931, she was embraced matrimonially by Seeger.

Crawford worked with John and Alan Lomax in the Archive of American Folk Song, and was celebrated as a pillar of the folk music revival of the 1930s.

Much of Crawford Seeger's reputation as a composer rests on the music she wrote in New York during the early 1930s, when her creative interests revolved around the possibilities of dissonant counterpoint and serial techniques. In this vein she composed a masterful String Quartet, "1931," which Virgil Thomson called "a distinguished, a noble piece of work." In her series of four *Diaphonic Suites* she experimented with "dissonating" extended melodic lines – maintaining unrelieved harmonic tension from the first to last note. She also wrote a handful of vocal works, among which are some marvelously evocative songs to Carl Sandburg's poems, of which "**Rat Riddles**" illustrates her method of exploiting the vivid, somewhat surreal poetry by setting it for *Sprechstimme* (a vocal line midway between song and speech in which, rather than actual notes, relative pitches – high and low – are indicated).

After 1935 Crawford Seeger redirected her energies from composition to the preservation and publication of American folk music. At the Library of Congress she worked with John and Alan Lomax in the Archive of American Folk Song, and through her transcriptions and arrangements of this extraordinary material she, along with her husband, her stepson Pete and her own two children, Mike and Peggy, was celebrated as a pillar of the folk music revival of the 1930s. During the 1940s her school programs and her collections, most notably *American Folksongs for Children* (1948), were roundly praised, while her interest in folk music led to her only major orchestral work, *Rissolty Rossolty*, an "American Fantasia based on folk tunes," commissioned in 1939 by CBS for its educational radio series American School of the Air. After a long hiatus Crawford Seeger resumed original composition, entering and winning a music competition with her Suite for Wind Quintet (1952), only to die soon afterward of cancer. Ultimately, her compositional output was small. But it was choice.

Among Nadia Boulanger's American students were other women who achieved positions of distinction as composers, among them Marion Bauer (1882–1955) and Louise Talma (1906–1996). Bauer, born in Walla Walla, Washington, had learned fluent French from her parents; when introduced to Boulanger by the French pianist and composer Raoul Pugno in 1906, she offered to give Boulanger English lessons in return for lessons in composition, and thus became Boulanger's first American student. She later achieved national prominence as a music critic, author and professor at New York University and Juilliard. Bauer's own music reaches out to

> Louise Talma's lifelong fascination with religious and philosophical texts inspired some of her most memorable works.

a wide range of idioms and influences, from the self-evident *Lament on an African Theme*, Op. 20a (1927), and the sleek modalities and dance rhythms of the Duo for Oboe and Clarinet, Op. 25 (1932), to the Straussian angst of the Symphonic Suite for Strings, Op. 33 (1940), and the teen-oriented blues and cakewalk references against a Rachmaninovian background of the *American Youth Concerto*, Op. 36, which she composed for the student orchestra of New York's High School of Music and Art in 1943.

Louise Talma, the first woman granted two Guggenheim fellowships, the first woman elected to the National Institute of Arts and Letters (1964), and the first American composer to have an opera – *The Alcestiad*, to a libretto by Thornton Wilder – produced by a major European house (Frankfurt, 1962), began as a neoclassicist, strongly influenced by her intimate study of Stravinsky's music with Boulanger at Fontainebleu, where she went each summer beginning in 1926, and where she later became the first American faculty member. In fact, the linear clarity of such works as the two Piano Sonatas (1943, 1944–5) and the ebullient Toccata for Orchestra (1944) led some pundits to call her "the female Stravinsky." Yet her song cycle *Terre de France*, to verses selected from Ronsard and other French poets, shows her basking in sultry impressionism. Her mature compositions are evidence of her increased interest in serial writing, which she applied freely, often in a tonal context, and with a lucid sense of order and architecture both in instrumental and in vocal forms. For example, **Seven Episodes**, for flute, viola and piano (1986–7), is founded on a tone row in which the first and last notes form a perfect fifth. Talma's lifelong fascination with religious and philosophical texts inspired some of her most memorable works, among them *La Corona*, choral settings of seven sonnets by John Donne (1954–5), the cantata *All the Days of my Life* (1963–5), and *The Tolling Bell*, a solo cantata for baritone and orchestra to texts by Shakespeare, Marlowe and Donne (1967–9). From 1928 to 1979 Talma was the doyenne of the music department at Hunter College, New York, where she left an indelible impression on countless students, the present author among them.

Website
track 48
www.naxosbooks.com

Like Copland and Virgil Thomson, Walter Piston (1894–1976), a Maine-born Harvard graduate, was another American in Paris, from 1924 to 1926. There he studied not only with Boulanger but with Paul Dukas (of *The Sorcerer's Apprentice* fame) before returning home to teach at Harvard, where he numbered Elliott Carter and Leonard Bernstein among his pupils. Piston's Harvard identity has often misled people to dismiss his music as merely academic, usually without listening to it. Indeed, Piston was a polished craftsman adept at any compositional technique, but his best music has plenty to delight broader audiences. His 1929 Suite for orchestra culminates in a magnificent nine-part canon, while the rhythmic vitality and blues-tinged atmosphere of the first movement bespeak his youthful days playing in dance bands. In 1938 he wrote his most familiar work, the ballet *The Incredible Flutist*, for Arthur Fiedler and the Boston Pops orchestra, later preserving its

Like Copland and Virgil Thomson, Walter Piston, a Maine-born Harvard graduate, was another American in Paris, from 1924 to 1926.

melodic appeal and vivacious humor in a concert suite from the score. No one could dismiss its brief "Spanish Waltz" movement as "academic." Nor could one call the beautiful **Fantasy**, for English horn, harp and strings (1953), or the extraordinary Concerto for String Quartet, Winds and Percussion (1976), the mere "scratchings" of a dull professor.

Piston's Second Symphony (1943) achieved considerable popularity among concert audiences, as did his Fourth (1950) and Sixth (1955) Symphonies. During his last twenty years he wrote a series of concertante works with particular soloists in mind, for instance the Cello Concerto (1966–7), for Mstislav Rostropovich, and the Flute Concerto (1971), for Doriot Anthony Dwyer, the celebrated principal flutist of the Boston Symphony Orchestra. Among his awards were Pulitzer prizes for his Third (1947) and Seventh (1960) Symphonies, and New York Music Critics' Circle awards for his Viola Concerto (1957) and his Fifth String Quartet (1962). Nevertheless, Piston's work habits militated against being prolific: while he left a solid legacy of music and of important and very readable textbooks on music theory, he tended to compose slowly, writing a single work a year and joking that he'd spend an hour writing a note and another hour deciding to erase it.

If Piston's music competed with his academic duties, the music of Robert Russell Bennett (1894–1981) was genuinely overshadowed by his work as one of the most prominent Broadway arrangers. The son of a Kansas City bandmaster, he had learned to play virtually every instrument well enough to substitute for absentees in his father's band. And because few Broadway composers could orchestrate their own scores, Bennett was working on twenty or more shows a season. But he had a greater objective than to make other composers sound good in the pit. Aided by two Guggenheim fellowships, Bennett studied with Nadia Boulanger in Paris and pursued further composition studies in Berlin, returning briefly to New York in 1927 to orchestrate Jerome Kern's *Show Boat*. In 1929 two of his symphonic works received $5,000 prizes in a competition sponsored

Robert Russell Bennett wrote that he had "put every emotional and patriotic thought" into *Abraham Lincoln*, which predates Copland's more familiar *Lincoln Portrait* by more than a decade.

by RCA Victor: *Abraham Lincoln: A Likeness in Symphony Form*
and *Sights and Sounds (An Orchestral Entertainment)*. A thorough
craftsman with a keen sense of drama, lyricism and humor (consider
his 1941 baseball-oriented Symphony in D "For the Dodgers"), Bennett
was committed to writing accessible symphonic music throughout
his career while maintaining a high profile as a commercial
orchestrator – his Second Symphony, written to mark the 125th
anniversary of the New York Philharmonic, was premiered in 1968.
Bennett later wrote that he had "put every emotional and patriotic
thought" into *Abraham Lincoln*, which predates Copland's more
familiar *Lincoln Portrait* by more than a decade. *Sights and Sounds*
comprises seven movements, each with a contemporary theme:
"Union Station," "Electric Signs," "Skyscraper," etc. The "Night Club"
movement is a sly foxtrot in symphonic terms, and incorporates
saxophones and a cornet with a "wa-wa" mute. No dance band
would actually sound like this, but the reference is clear.

Meanwhile, the 1930s witnessed Aaron Copland's move from
the dissonance of his Symphony, for organ and orchestra (1924),
through the jazz influence of his Piano Concerto (1926), to the rigors
of his *Short Symphony* (1933). Having attended dance performances
by Isadora Duncan and the Diaghilev ballet troupe in his teens,
Copland was drawn to dance from the start of his career. It was an
affinity perfectly timed with the rising new interest in modern dance
and ballet that was gripping the country's major cultural centers
during the 1920s, 1930s and 1940s. Although his ballet score from
Paris went unperformed, Copland soon incorporated the music into
A Dance Symphony, completed in 1925, and received a prize awarded
by the Victor Talking Machine Company (an ancestor of today's
BMG label). Leopold Stokowski conducted the premiere with the
Philadelphia Orchestra in 1931. Three years later choreographer
Ruth Page performed Copland's ballet *Hear Ye! Hear Ye!* in Chicago.

Copland's interest in composing further dance scores paralleled
his determination not only to make his music more accessible to
audiences but to forge a personal American-sounding voice. Already
fascinated by jazz and popular styles, he looked for inspiration to
American and Latin American folk music as well, and the works that
emerged from this period of assimilation, including *El salón México*

(1936, choreographed by Doris Humphrey in 1943) and *Danzón Cubano* (original two-piano version, 1942; orchestral version, 1946), became some of his most popular ones.

With his ballet score for **Billy the Kid** (for choreographer Eugene Loring, 1938), and the orchestral suite he derived from it in 1939, Copland arrived at his most popular idiom: with its wide melodic intervals and haunting, often lonesome-sounding instrumentation (exploiting horns, strings and timpani strokes), *Billy the Kid* was immediately recognized as distinctively American, capturing the spirit of the Old West in a completely up-to-date manner. Copland continued to mine this American vein in his ballets *Rodeo* (for Agnes De Mille, 1942) and *Appalachian Spring* (for Martha Graham, 1944, which garnered both a Pulitzer Prize and the New York Music Critics' Circle Award). He also found it the obvious idiom for his opera *The Tender Land*, deliberately conceived as a folk piece, about a midwestern farming family (1954).

Choreographers turned to other Copland works for dance scores, among them Anthony Tudor, who used the *Music for Theatre* for his ballet *Time Table*; Doris Humphrey, who used the 1941 Piano Sonata for her ballet *Day on Earth* (1947); and Pauline Koner, who choreographed the *Dance Symphony* in 1963. Copland's superb **Clarinet Concerto**, commissioned by Benny Goodman in 1947, was transformed into *The Pied Piper* by Jerome Robbins in 1951. And in 1963 Copland himself conducted the premiere of *Dance Panels*, in

The Card Scene from the Ballet Caravan premiere production of Copland's Billy the Kid *at the Chicago Opera House, 1938*

seven movements, choreographed by Heinz Rosen to inaugurate the new National Theatre in Munich.

Ballet was by no means Copland's sole concern. In 1942 he unveiled another work that was to become a perennial box-office attraction, *A Lincoln Portrait* – the text (arranged by Copland himself from Lincoln's speeches and letters) eliciting one of the composer's most eloquently simple scores. His film scores formed another important body of work, among them *Of Mice and Men* (1940), *Our Town* (1940), *The Red Pony* (1948) and *The Heiress* (1949, a screen adaptation of Henry James' *Washington Square*, for which Copland won an Academy Award). From these pieces, as well as his incidental music for such plays as **Quiet City** (1939), Copland fashioned orchestral suites that kept the music in the concert repertoire.

> Copland's film scores formed another important body of work, among them *Of Mice and Men* (1940), *Our Town* (1940), *and The Red Pony* (1948).

Website
track 159
www.naxosbooks.com

After having composed music in virtually every genre, from instrumental solo to symphony and opera, Copland eventually turned to a variety of more complex idioms. Nevertheless he remained essentially a communicator, not only through his music but through his writings, including such classic books as *What to Listen for in Music* (1939), *Copland on Music* (1960) and *The New Music* (1960, and revised thereafter). He taught composition, and headed the faculty at the Berkshire Music Center at Tanglewood from 1940 to 1965, and he also lectured and taught courses at Harvard and at the New School for Social Research in New York. After 1955 he enjoyed considerable acclaim as a conductor.

> Copland was a generous supporter of other composers' work. Today his former home is preserved as Copland House; it is a center of musical learning.

Having received numerous awards and prizes, Copland was himself a generous supporter of other composers' work. Today his former home in Cortland, New York, is preserved as Copland House; it is a center of musical learning, offering concerts by resident artists and ensembles as well as the Aaron Copland Awards, which support residencies to enable emerging and mid-career composers to work for a period "free from the distractions of daily life."

Copland's immense popularity today as *the* most American-sounding composer of his generation should not obscure the legacy of others among his contemporaries whose music is equally individual and unmistakably American. Roy Harris (1898–1979), for example, was inhaling the air of America's open West from the moment of his birth. Born on farmland his family had claimed in one of the Oklahoma land rushes, he later moved with them to California, where he asserted he had been influenced from early childhood by the sounds of nature and by the whistles of distant passing locomotives. While a student Harris was introduced to Walt Whitman's poetry, which he later used for many vocal texts. During his professional career he devoted considerable time to teaching in a wide variety of successive college posts.

Over the course of four decades Harris composed more than 200 works, securing his initial recognition while he was still in Paris with the performance in 1927 of his Concerto for Piano, Clarinet and String Quartet. Its success led to a Guggenheim Fellowship that prolonged his studies in France. He returned to the US unexpectedly, on a stretcher, after breaking his back in a serious fall on a staircase. Imprisoned in a plaster cast and flat on his back for six months, he learned to read and write music without relying on a piano, and during this convalescence he composed his First String Quartet.

During the ensuing years Harris gained the attention of Serge Koussevitzky, conductor of the Boston Symphony Orchestra, who commissioned his First Symphony. The score was nearly lost before the premiere when the valise containing the manuscript and orchestral parts was stolen from Harris's parked car while he was visiting New York. Happily the thief, disappointed at finding only a suitcase full of music and not money, tossed his swag at the entrance of a subway station, where the police recovered it. The premiere of this *Symphony 1933* clinched Koussevitzky's faith in Harris as an "unmistakably American" voice, and he subsequently conducted the performances of Harris's Second (1934), Third (1938) and Fifth (1942) Symphonies, and recorded the First, Third and Fifth. Harris would eventually write thirteen symphonies, culminating with the choral *Bicentennial Symphony* (1975–6).

Koussevitzky called the one-movement Third Symphony "the first truly great orchestral work produced in America," though not every critic was delighted by Harris's boundless musical energy, one of them dismissing the piece as sounding "like a lot of people moving furniture around." Nevertheless, with its broad melodies riding upon lonely open fourths and fifths in the harmony, it is the most frequently played of all Harris's symphonies. The choral Fourth, or "Folk Song," Symphony was given its premiere by the Cleveland Orchestra under the composer's friend Artur Rodzinsky in 1941, and moved one critic to write that "forty-five minutes swept by like a second and left one listener with the excited consciousness of having heard something like the American continent rising up and saying hello." Choral music was Harris's other primary focus, and here he gave voice to his deep love of Whitman's poetry, which inspired his *Whitman Triptych* (1927), *A Song for Occupations* (1934), *Symphony for Voices* (1936), *American Creed* (1940), *Walt Whitman Suite* (1944), and later works for choir, solo voices and instruments. Harris also wrote chamber music, of which his Piano Quintet (1939) remains the most highly regarded.

> Roy Harris's ear was keenly attuned to what he perceived as the "American" qualities in folk song and popular music of his day.

Harris's training with Nadia Boulanger in Paris endowed him with a liking for uncluttered instrumental textures and an overall clarity in his orchestral writing. His style springs from America's indigenous folk culture, and his ear was keenly attuned to what he perceived as the "American" qualities in folk song and popular music of his day. In 1940 he wrote that folk song is all about:

> singing and dancing your heart out for yourself and the people you were born among – whose daily lives you share through the seasons, through thick and thin. From the hearts of our people they have come – our people living, loving, bearing, working, dying. These songs are as the people whom they express – salty, hilarious, sly, vulgar, gay, sad, weary, heroic, witty, prosaic, and often as eloquent as the silent poor burying their dead. They constitute a rich legacy of time-mellowed feelings and thoughts

chosen through usage from the experiences of people who lived here and helped make America what she is today.

Harris genuinely enjoyed listening to his own music, and Walter Piston once observed of him that "his personality is contagiously enthusiastic, and his honest appreciation of the beauties of his own work is refreshing." One dominant quality in much of Harris's music is a sense of boisterousness. In his driving rhythms we feel the impulsive motion of people untrammeled by the restraints of urban civilities. In the strength of his songful melodies, with their wide and ardent intervals, in the vastness of

Harris's Ninth Symphony was inspired by the preamble to the United States Constitution and passages from Walt Whitman's poetry.

his modal harmonies, and in the way his music strides confidently forward, he embodies the wide-open spaces of America's countryside when farming towns and villages were yet untouched by suburban sprawl. These qualities are graphically illustrated by the opening movement of the **Ninth Symphony**, inspired by the preamble to the United States Constitution and passages from Whitman's poetry, and composed for the Philadelphia Orchestra, which gave the premiere in 1962. If there are visual counterparts to this sinewy, vital music, they are the paintings and murals of Thomas Hart Benton, whose earthy, hot-blooded men and women project a similar lust for life.

Website
track 160
www.naxosbooks.com

Randall Thompson and Roger Sessions, two students of Ernest Bloch, also rose to central positions on the American scene during the interwar years. Thompson (1899–1984) became one of the nation's leading choral composers, and his basically diatonic, vigorously melodic style, often with antiphonal effects, made his works exceptionally popular with choral societies. Among the most celebrated are *Alleluia* (written for the opening of the Berkshire Music Center in 1940, and performed there every summer since then), *Frostiana* (1959, to poetry by Robert Frost) and *The Testament of Freedom* (1943, based on texts by Thomas Jefferson). Thompson, who served as director of the Curtis Institute of Music and eventually joined the faculty of his alma mater, Harvard, was also endowed with a rich sense of humor that yielded one of his most delightful choral works, *Americana* (1932), in which he set a variety of texts gleaned from the colonial periodical *American Mercury*. Among his non-choral works, his Second Symphony (1931) enjoyed a place in the orchestral repertoire for several decades, and deserves revival.

Sessions (1896–1985) became a highly influential teacher, successively at Boston University, Princeton University, the University of California at Berkeley, Harvard University and the Juilliard School, and in the course of his academic career he numbered David Diamond, Milton Babbitt, Hugo Weisgall and the fascinating expatriate composer-author Paul Bowles among his students. Though born in Brooklyn, New York, he was descended, like Carl Ruggles, from prominent New England families, and the regional strain of indepen-dence ran in his blood. Sessions' First Symphony (premiered by the Boston Symphony Orchestra in 1927) embraces a buoyant neoclassical idiom that flows along in the manner of Bloch's rhapsodic style. As he progressed,

> Roger Sessions wrote his Second Symphony between 1944 and 1946 and dedicated it to the memory of Franklin D. Roosevelt, who had died suddenly in 1945.

however, his personal voice emerged in works such as the First Piano Sonata (1930) and the First String Quartet (1936) – increasingly complex, emphasizing richly chromatic polyphony spiced with unresolved dissonances, yet with a distinctive, often powerful lyricism. Copland declared the First Piano Sonata "a cornerstone upon which to base an American music." The Second Piano Sonata, entirely atonal, followed in 1946, and the Second String Quartet in 1951. Sessions' Violin Concerto (1935) was initially regarded as "impossible to play," but violinists learned it, just as soloists would later tackle his Concerto for Violin and Cello (1970–1), much to their satisfaction.

Sessions wrote his Second Symphony between 1944 and 1946 and dedicated it to the memory of Franklin D. Roosevelt, who had died suddenly in 1945. Musically, it departed provocatively from his First. Written nominally in a key of D minor and laden with dissonance, it presents a series of four movements during which musical events happen in rapid succession. The emotional center of the symphony is the third movement, *Adagio, tranquillo ed espressivo*, with notably eloquent writing for muted violas, clarinet and piano, on which Sessions was working when he learned that F.D.R. had suffered his fatal stroke. After the premiere, with the San Francisco Symphony under Pierre Monteux, *Time* magazine declared the symphony "hard work for musicians and audience alike," while Alfred Frankenstein of the *San Francisco Chronicle* hailed it as "big ... challenging ... important ... [a] fiendishly difficult ... complex of forceful and fruitful ideas which can be studied for a long time before they yield all their secrets." The Second Symphony received the Naumburg Award and the New York Music Critics' Circle Award in 1949 and 1950 respectively. Nevertheless, even today, when Sessions is regarded as one of the most important American composers of the twentieth century, neither this monumental work nor any of his eight symphonies is widely familiar. Nor, for that matter, is the powerful cantata he fashioned from Whitman's Lincoln threnody, *When Lilacs Last in the Dooryard Bloom'd*, which was premiered at the University of California at Berkeley in 1971, or his monumental opera *Montezuma*, which occupied him for a quarter century before its completion in 1962.

The composer himself observed that his main goal was "to write good music" rather than strive to reach the public. And although his work helped define a twentieth-century American musical idiom, Sessions observed that "I am not trying to write 'modern,' 'American,' or 'neo-classic' music; I am seeking always and only the coherent, and living expression of my musical ideas."

13 Lighter Hearts of the 1920s and 1930s

Running parallel to the serious concert works composed in a variety of modernist styles during the interwar years was a more popular stream of lighter instrumental music that found an immediate audience. Positioned somewhere between fully fledged "art music" and outright "pop," the works of composers such as Zez Confrey and Ferde Grofé perpetuated in twentieth-century terms what was still a living tradition of program, or descriptive, music stretching back to Beethoven and Berlioz. At the same time this repertoire drew on the appealing tunefulness of salon music, opera, jazz and a variety of ethnic musical idioms. Gershwin's *An American in Paris* (1928) and *Cuban Overture* (1932) and Copland's *El salón México* (1936) are examples now firmly in the standard concert repertoire.

One of the most successful of the era's "light symphonists" was Ferdinand Rudolf von Grofé (1892–1972), a New Yorker of Franco-German extraction who went by the less sonorous diminutive of Ferde. In 1920, after playing viola in the Los Angeles and San Francisco Symphony Orchestras, Grofé joined Paul Whiteman's band as pianist and arranger. Four years later he secured his reputation as a deft orchestrator with his arrangement of Gershwin's *Rhapsody in Blue*.

> A more popular stream of lighter instrumental music found an immediate audience.

Grofé had composed original music since his youth, and after his triumphant association with Gershwin he wrote a long series of descriptive tone poems, beginning with *Broadway at Night*.

Ferde Grofé with George Gershwin, S.L. Rothafel and Paul Whiteman
by a piano at the Roxy Theatre, New York, ca. 1930

The tone poems remain his chief legacy, especially the descriptive, multi-movement suites: *Mississippi*, first performed by Whiteman and his band in 1926; *Grand Canyon Suite* (1931), his most famous work, especially the movement "On the Trail," with its jog-trot rhythm and braying mule; *Hollywood Suite* (1937); *Death Valley Suite* (1949); *Hudson River Suite* (1955); and **Niagara Falls Suite**

(1961). This last makes an interesting comparison with William Henry Fry's symphony essay on the same subject, written a century earlier. Every natural and mechanical stimulus, from sunsets and thunderstorms to bird songs and bicycle pumps, offered Grofé musical ideas, and his colorful sense of Americana appealed even to listeners with no knowledge of standard concert repertoire.

Paul Whiteman's "Experiment in Modern Music" concert in 1924 helped establish Grofé and Gershwin. Also on the program was pianist Zez Confrey, who played a medley of popular songs followed by *Kitten on the Keys*, one of the piano novelties by which he earned his own measure of immortality.

With his good looks and brilliantined hair, Zez (Edward Elzear) Confrey (1895–1971) was every inch the "bright young person" of the "roaring twenties," a figure right out of F. Scott Fitzgerald. More importantly, he was a born pianist. His studies at Chicago Musical College left him well versed in classical music, and his early work in the Chicago dance orchestra he formed with his brother sharpened his ear for up-to-date style. After recording with that orchestra in 1918 for the Victor Talking Machine Company, Confrey was hired to record novelty pieces for the QRS Piano Roll Company and later the Ampico Corporation, whose reproducing pianos were among the finest made. In 1921 he signed a publishing contract with Mills Music, for which he wrote a series of pieces that are as evocative of the 1920s and 1930s as Scott Joplin's rags are of the 1890s and 1900s. Characteristically their catchy titles were often explanatory, such as *Dizzy Fingers*, *Coaxing the Piano*, *Dumbell*, *Stumbling*, etc., and their tuneful syncopations made them phenomenal bestsellers, both as sheet music and on record.

> Leroy Anderson was an arranger before emerging as one of the most popular of all light orchestral composers.

Like Ferde Grofé, Leroy Anderson (1908–1975) was an arranger before emerging as one of the most popular of all light orchestral composers. Following studies at the New England Conservatory and Harvard (with Walter Piston), and postgraduate work in Scandinavian philology and German, he joined the Harvard faculty as organist, choirmaster, and director of the University Band, though he also taught at Radcliffe College. Meanwhile, his dance-band arrangements attracted the attention of Arthur Fiedler, conductor of the Boston Pops, who engaged Anderson as the orchestra's arranger in 1935. With his keen ear for every musical style, from baroque dances to jazz, and a sense of humor that lent itself to witty musical parody, Anderson began writing short orchestral pieces for Fiedler in 1938. The first, *Jazz Pizzicato*, for strings, became an immediate hit, and was followed by *Jazz Legato*.

After his military service during World War II, Anderson published *Promenade*, the first of a long series of piquant orchestral miniatures that became familiar worldwide, among them *The Syncopated Clock*, *Fiddle-Faddle*, *Sleigh Ride*, *Forgotten Dreams*, *The Waltzing Cat*, *The Typewriter* and *Blue Tango*. Beyond Fiedler's repertoire, Anderson's pieces, through lucrative licensing agreements, entered the realm of commercial mood music and were played as radio and television themes, as background music to advertising, and even (dare we acknowledge it?) as elevator music.

14 Perpetuating the Romantic Tradition

Despite the clarion call of modernism and experimentation that resounded through the 1920s and beyond, some major figures still strove to maintain late-Romantic ideals, but in a fresh language that did not sound outmoded. Among these were the long-lived John Alden Carpenter, Howard Hanson, William Grant Still, George Frederick McKay, Leo Sowerby, Samuel Barber and Gian Carlo Menotti.

Carpenter (1876–1951) was an almost exact contemporary of Ives and, like Ives, was a successful businessman (vice-president of the family shipping firm) who composed as an avocation. Nevertheless he was one of America's most prominent composers during the 1920s, his works performed repeatedly by major orchestras at home and, even more tellingly, in Europe. A student of Paine at Harvard, he also studied briefly with Sir Edward Elgar. When in 1914 Carpenter finished his suite *Adventures in a Perambulator*, conductor Frederick Stock quickly slated it for performance by the Chicago Symphony Orchestra, thus securing Carpenter's reputation. The six movements each describe what a child would see while being wheeled around in a stroller (or "pram"). Carpenter's own descriptive notes for the piece are written from the child's viewpoint and convey the spirit of Robert Louis Stevenson's *A Child's Garden of Verses*, while the orchestration and subtle harmony suggest his affinity for Debussy, especially in the movement "The Lake:" "... Waves and sunbeams! Blue water – white clouds – dancing, swinging! A white sea gull in the air. This is My Lake." Carpenter lends immediacy to the movement "The Hurdy-Gurdy" with passing quotes of Irving Berlin's "Alexander's Ragtime Band," Eduardo di Capua's "O! Marie" and other popular tunes of the day.

Carpenter used elements of ragtime and Spanish rhythms in his Concertino, for piano and orchestra (1915), which also boasts a movement in 5/8 time. He successfully exploited further jazz elements in his ballets *Krazy Kat* (1921), based on the widely read comic strip and thus a notable adaptation of popular culture in a classical genre, and *Skyscrapers* (1926). The latter, commissioned by impresario Serge Diaghilev and performed at the Metropolitan Opera House, was Carpenter's most modernist score to date, embodying his aim to "reflect some of the many rhythmic movements and sounds of modern American life." Indeed, at the time it was widely heralded as the first symphonic work descriptive of contemporary American civilization, though from today's viewpoint this suggests the refusal of mainstream critics to acknowledge earlier avant-garde works such as Varèse's *Amériques* or Antheil's *Ballet mécanique* as music at all. Though Carpenter's First and Second Symphonies date from 1940 and 1947 respectively, in fact the former is a revision of an earlier First Symphony (1917) which the composer undertook at Stock's request for a work to mark the Chicago Symphony Orchestra's golden jubilee. The Second Symphony was initially an orchestration of the 1934 Piano Quintet, and received its premiere by the New York Philharmonic under Bruno Walter in 1942. Carpenter's 1947 revision was premiered by Fritz Busch and the Chicago Symphony at the Ravinia Festival in 1949, and, if a quiet sense of retrospection is the most salient characteristic of both symphonies, we can agree with Virgil Thomson's appraisal of the Second as "opulent and comfortable, intelligent, well-organized, cultured and firm without being either ostentatious or unduly modest."

Howard Hanson (1896–1981), a native of Nebraska, achieved major status as composer, conductor, and director of the Eastman School of Music in Rochester, New York (1925–64). A winner of the American Prix de Rome in 1921, he spent three years at the American Academy in Rome. Here, he composed the first of his seven lush and

Website
track 60
www.naxosbooks.com

colorful symphonies, the "**Nordic**," which reflected his Scandinavian ancestry. The influence of Sibelius, Rachmaninov and Richard Strauss is immediately discernible in the stirring final movement, and it remained strong in Hanson's subsequent works, which he wrote in an idiom distinguished by rich harmony, singing melody and superb orchestration: he pointedly called his Second Symphony "Romantic," and it remains among his most frequently performed scores. While open to occasional experiments with pungent tonal relationships, Hanson steadfastly avoided modernist dissonance or avant-garde instrumentation. Thus a relatively late work, his 1970 piano arrangement of the brief "Fireworks" movement from his 1963 orchestral suite *For the First Time*, sounds like a bridge between influences as disparate as Grieg and Stravinsky.

Website
track 164–165
www.naxosbooks.com

Hanson's **Merry Mount**, based on Nathaniel Hawthorne's novel of witchcraft and sexual obsession in Puritan New England, was produced by the Metropolitan Opera in 1934. With its superb choruses, vivacious dances and impassioned melodies, not to mention a climactic nightmare sequence, during which the opera's hero, a troubled Puritan minister, dreams of damnation for making love to the Philistine goddess Astoreth, the opera made a deep impression at its premiere, but suffered

Hanson was a sincere and lifelong promoter of music by his many American contemporaries.

the usual fate of American opera at that time and failed to enter the repertoire. In 1938 Hanson arranged from it a five-movement suite, including the brief but infectious "Children's Dance." The suite proved to be one of his most popular orchestral works, and its impassioned "Love Duet" movement shows that the soaring musical vernacular of Hanson's Hollywood contemporaries Erich Wolfgang Korngold and Max Steiner clearly emerged from the same wellspring.

As a conductor of the Rochester (New York) Symphony Orchestra and of the orchestra of Rochester's Eastman School of Music, Hanson was a sincere and lifelong promoter of music by his many American contemporaries, among them William Grant Still (1895–1978). The son of a Mississippi town bandmaster and a teacher, Still grew up in a cultivated musical home in Little Rock, Arkansas. In 1935 he became the first African American to have a symphony performed by a major American orchestra when the New York Philharmonic performed his First Symphony, "Afro-American." The next year he became the first African American to conduct a major orchestra (the Los Angeles Philharmonic) and in 1955 the first to conduct an orchestra in the South (New Orleans Philharmonic). His *Troubled Island* was the first opera by an African American mounted by a major company (the New York City Opera, 1949), while his *Bayou Legend* was the first African-American opera to be televised (Public Broadcasting, 1981). His postgraduate studies with Chadwick and with Varèse during the 1920s, and his work as an arranger for W.C. Handy and as a player in dance orchestras, endowed Still with exceptional stylistic versatility on a level with Gershwin. Indeed the two men admired and influenced each other. After experimenting with avant-garde techniques, Still adopted a more conservative style. Just as Joplin had aimed to compose genuine ragtime opera, Still directed his much more sophisticated technique toward synthesizing a truly symphonic form of Negro music. In his **"Afro-American" Symphony** he adroitly treats a specific African-American musical genre in the first three movements, linking each with a characteristic emotional state: blues and longing; Negro spiritual and sorrow; ragtime and jazz and humor. The finale, entitled "Aspiration," links all three together with a fine, hymn-like theme. In the first movement Still subjects his limber blues melody to full-blown Lisztian thematic transformation. Premiered by Hanson at Rochester in 1931, the symphony clinched Still's international reputation as a composer of music thematically rich, technically refined and immediately appealing, attributes that apply equally to his three-movement tone poem *Africa* (1930), his operas, and his other works for orchestra and symphonic band.

George Frederick McKay composed orchestral music inspired by his Pacific Coast surroundings with their mountainous backdrop.

Website
track 61
www.naxosbooks.com

Like Howard Hanson, George Frederick McKay (1899–1970) was a distinguished teacher, and during his forty-one years as Professor of Music at the University of Washington his pupils included William Bolcom and John Cage. Based in the Northwest, McKay composed orchestral music inspired by his Pacific Coast surroundings with their mountainous backdrop. While not strictly programmatic, his works often have suggestive or illustrative titles – for example, the nine-movement suite *Harbor Narrative* (1934), the suite *From a Moonlit Ceremony* (1945), incorporating songs and dances he collected while visiting the reservation of the Muckleshoot Indians, near Mount Rainier, and the *Symphony for Seattle* (1951).

Leo Sowerby (1895–1968) also put a twentieth-century spin on nineteenth-century traditions as one of the great organists and organ composers of his time. And if Hanson took his cue from Sibelius *et al.*, Sowerby took his from César Franck, observing in his own music the French principles of formal and tonal clarity championed by Franck, Saint-Saëns and Louis Vierne. Based for most of his life in Chicago as organist and teacher, in 1962 he became director of the College of Church Musicians at the National Cathedral in Washington, DC. Sowerby enjoyed a fruitful working relationship with E. Power Biggs, America's pre-eminent organ virtuoso of the mid-twentieth century: Biggs gave the first performance of Sowerby's Organ Concerto in C major, with the Boston Symphony Orchestra, in 1938, and Sowerby composed the *Classic Concerto* (1944) and **Festival Musick** (1953–4) for him. The latter work, for organ and brass, is prime Sowerby, and the opening movement, "Fanfare," provides a vivid example of his spacious organ writing and the piquant blend of medieval modality and tangy dissonance that defines his mature idiom. Sowerby was a niche figure oriented primarily toward organ and sacred music. His choral music is widely acclaimed, especially his majestic setting of St Francis of Assisi's *Canticle of the Sun*.

Website
track 62
www.naxosbooks.com

Like Sowerby, Samuel Barber (1910–1981) received early recognition. A child prodigy, he composed an operetta at the age of seven and was carefully guided by his aunt Louise Homer, a contralto at the Metropolitan Opera, and her husband, Sidney Homer, a pupil of Chadwick who composed very popular art songs. Barber, an excellent baritone, was trained as a singer, conductor (with Fritz Reiner) and composer at Philadelphia's Curtis Institute of Music, where his classmates referred, tongue-in-cheek, to "the three Bs" of classical music – Bach, Beethoven and Barber. His extensive European travel

At Philadelphia's Curtis Institute of Music, Samuel Barber's classmates referred, tongue-in-cheek, to "the three Bs" of classical music – Bach, Beethoven and Barber.

Gian Carlo Menotti (left) with Samuel Barber,
photographed while visiting St Wolfgang, Austria in 1944

contributed profoundly to a Romantic aesthetic revolving around genuine emotional expression, wonderfully idiomatic vocal melody, highly flavorful "post-Straussian" chromatic harmony, and a keen sensitivity for poetry and literature, which he channeled into his many songs and choral pieces as well as his two operas, *Vanessa* (1956–7) and *Antony and Cleopatra* (1966, revised 1974).

Among Barber's earlier works to enter the repertoire were his sparkling overture *The School for Scandal* (1931), his thoughtful setting of Matthew Arnold's *Dover Beach*, for baritone and string quartet (1931), and his one-movement Symphony No. 1 (1936). In 1938 Arturo Toscanini conducted Barber's *First Essay for Orchestra* and the *Adagio for Strings* in an NBC Symphony broadcast, and by the time his Violin Concerto appeared in 1939 Barber was taking his place among those American composers to be most often programmed over the next four decades. "There's no reason music should be difficult for an audience to understand," he said in an interview later in life. Hence, in addition to those already cited, many of his works are still performed – especially the superb Piano Concerto (1962, which won a Pulitzer Prize), the Piano Sonata (1949), the song cycles *Knoxville: Summer of 1915* (1947) and *Hermit Songs* (1952–3), and *Medea's Meditation and Dance of Vengeance* (a 1953 revision of his earlier ballet *Medea*). In 1954 the Boston Symphony unveiled his *Prayers of Kierkegaard*, for soprano, chorus and orchestra, a profoundly moving contemporary oratorio.

Barber had met the Italian-born Gian Carlo Menotti (1911–2007) at Curtis, and their close personal and professional relationship was exceptionally fruitful. Each stimulated the other intellectually. Barber's *Capricorn Concerto* (1944), scored for the same ensemble as Bach's Brandenburg Concerto No. 2 – flute, oboe, trumpet and strings – was inspired by Capricorn, the house he and Menotti owned in Mount Kisco, New York, with themes representing himself, Menotti and Menotti's adopted son, Chip. The music shifts back and forth between linear baroque-style textures and more straightforward melody, and the final movement, with its trumpet fanfare, is an outright salute to Bach.

Menotti wrote the libretto of Barber's witty nine-minute opera for four soloists and orchestra, *A Hand of Bridge* (1959), in which the characters alternate dry recitative during their bridge-playing with quasi-aria solos that peer into their inner thoughts. Menotti was also librettist of Barber's first full-length opera, the romantic **Vanessa** (Metropolitan Opera, 1958), which garnered Barber's second Pulitzer Prize and became a classic repertoire work. The orchestral intermezzo is often played as a concert piece.

Menotti helped promote Barber's music through performances at the annual Spoleto Festival, which he founded in Italy and the United States. Barber's third opera, *Antony and Cleopatra*, based on Shakespeare's drama, was produced by the Metropolitan to inaugurate its new house in Lincoln Center in 1966. However, after a hair-raising rehearsal period dogged with mechanical problems in the new theatre, the opera itself was soundly derided by the press. Thereafter, though Barber made extensive revisions to the opera, he became increasingly reclusive; he accepted fewer and fewer commissions and eventually died sad and alone. He left behind a final, unfinished work, **Canzonetta**, the single movement of a projected oboe concerto. Completed by his only pupil, Charles Turner, it is a beautiful score that represents a summation of the mingled late-Romantic and modernist idioms out of which Barber forged his musical immortality.

Gian Carlo Menotti himself was the most successful mid-twentieth-century American opera composer, his music fusing emotional melody descended from the verismo of Puccini and Mascagni with more modern harmony and rhythm. Admittedly his works after 1960 met with increasing criticism, but those of the 1940s and 1950s have become standard repertoire, especially among university opera theatres. These include *The Old Maid and the Thief*, *The Medium*, *The Telephone*, *The Consul*, *The Saint of Bleeker Street* (a Pulitzer Prize winner) and *Amahl and the Night Visitors*. This last, written for television, has become a perpetual Yuletide favorite of regional opera companies since its first broadcast in 1951.

15 America Goes to War: The 1940s

On Sunday morning, December 7, 1941, Japanese airplanes attacked the US Pacific Fleet at Pearl Harbor, Hawaii. Within twenty-four hours the Japanese air force made further attacks on US bases in the Philippines, Guam and the Midway Islands. President Franklin D. Roosevelt addressed a joint session of Congress, declaring December 7 "a day that will live in infamy" and asking for a declaration of war against Japan. America joined its allies in the war that had begun with Germany's attack on Poland in September 1939. "We did it before, and we can do it again," went a popular song of the time, referring to the allied victory in World War I. Then, America's participation had lasted just eighteen months. This time its fight would be longer and bloodier.

The 1940s were rich in new and memorable orchestral music, with works such as Copland's ballets *Rodeo* and *Appalachian Spring*, his *Lincoln Portrait*, and his *Fanfare for the Common Man* coming immediately to mind. The unifying element in these scores is the composer's use of actual folk melodies (e.g., the hymn tune "Simple Gifts" in *Appalachian Spring*) or themes written in a folksy style. Works such as these focused on their audiences' American identity, much as the magazine illustrations of Norman Rockwell expressed it in visual terms. Similarly, Rodgers and Hammerstein's *Oklahoma!* ushered in a new era on Broadway when it opened in 1943 – with its picnics,

In the 1940s, many composers used actual folk melodies or themes written in a folksy style, focusing on their audiences' American identity.

barn dances and fringe-topped surrey, the show looked nostalgically at a less threatening time in American history while addressing the darker psychology of its chief protagonists.

Not all Americana evoked the old West or South. The *William Billings Overture* (1943) by William Schuman (1910–1992) evoked old New England by ringing ingenious changes upon a psalm tune by the pioneering musical Bostonian. His *New England Triptych* (1956) treats three of Billings' tunes contrastingly: the third movement, "Chester," presents the hymn straight, then in rousing martial variations inspired by its subsequent use as a marching song by Washington's Continental Army.

Considering Schuman's stature among America's finest symphonists, it is surprising that he only discovered classical music when he was almost twenty: coerced into attending one of Toscanini's New York Philharmonic concerts, the former high-school dance-band leader made his first acquaintance with works by Robert Schumann, Wagner and Kodály, and saw the light.

William Schuman became the first American composer to win the Pulitzer Prize.

Upon hearing Roy Harris's *Symphony 1933*, he tracked down the composer at the Juilliard School, where Harris was then teaching, and became his student. Harris encouraged Schuman to think big, and Harris's taste for rhapsodic forms and for expansive chromatic melodies riding over piquant accompaniments with several chords clashing at once rubbed off on the student, who blended this with his own penchant for bold, agile, often zig-zagging themes set against brass, cymbals and other metallic percussion that gave an adamantine gleam to his orchestration.

Although he later withdrew the first two of an eventual ten symphonies, a radio broadcast of Schuman's Second Symphony (1939) and the subsequent performance of his *American Festival Overture* (1939) served as his consecration as a major American composer. His Third Symphony (1941) became his most frequently played symphony, its two parts based on baroque forms – Passacaglia and Fugue, Chorale and Toccata, though it would never be mistaken for Bach. With this work he also became the first American composer to win the Pulitzer Prize (Gershwin's *Of Thee I Sing* had won a Pulitzer only for its book, not for its score). Schuman's Symphony

William Schuman, New York, 1981

for Strings (1943) resounds with pungent bichordal harmony; his Fourth Symphony, composed in 1941 and premiered in January 1942, shortly after Pearl Harbor was attacked, maintains an optimistic viewpoint, as does his rollicking *Circus Overture* (1944). However, the Sixth Symphony (1946) expresses the pessimism of mankind worn out by world war and newly thrust into the atomic age. Pessimism also colors Schuman's Seventh (1960) and Ninth (1968) Symphonies – the latter subtitled "**Le Fosse ardeatine**" in memory of the Ardeatine Caves near Rome, where Nazi soldiers shot some 335 Italian civilians to avenge the killing of thirty-five SS troops by Roman guerillas. With its softly clashing harmonies and sudden outbursts of instrumental rage, its last movement, "Postludium," conveys the composer's shock and sorrow over what he had seen there on a visit in 1967.

Website
track 64–66
www.naxosbooks.com

Schuman also wrote important chamber and choral music and directed his all-American spirit to the stage, with his baseball opera *The Mighty Casey* (1953, based on Ernest Thayer's 1888 poem *Casey at the Bat*), and to the band shell, with several large-scale works for wind band, including *George Washington Bridge* (1950). Apart from his major position as a composer, Schuman was one of American music's most adroit statesmen, wielding considerable power and influence as president of the Juilliard School and later of Lincoln Center.

The treasury of America's wartime music brims with repertoire that proves remarkably appealing now. Among the most powerful expressions of grief and anxiety over the condition of the world at that time are the Second, Third and Fourth Symphonies of David Diamond (1915–2005), yet another pupil of Boulanger. For instance, the opening movement of his **Second Symphony** (1942), marked *Adagio funebre*, is a wrenching funeral march, bridging the sorrowful rhetorics of Mahler and Shostakovich. Its melodic string lamentation is punctuated by shattering strokes on the bass drum and cymbals, and the composer employs emphatic doublings of trumpet and brass. The four movements present a series of striking contrasts: movements one and three, each lasting nearly a quarter hour, are despairing in tone; movements two and four are each much shorter. The second, *Allegro vivo*, is an angry

Website
track 161
www.naxosbooks.com

scherzo, its primary rhythmic motif tossed from instrument to instrument. However, the finale, *Allegro vigoroso*, is completely optimistic, its ebullient themes as American in sound as anything by Copland.

Diamond's three-movement Fourth Symphony (1945) is far briefer, and reflects his pondering over the relationship between birth, sleep and death. The elegiac second movement, *Adagio – Andante*, presents a noble brass chorale as the frame for a middle section whose quiet modal grandeur is successively unfolded by the woodwind and string choirs.

The treasury of America's wartime music brims with repertoire that proves remarkably appealing now.

Even in ensuing decades, when he adopted twelve-tone techniques in his later symphonies and choral works, Diamond never abandoned the idiomatic approach to instruments and voices that appeals to audiences as much as to musicians.

Diamond's wartime symphonies are matched in color and vitality by Paul Creston's first three symphonies (of an eventual five), completed respectively in 1940, 1944 and 1950. Creston (1906–1985), born Giuseppe Guttoveggio, the son of a Sicilian immigrant, had studied piano and organ in New York with the Italian-born Pietro Yon, organist and choirmaster of St Patrick's Cathedral and composer of the popular Christmas song "Gesu Bambino." But he essentially taught himself composition. His Italian heritage is apparent in his music's warmth, melodic verve and expressive harmony: it is no wonder that he marked the opening movement of his magnificent

Emotion is at the heart of Paul Creston's First Symphony, whose movements are in four contrasting states of mind.

Second Symphony "with deep emotion." Emotion is equally at the heart of Creston's First Symphony, whose movements are in four contrasting states of mind ("Majesty," "Humor," "Serenity" and "Gaiety"), and it also charges the sensitive instrumental treatment of the life of Christ that forms his Third Symphony and the tone poem *Out of the Cradle*, Op. 5 (1934), inspired by "Out of the Cradle Endlessly Rocking," from Whitman's *Leaves of Grass*. Creston's masterful orchestral technique and the sense of virtuoso style also imbue his towering **Fifth Symphony**, Op. 64 (1955–6), his fifteen concertos and more than thirty other symphonic scores, among

Website
track 67–69
www.naxosbooks.com

them the neo-baroque *Partita*, Op. 12 (1937), the atmospheric *Invocation and Dance*, Op. 58 (1953), and the vivacious *Toccata*, Op. 68 (1957).

Norman Dello Joio (b. 1913) was another Italian American (the family name was properly spelled Dello Ioio) who rose to celebrity during the war years. The son of an organist and vocal coach whose clients included stars of the Metropolitan Opera, he had a melodic sense shaped by intimate exposure to the smooth, gratifying cantabile inherent in vocal and organ repertoire. At Yale and Tanglewood his teacher and mentor Paul Hindemith pointedly told him, "Your music is lyrical by nature, don't ever forget that." He didn't, and throughout his long career – past ninety at the time of this writing, he still undertakes commissions for new works – his music has glowed with a melodic impulse to rival that of Samuel Barber. Although he ultimately declined to follow his father and godfather (coincidentally Creston's teacher, Pietro Yon) into a career in the choir loft, he has often been attracted to sacred texts or subjects with religious overtones, such as his Magnificat, which won the Town Hall Composition Award in 1943. His opera *The Trial of St Joan* (1950), telecast by NBC in 1956 (as *The Trial at Rouen*), won a New York Music Critics' Circle Award in 1959, and his *Meditations on Ecclesiastes*, for string orchestra (1956), won a 1957 Pulitzer Prize. Dello Joio wrote some twenty chamber works, striking concertante scores for piano, flute, harp, clarinet and harmonica, music for television, and over forty choral works, including a cantata setting

> At Yale and Tanglewood his teacher and mentor Paul Hindemith pointedly told Norman Dello Joio, "Your music is lyrical by nature, don't ever forget that."

of Whitman's *Mystic Trumpeter* (1943), *Psalms of David*, for chorus, brass, strings and percussion (1950), and a Mass for chorus, cantor, congregation, organ and brass ensemble (1976). His sonorous three-movement *Triumph of St Joan Symphony* (1951), based on material from his opera, is truly memorable, while the witty *Homage to Haydn*, for orchestra (1969), would offer a very welcome alternative to Prokofiev's more familiar "Classical" Symphony.

Other interesting composers were working during this period and into the postwar era, including Ulysses Kay, Robert Ward, Robert

Palmer, William Bergsma, Vincent Persichetti and Peter Mennin, the last of whom succeeded William Schuman as President of Juilliard. During the 1930s and 1940s, when American radio stations boasted house orchestras to provide live music on a large scale, a number of composers worked in the lighter symphonic manner of Ferde Grofé, consciously producing orchestral music with recognizably American themes. Among these modern "nationalists" were figures such as Ernst Bacon (1898–1990), another student of Ernest Bloch, whose works include the suites *Country Roads Unpaved* (1936) and *From these States* (1943); Don Gillis, who was a production director for NBC Radio as well as composer of symphonies, notably the tongue-in-cheek *No. 5½*, and orchestral pieces such as *The Panhandle*, *Portrait of a Frontier Town* and *Citizen Tom Paine*; and Elie Siegmeister (1909–1991), a student of Riegger and of Nadia Boulanger who published collections of American folk songs and achieved a significant reputation

> Though sometimes compared to Gershwin because of the way in which he freely adapted pop idioms in his concert music, Morton Gould was rigorously schooled in the craft of composition.

as a professor at Hofstra University and a highly accessible author of music texts for lay readers, as well as being a composer of music that sought to "express the social values of the people." His considerable legacy includes such works as the *Walt Whitman Overture* (1939), the *Western Suite* (1945), a splendid Clarinet Concerto in which he deploys elements of jazz, blues and swing within a thoroughly classical framework, symphonies, choral music, piano music, chamber music, and a not inconsiderable body of operas and other dramatic music.

By and large the leading name in this most approachable group is that of Morton Gould (1913–1996), a popular conductor as well as a composer blessed (though some say cursed) with a common touch that did not compromise his sophisticated craftsmanship. Though sometimes compared to Gershwin because of the way in which he freely adapted pop idioms in his concert music, Gould was rigorously schooled in the craft of composition, completing his academic training at the Institute of Musical Art and New York University at the age of fifteen. His *Chorale and Fugue in Jazz* (1931) first gained him attention when Stokowski conducted it with the Philadelphia Orchestra in 1936. Thereafter he brought out four symphonies, modestly styled *American Symphonettes*, which remain standard works today, especially the "Pavane" movement of the first (1936) and the entire fourth, or *Latin American Symphonette* (1944). His *Foster Gallery* (1939) inventively gives a baker's dozen of songs by Stephen Foster a full symphonic treatment equivalent to Britten's *Variations on a Theme by Purcell* and Hindemith's *Metamorphoses of a Theme by Weber*, while his *American Salute* (1942) similarly expanded on Patrick Gilmore's Civil War song "When Johnny Comes Marching Home." A great morale-booster immediately after Pearl Harbor, it became an American classic.

Gould's nationalism, deft humor and sophisticated instrumental technique yielded a panoply of works with immediate appeal: the *Cowboy Rhapsody* (1940), the fine ballet **Fall River Legend** (1948, based on the murderous tale of axe-wielding Lizzie Borden), the Viola Concerto (1943) and Concerto for Tap Dancer and Orchestra (1952), the *Jekyll and Hyde Variations*, for orchestra (1957), and the *American Ballads* and *Symphony of Spirituals* (both 1976) only skim the surface of his output for which he was showered with honors and awards.

Walter Piston composed his **Second Symphony** in 1943, as the tide of the war was turning, and its deft balance of heroic, lyrical and march-like gestures (recalling Ives' jauntier manner) bespeaks the composer's ability to express American optimism without resorting to jingoist bombast. The *Adagio* is pure nostalgia, with its heart-wrenchingly beautiful solos for clarinet and flute, while the finale asserts itself with unbridled vigor and admirable contrapuntal panache.

World War II ended in two stages: Germany fell in May 1945 (not long after the sudden death of President Roosevelt on April 12), and the planned Allied invasion of Japan was averted by President Harry S. Truman's decision to drop atomic bombs on Hiroshima and Nagasaki in August. Victory in the Pacific had thereby come at a great cost, for the world had entered the atomic age, engendering all the fears that haunt us to this day. Thus if Piston could wax nostalgic in 1943, so could Samuel Barber in 1947, with **Knoxville: Summer of 1915**, his touching evocation of small-town life. It is a "lyric rhapsody" for soprano and orchestra (text by James Agee) that ranks with the finest songs of Brahms and Fauré.

Website
track 70–85
www.naxosbooks.com

Website
track 86–88
www.naxosbooks.com

Website
track 89
www.naxosbooks.com

16 Exploring the Frontiers of Sound

During the late 1940s and into the postwar decades, cutting-edge composers set their sights on creating music that moved further and further away from traditional Western harmony, melody, rhythm, form and instruments. Encouraged by universities (where many of them held teaching positions) and funded by a variety of grants, fellowships and other academic resources, this postwar avant-garde effectively declared their independence from the old-line criterion of audience approval, determining that only their peer group of like-minded composers was eligible to judge their work.

Aesthetic descendents of Charles Ives, composers such as George Perle (b. 1915), the mathematician-turned-musician Milton Babbitt (b. 1916) and the iconic John Cage, expanded the accepted definition of music as they probed the very nature of sound, exploring new ways to use all manner of sounds and to arrange them into recognizable compositions. Even the traditional way of performing music was questioned, especially as composers began to research the incredible possibilities of electronic music: not only did electronic sources add almost limitless varieties of sound to the aural palette, they also called for new forms of musical notation divorced from traditional notes on a staff. Electronic music raised questions as to the nature, not to mention the necessity, of a musical score, and questions concerning the relationship between the composer, the performer, the listener and the musical work. It even raised questions about what abilities were necessary to compose music, or even to experience it: the sight-reading skills needed to "listen" to the printed score of the most complex Richard Strauss tone poem were of little use when a new piece of electronic music existed only on a computer print-out and magnetic tape.

Admittedly, one challenge posed by experimental music has been that it often represents aesthetic philosophies that demand explanation if the listener is to understand what he or she is hearing. While a piece by Copland or Schuman or any of the mainstream figures falls within most informed listeners' expectations of what concert music ought to sound like, many experimental pieces definitely sound strange at first hearing – and this does not mean ugly or even unpleasant, just strange. Therefore, such pieces require listeners to approach them with open minds, receptive to sounds and time frames that transcend most familiar preconceptions.

Although most experimental composers were quite well trained in traditional musical techniques before they struck out in their new directions, one exception was the extraordinary Harry Partch (1901–1974). As a composer, Partch was primarily self-taught. He lived as a hobo during the 1930s, collecting experiences and folk materials, among them graffiti scrawlings, which he later used in such works as *Eight Hitchhiker Inscriptions from a Highway Railing at Barstow, California*, for chorus and instruments (1941, revised 1968). He also kept a series of journals of his peripatetic adventures, including drawings, notated transcriptions of speech-music, narratives of his thoughts and homoerotic fantasies, which he entitled *Bitter Music*. Furthering the idea of quarter-tones (which Ives had used as early as 1903) and other, smaller "microtones," Partch continually worked at dividing the octave into an increasing number of unequal steps, eventually reaching forty-three. He also invented a battery of new instruments to play his microtonal compositions. In this "instrumentarium," as he called it, were chordophones (plucked or struck with mallets) such as adapted guitars, kithara, surrogate

> Most experimental composers were so far off the beaten path of mainstream concert programming that the majority of audiences weren't even aware of their activities.

kithara and crychord; tuned idiophones, taking in diamond marimba, marimba eroica, quadrangularis reversum, gourd tree, cloud-chamber bowls and spoils-of-war (metal and wood, including whang gun); and aerophones, notably chromelodeons (modified reed organs) and his bloboy [sic] of pipes and bellows.

Partch's compositions, reflecting broad literary tastes ranging from Western classics to Eastern and African traditions, include treatments of Shakespeare (the Potion Scene from *Romeo and Juliet*, 1931), Sophocles via W.B. Yeats (*King Oedipus*, 1933, and revised thereafter) and Lewis Carroll ("O Frabjous Day" and "The Mock Turtle Song"). Among other works are *Rotate the Body in All its Planes (A Ballad for Gymnasts*, 1961), which was based on his earlier *Revelation in the Courthouse Park* (after Euripides' *Bacchae*, 1961), as well as *And on the Seventh Day Petals Fell on Petaluma* (1963–6) and *Delusion of the Fury: A Ritual of Dream and Delusion*, after Japanese and African sources (1965–6).

Most experimental composers were academically cloistered or so far off the beaten path of mainstream concert programming that the majority of audiences weren't even aware of their activities. The most inventive and influential composer of this time was John Cage (1912–1992), who had studied composition with Henry Cowell before taking Arnold Schoenberg's course at the University of California, Los Angeles.

As early as the 1930s, Cage took Cowell's piano technique beyond the tone clusters produced by fists and forearms on the keys and the striking and plucking of the piano strings. Necessity proved the mother of invention: he had been working with a Seattle dance group and needed percussion instruments for a dance with an African flavor. The theatre had only a small grand piano, and neither wings nor a pit. "At the time I either wrote twelve-tone music for piano or I wrote percussion music," Cage recalled in an autobiographical essay. "There was no room for the instruments and I couldn't find an African twelve-tone row. I finally realized I had to change the piano ... by placing objects between the strings.

> A piece by Copland or any of the mainstream figures falls within most informed listeners' expectations of what concert music ought to sound like, but many experimental pieces definitely sound strange at first hearing.

The piano was transformed into a percussion orchestra having the loudness, say, of a harpsichord."

In Cage's "prepared piano" coins, screws, rubber, felt or paper strips, and other non-musical objects are applied to the piano strings to change their sound. Depending on the applied objects, the prepared piano can plink, plunk, chime, tingle like a hi-hat cymbal,

Photograph by Malcolm Crowthers

John Cage

or sound like a lute, a dulcimer or a clavichord. In brief, it is able to produce an almost limitless variety of pitched and unpitched sounds. For example, Cage's **Totem Ancestor** (1942) presents a fascinating array of timbres and unexpected rhythms, not to mention a complete sense of atonality – but atonality without the dissonance with which it is frequently associated.

The effect of this new twist on the good old concert grand startled listeners when Cage introduced it. During the 1940s Cage achieved considerable notoriety through performing his own works for prepared piano. By the 1950s the use of a prepared piano was acknowledged as a legitimate musical technique and was adopted by other composers. Meanwhile Cage had many more avenues to travel.

After moving to New York from his native California, Cage embarked on a fruitful collaboration with the choreographer Merce Cunningham, for whom he wrote a number of dance works, including the aforementioned *Totem Ancestor*. Much of his music lends itself to dance because of its rhythmic energy. Indeed, Cage had emphasized rhythm in his works while still a pupil of Schoenberg, soon after realizing that he had little feeling for conventional harmony, and this emphasis yielded, among other purely rhythmic explorations, his beguiling series of *Constructions* – *First* (1939), *Second* (1940) and *Third* (1941) – for different percussion ensembles.

> Much of John Cage's music lends itself to dance because of its rhythmic energy.

During the 1950s, profoundly influenced by his study of Zen Buddhism, Cage deliberately began to write music devoid of expression or communication, intended instead "to quiet the mind, thus making it susceptible to divine influences." He investigated the possibilities of pre-recorded sounds distorted by microphones or generated electronically by synthesizers (whose immediate antecedents were electric organs). Dramatically influenced by the experience of hearing his own nervous and circulatory systems while in a soundproof chamber, he realized that silence is only the difference between intentional and unintentional sounds. Also influenced by Robert Rauschenberg's blank white paintings, he looked to silence as music. Thus, in Cage's three-movement piece

4'33" (1952), the performer remains silent for the titular duration while the audience hears only the ambient sounds in the hall. In the same period in which he was advocating that his listeners regard their environment at any given moment as music, Cage also produced the first well-known aleatory work, *Music of Changes* (1951) for piano.

Aleatory music, in its broadest sense, is music whose components are partly or entirely left to chance. In *Music of Changes* the pitches are noted exactly, but their duration and frequency of occurrence (i.e., rhythm) are decided by the *I-Ching* (Book of Changes), the ancient Chinese formula for arriving at random numbers by throwing coins or sticks. Cage explored various ways of applying aleatory principles to his music. For example, in Concert for Piano and Orchestra (1958) eighty-four different "sound-aggregates" can be played in their entirety or in part, and in any sequence. The orchestral parts are similarly left to chance, and the work includes a soprano "aria," which may be sung or not sung.

In addition to music, Cage wrote poetry and prose, and he drew and worked in watercolor, lithography and etching, allowing each discipline to meld with the other.

Cage's early training in art and architecture also came into play in ensuing years. In addition to music, he wrote poetry and prose, and he drew and worked in watercolor, lithography and etching, allowing each discipline to meld with the other. For instance, after creating a series of prints called *On the Surface*, Cage composed *Thirty Pieces for Five Orchestras* during which he discovered that, in order for the musical work to correspond with the visual one, "a horizontal line that determined graphic changes had to become a vertical line in the notation of music. Time instead of space."

Throughout his long and creative life, Cage never stopped exploring, never stopped experimenting. A born showman with an engaging sense of humor (and a ready smile), he was always serious about his work, but he never made the mistake of taking *himself* too seriously.

At every stage of his mature career, Cage influenced other experimental composers, especially the French-born Christian Wolff, Earle Brown and Morton Feldman. Wolff and Feldman were greatly attracted by Cage's idea of liberating sounds from the interrelationships that normally occur in the ordered arrangements and sequences of musical composition. Brown and Feldman both drew considerable inspiration from their personal relationships with the contemporary art world.

Christian Wolff (b. 1934), who teaches at Harvard and Dartmouth, evolved a musical language based on highly limited numbers of pitches, with formal structures derived from arithmetical progressions of rhythmic values and expressive deployment of rests. For instance, his Trio for flute, cello and trumpet (1951) contains only four different pitches, while his Duo for violin and piano (1961) contains three. Consequently, Wolff's compositions often contain more passages of silence than passages of sound. In some of his chamber works he leaves not only the duration of sounds or tones

> Earle Brown was profoundly influenced by the sculptor Alexander Calder, whose mobiles constantly change shape.

unspecified but also the instrumentation, for example in the Septet for any instruments (1964). In some works, performers themselves are intended to react to one another according to unforeseen cues, less as musicians following a specific score than as players on a field passing a ball from one to the other. Wolff's overall aim has been to encourage a sense of liberating interdependence between his players. His music has been used by the choreographer Merce Cunningham and the dancer Lucinda Childs.

Earle Brown (1926–2002) was profoundly influenced by the sculptor Alexander Calder, whose mobiles constantly change shape as their balanced elements slowly move about in mid-air. Inspired by this, Brown arrived at the notion that a musical work could be played several times, it being slightly different each time but always remaining the same work. His *Folio* (1952–3) incorporated the score of *1953* for piano, his initial work composed according to this "mobile" plan. He later expanded this into *Twenty-Five Pages*, for one to twenty-five pianos: the score's twenty-five pages can be played in any sequence; as in conventional piano music, the notes are written on two-stave systems, but the staves can be played in either bass or treble clef, the duration of each system being left up to the performer. *December 1952* is the composer's most famous work:

the music is written on a single page with no staves. Instead of notes, Brown drew a composition of horizontal and vertical lines, some longer, some shorter, some thicker, some thinner. The lines suggest direction, dynamic level, duration and pitch, and the performer, holding the page in any position, is meant to "track" his way around it, selecting his own sequence of auditory events. The page itself suggests a painting by Piet Mondrian, and indeed it was exhibited as a piece of graphic art. Brown's work, which includes such recent compositions as *Tracking Pierrot*, for chamber ensemble (1992), *Summer Suite*, for variable keyboard (1995), and *Special Events*, for cello and piano (1999), also incorporated ideas he derived from abstract expressionist painting, surrealist poetry and neo-dadaism.

Morton Feldman (1926–1987) had already studied composition successively with Wallingford Riegger and Stefan Wolpe when he met Cage in 1949. Cage encouraged him to discard the rules when composing and just follow his musical instincts. Passionately drawn to abstract expressionism during the 1950s (apart from Cage, he numbered painters Jackson Pollock, Mark Rothko, Willem de Kooning and Robert Rauschenberg among his friends), Feldman created a physical sonic world for his musical expression, one that reflected the kinetic visual energy he perceived in their works, along with the parallel "action-painting" concept of "predetermined indeterminacy" (i.e., Pollock flung paint from brush to canvas, knowing that chance played a great part in determining the precise areas of the canvas on which the paint droplets would land). Feldman's adaptation of this principle resulted in scores such as *Projection No. 2*, written in graph notation, from which the players were to choose a certain number of notes for their musical "action" (hence indeterminacy) from within a predetermined time structure and range (high, middle, low). Feeling that this method allowed the performers too great an improvisational latitude, Feldman wrote in precise notation during the mid-1950s, only to return to graphic notation for two orchestral works, *Atlantis* (1958) and *Out of Last Pieces* (1960). Subsequently he composed several instrumental works

Morton Feldman's goal was to create an environment in which the listener experienced the music from "inside" a composition.

collectively titled *Durations*. In these, the pitches and tempi were precisely notated, but the players were allowed to determine the *durations* of the pitches within a given tempo. With *On Time and the Instrumental Factor* (1969) Feldman resumed composing in strict notation of pitch, rhythm and dynamics.

During the late 1970s Feldman was preoccupied with expanding the length of his compositions. "Up to an hour, you think about form," he observed, "but after an hour and a half, it's scale. ... Before, my pieces were like objects; now they're like evolving things." Thereafter, Feldman composed increasingly long works – for instance, *Patterns in a Chromatic Field*, for cello and piano (1981), runs non-stop for over an hour, while the String Quartet II (1983) lasts five hours. His goal was to create an environment in which the listener experienced the music from "inside" a composition. And to his characteristic idiom of atonality, low dynamic levels and extremely spare textures he added minimalist repetition. By repeating individual motifs or groups of motifs as many as a dozen times and more, Feldman intended to disorient the listener's memory, stressing the static nature of particular musical gestures while de-emphasizing any patterns created by the repetition. Feldman's eighty-minute Piano and String Quartet (1985) is a delicate encapsulation of these ideas – the work is essentially a series of quiet, enigmatic arpeggios on the piano, answered by quiet, enigmatic chords by the string quartet. Throughout, Feldman makes subtle alterations to the harmony – a tone here, a tone there – so that, as you listen, you realize that the repetition is never entirely exact. The effect is truly dream-like, timeless, akin to the subtle shift of late-afternoon sunbeams through a window blind.

The intricate, repetitious patterns of textiles provided another source of inspiration: Feldman's last orchestral score, *Coptic Light* (1986), contains more than twenty instrumental layers, each repeating a simple pattern. It was suggested by the dense textures of early Coptic textiles housed in the Louvre, Paris.

Conlon Nancarrow (1912–1997) was another fascinating outsider, though his politics helped to isolate him as much as his music. In 1937, having already become a member of the Communist

Party, he joined the Abraham Lincoln Brigade to fight the Fascists in the Spanish Civil War. On his return two years later, the US government treated him with suspicion. By 1940 growing anti-communist activity forced him to leave for Mexico City, where he lived for the rest of his life, eventually taking Mexican citizenship.

Having played trumpet in jazz orchestras, Nancarrow studied privately with Walter Piston, Roger Sessions and the pioneering modernist conductor and scholar Nicolas Slonimsky. Jazz and J.S. Bach were his two overriding inspirations, and an exhilarating mixture of bluesy syncopation and neo-baroque counterpoint distinguishes much of his work, from compositions such as the Blues (1935), Prelude (1935) and Sonatina (1941), all for piano, to the marvelously disjointed *Tango?* (1983), also for piano, and the insouciant Piece No. 2 for Small Orchestra (1986). Together with his delight in the fast jazz tempos of his favorite pianists Art Tatum and Earl Hines, Nancarrow's lifelong exploration of rhythm and its complexities led him to transcend the technical limitations of even the best players. In his **Toccata** for violin and player piano (1935), for example, he composed lightning-fast repeated notes and passage-work that, while easily played on a violin, are impossible for a pianist to execute on a keyboard. His solution was to transcribe the piano part in punched holes on a player piano roll, and in performance the violin is accompanied by a player piano.

Between 1948 and 1992 Nancarrow wrote a series of fifty-one Studies for Player Piano, many of which exploit a technique that became his calling card: tempo canon. His brief **Study No. 15** (1950s), one of a few transcribed for piano duet by Yvar Mikhashoff, is a prime example of the technique. In this two-part tempo canon, both parts play the same thematic material (as in a normal canon), but in different tempos, at a ratio of 4:3. The upper part starts out in the faster tempo, the lower part in the slower one. After the upper part completes its statement of the theme, it begins again at the slower tempo. Meanwhile the lower part, upon completing its statement of the theme, begins again at the faster tempo. Soon it overtakes the now slow upper part and, by virtue of their mathematical balance, both parts end together.

CD
track 15
www.naxosbooks.com

Website
track 90
www.naxosbooks.com

Ironically, by concentrating on writing for player piano, thereby eschewing live performance, Nancarrow placed himself outside the concert and mainstream music-publishing circuits – even among avant-garde circles. Thus his music, even the early works, remained unknown until his student, the composer and publisher Peter Garland (b. 1952), published Nancarrow's scores in his periodical *Soundings*. At the same time, the Player Piano Studies began to appear on recordings, and after forty years Nancarrow's music began to attract a following, especially among younger composers – it is no coincidence that a work such as John Adams' piano concerto *Century Rolls* (composed for Emanuel Ax) exhibits the same joyous energy as Nancarrow's Toccata. Nancarrow began to receive commissions for live-performance works, as well as invitations to appear at European music festivals, and in 1983 he received the MacArthur Foundation "genius" award of $300,000.

17 The Melting-Pot of American Opera and Musical Theatre

After World War II music for the American stage underwent a gradual blurring of the lines between opera and musical theatre. Apart from the nature of the music itself, this blurring was fostered by regional opera companies absorbing classic Broadway musicals alongside their operettas. American opera composers imparted a distinctive American flavor both through their musical style and through their chosen subjects.

Certainly George Gershwin's *Porgy and Bess* is the American opera most firmly established in the standard repertoire, alongside the works of Verdi, Wagner and Puccini. It is known even to people with little interest in opera. Conceived for a cast of black singers at a time of rampant segregation in the US, when white entertainers in blackface were still acceptable on stage, the score is hardly an ethnographically accurate representation of African-American folk music. Gershwin observed, "The recitatives I have tried to make as close to the Negro inflection in speech as possible." No one should mistake the sultry melody of "Summertime" for a genuine antebellum lullaby or Porgy's "I got plenty o' nuttin'" for an authentic plantation tune, yet even to ears familiar with black music, from ragtime to rap, the appropriateness of Gershwin's music to the characters and story of the opera is undeniable.

Moreover, Gershwin's biographer Joan Peyser points out that, beneath the loveliness of Gershwin's melodies, the score is remarkable for its background textures of intricate counterpoint and twelve-tone writing, quoting such authorities as Gershwin's friend, the pianist Oscar Levant, and composers Morton Gould and Elie Siegmeister, on the admirable qualities of such passages as the fugue in the crap game and murder scene: "I took another look at the fugue in the murder scene of *Porgy and Bess*," wrote Siegmeister to Peyser in 1990, "and found it to be a very respectable, traditional

> George Gershwin's *Porgy and Bess* is the American opera most firmly established in the standard repertoire, known even to people with little interest in opera.

fugue – with jazz subject and countersubject – fully developed. ... I can think of no other full-fledged fugues in opera except the one in *Falstaff* – and Gershwin's is, I think, far more dramatic."

Generally, American operas with compelling stories and harmonious, melodic scores have proved more durable than operas with serial, electronic or otherwise experimental music. Among the former, Gian Carlo Menotti's earlier operas have been regularly revived because their music "speaks" to listeners. So does Samuel Barber's *Vanessa*, which he wrote to Menotti's libretto. Barber's *Antony and Cleopatra*, revised by the composer after its initial failure at its premiere at the Met in 1966, has been critically and positively reassessed in recent years.

Like Menotti, Dominick Argento (b. 1927) has roots in the Italian tradition, and his music packs an appropriate emotional wallop in a drama such as *The Aspern Papers* (1987), based on Henry James' novella. His comedies are equally adept, among them *The Boor* (1957, based on Chekhov's play *The Bear*) and his most popular opera, the enigmatic *Postcard from Morocco* (1971).

Striving for American flavor, composers often turned to American stories for their libretti. Virgil Thomson, having puzzled his audience with the surreal *Four Saints in Three Acts* in 1934, looked to American history for his second opera, *The Mother of Us All*, which premiered at Columbia University in 1947. Nominally, it concerns the life of Susan B. Anthony, the nineteenth-century pioneer of women's voting rights. Gertrude Stein's libretto plays fast and loose with history, and the plot is typically vague. Thomson's eminently listenable score incorporates period ballads, hymns and march tunes.

Douglas Moore (1893–1969), a former student of Parker at Yale, wrote *The Ballad of Baby Doe* in 1956. It dramatizes the history of "Baby Doe" Tabor during the Colorado silver boom with lyrical music, richly evocative of the raw-boned West. Aaron Copland's

Thomas Pasatieri, a prolific opera composer, writes in an expressive, vocally idiomatic style particularly gratifying to singers.

The Tender Land was written for NBC television, which commissioned and then rejected it. The New York City Opera ultimately premiered the work in 1954. As in the composer's ballets, the setting is rural American, and the most memorable set-pieces are those most obviously tinged with Copland's Americana idiom, especially "Stomp your Foot," the toe-tapping square dance in Act II.

Like Gershwin and Menotti, Marc Blitzstein (1905–1964) straddled the line between the opera house and Broadway. After completing in 1937 a controversial socialist musical, *The Cradle Will Rock*, he turned to Lillian Hellman's haunting drama of greed and betrayal in a post-Civil War southern family, *The Little Foxes*. As *Regina*, it was produced on Broadway in 1949, but the audiences found it too operatic to be a musical, and vice versa. Today we know better: the score gets under your skin and stays there.

Other works in this genre do the same. Carlisle Floyd (b. 1926) set the biblical tale of Susannah and the Elders in the southern backwoods in *Susannah* (1955), and his *Of Mice and Men* (1970) is based on John Steinbeck's novel of the same title. *Desire under the Elms* (1975), styled a "folk opera" by its composer, Edward Thomas (b. 1924), illuminates Eugene O'Neill's violent tragedy

Jazz plays a legitimate dramatic part in *Trouble in Tahiti* and *A Quiet Place*, Leonard Bernstein's studies of suburban malaise.

of lusty youth repressed by a father's greed. Thomas's vivid score draws upon the pastoral traditions of Copland and Barber, with effective nods at verismo. O'Neill's *Mourning Becomes Electra* found a musical voice when it was transformed into an opera by Marvin David Levy (b. 1932). The work made a considerable splash at its 1967 premiere at the Met, and, revised in 1998 and 2003, it continues to enjoy important revivals. Similarly, *Summer and Smoke* (1970), by Lee Hoiby (b. 1926), adapts Tennessee Williams' play about repressed desire, using lush, expressive music. Thomas Pasatieri (b. 1945), a prolific opera composer, also writes in an expressive, vocally idiomatic style particularly gratifying to singers. Of his pieces, commissioned by the Houston Grand Opera, Baltimore Opera and Michigan Opera Theatre, the most successful have been *The Seagull* (1974), after Chekhov, and *Washington Square* (1976), after Henry James. The continued accessibility of his music is evident in his recent orchestral song cycle *Letter to Warsaw* (2003). It sets texts by the Polish cabaret singer Pola Braun, who was murdered in Majdanek concentration camp in 1943.

Since the 1970s, new American opera commissions and more frequent performances and recordings have raised the consciousness and fostered a greater receptiveness among audiences to new works, as well as to revivals and reappraisals of older pieces. Leonard Bernstein's *Candide* is a good example of the latter case. Its 1956 Broadway premiere

> Leonard Bernstein's *West Side Story* is a pivotal work of musical theatre and as iconic as *Porgy and Bess*.

was unsuccessful, but after considerable revision by the composer a new production by Hal Prince arrived on Broadway in 1974, and *Candide* was established in earnest. Today, though there is still no definitive version of the score, it is standard fare of opera companies in America and abroad, with few questions asked about whether it is an opera, an operetta or a musical. To some extent the same holds true for Bernstein's **West Side Story**, a pivotal work of musical theatre and as iconic as *Porgy and Bess*. Premiered in 1957, the score includes a variety of musical influences – jazz, Latin, vaudeville ("Gee, Officer Krupke") – and, of course, Bernstein's own brand of soaring romantic melody. With masterful balance, he blends several of these in the Act I Quintet, during which the rival Jets and Sharks gangs plan their "Rumble" while Tony and Maria sing of their impatience to be together again, in "Tonight."

With Bernstein, the line between opera and musical theatre is always hazy: *On the Town* (1944) and *Wonderful Town* (1953) are unmistakably Broadway, but his two operas, *Trouble in Tahiti* (1952) and its sequel *A Quiet Place* (1983), incorporate the smoky, loose-shouldered jazz idiom he loved. That jazz element plays a legitimate dramatic part in both studies of suburban malaise, and the orchestral fabric of recurring leitmotifs in the later score is as sophisticated as any of Bernstein's symphonic works.

Website
track 91
www.naxosbooks.com

In recent decades Philip Glass (b. 1937) and John Adams (b. 1947) have been pre-eminent in American opera. Glass made his mark with *Einstein on the Beach* (1976), on which he collaborated with the controversial designer-director Robert Wilson. *Einstein* is nominally concerned with the formulator of the theory of relativity, though it does not follow a conventional narrative. This work led to two more operas revolving around epochal figures in history: *Satyagraha* (1980), to a Sanskrit libretto, treats Mahatma Gandhi's early years, while *Akhnaten* (1983) examines reaction to religious orthodoxy, centering upon the titular Egyptian pharaoh. The text of *Akhnaten*, by Glass and several associates, could stand as a definition of the word "eclectic," since it incorporates Egyptian, Akkadian and Hebrew texts, along with narrative passages in "the language of

Philip Glass and Robert Wilson in May 1976, New York,
planning Einstein on the Beach

the audience" and excerpts from Fodor's and Frommer's guides to Egypt. In later operas, such as *The Voyage* (1992) and *La Belle et la Bête* (1994, a treatment of Cocteau's *Beauty and the Beast*), Glass moved away from minimalist note-spinning to more conventional melodic writing.

Adams enjoys a similar performance track record. Pulsing minimalist sequences, engaging cross-rhythms, and often dense contrapuntal textures are at the center of his style; but so is finely honed melody, which he exploits in his operas *Nixon in China* (1987) and *The Death of Klinghoffer* (1991). Adams styled his third major theatre piece, **I Was Looking at the Ceiling and then I Saw the Sky** (1995), a "song play" rather than an opera. Written in collaboration with the poet and prominent civil rights advocate June Jordan (1936–2002), it dramatizes the experiences of seven young Angelinos of different ethnic and social backgrounds before and after the 1994 Los Angeles earthquake. However, while the piece is entirely sung, without dialogue, the vocal forces are pop in style rather than operatic, the language colloquial, and the accompaniment a pop-rock band of keyboards, clarinet, saxophone, guitar, bass and percussion. Adams deliberately eschews operatic continuity, presenting instead a quasi-narrative cyclical series of catchy, self-contained numbers whose respective styles embrace a succession of gospel, Latin, pop and various jazz and rock idioms, albeit distilled through the composer's sophisticated musical intelligence. The finale, a pop-passacaglia reprising the mellifluous opening ensemble, encapsulates it all quite vividly.

In October 2005 Adams unveiled his latest opera, *Doctor Atomic*, in a widely heralded production at the San Francisco Opera. The libretto, by the iconoclastic stage director Peter Sellars (who had also staged the premieres of both *Nixon* and *Klinghoffer*), draws entirely upon contemporary documents

John Adams' opera *Doctor Atomic* focuses on the mercurial physicist J. Robert Oppenheimer.

to dramatize the events surrounding one of the most epochal events in modern history, the testing of the first atomic bomb in 1945. It focuses on the leader of the latter's top-secret development team, the mercurial physicist J. Robert Oppenheimer. Adams' characteristically inventive score reveals how far he has transcended his minimalist origins as it probes the psychological and moral complexity of the event and its participants: to end a world war, mankind unleashed the means to its own annihilation. While his essentially lyric vocal writing follows the cadences of normal speech (sometimes verging on the easiness of gentle nightclub balladry), he evokes the ominous spirit of the time by weaving amplified snatches of period radio broadcasts and sounds of droning aircraft and crashing steel into the pulsing rhythms, kaleidoscopic instrumental color and expressive dissonance of his symphonic orchestration. Significantly, in an era of skyrocketing production costs, *Doctor Atomic* was commissioned jointly by the San Francisco Opera, the Lyric Opera of Chicago and the Netherlands Opera, thus ensuring future performances in other venues after the world-premiere run.

In 1991 John Corigliano (b. 1938) brought out *The Ghosts of Versailles*, commissioned by the Metropolitan Opera. Inspired by *La Mère coupable* (the dark-hued final play in Pierre Beaumarchais' "Figaro" trilogy), it takes up where Rossini' *The Barber of Seville* and Mozart's *The Marriage of Figaro* leave off – relating the trials of Count Almaviva's household when the French Revolution explodes around them. Writing in a contemporary idiom, Corigliano produced a score full of affectionate allusions to Mozart, Rossini, Richard Strauss and Puccini.

American literature and drama have continued to inspire new operas right into the present century, including William Bolcom's *McTeague* (1992, after Frank Norris's novel) and *A View From the Bridge* (1999, adapted from Arthur Miller's play), André Previn's *A Streetcar Named Desire* (1997), Mark Adamo's *Little Women* (1998), John Harbison's *The Great Gatsby* (1999), Jake Heggie's *Dead Man Walking* (2000, after the book by Sister Helen Prejean), and Scott Eyerly's *The House of the Seven Gables* (2000). Tobias Picker's *Emmeline* (1996), based on Judith Rossner's bleak novel, is a reversal of the Oedipus myth, set against the harsh background of an 1840s New England mill town. Picker's *An American Tragedy*, after Theodore Dreiser's novel, commissioned in 2000 and premiered at the Metropolitan

Opera in 2005, shows how his genuinely lyrical impulse, powerful vocal writing and masterful orchestral sense continue to respond positively to tales of sorrow, loneliness and spiritual poverty.

This focus on American operas with American themes should not obscure the many American operas based on European classics. Among these are Robert Kurka's satirical *The Good Soldier Schweik* (1958, founded on Jaroslav Hašek's eponymous novel), electronic/ microtonal composer John Eaton's *The Tempest* (1985), *Peer Gynt* (1993) and *Don Quixote* (1999–2000), Lowell Liebermann's *Picture of Dorian Gray* (1995), Picker's *Thérèse Raquin* (1999–2000, dramatizing Zola's novel), Stephen Paulus's *Heloise and Abelard* (2001), Heggie's *The End of the Affair* (2003, revised 2004–5, after Graham Greene's novel), and Adamo's *Lysistrata*, to his own adaptation of Aristophanes' comedy, which received its premiere at the Houston Grand Opera in 2005. At the time of writing, Steven Hartke's new opera, *The Greater Good, or the Passion of Boule de Suif*, based on Maupassant's story "A Ball of Wax," is being prepared for its premiere in summer 2006 at the influential Glimmerglass Opera.

> As "art" music, operas have never been expected to succeed commercially, so composers have not felt obliged to court audience popularity.

Despite the number of American operas written and produced during the last half-century, musical theatre has had an easier time maintaining its recognizable profile, for several reasons. First, notwithstanding the efforts of American composers, the standard opera repertoire in the US has traditionally been dominated by the European works demanded by the public. Second, American opera has never had a truly identifiable home base, the way Italian opera is identified with La Scala and Wagner's work is identified with Bayreuth. Third, with a few exceptions, American operas have a more difficult time entering the standard repertoire after their premieres because the opera-loving public doesn't expect or demand to hear them regularly. Moreover, as "art" music, operas have never been expected to succeed commercially, so composers have not felt obliged to court audience popularity. By contrast, the American musical has been firmly identified with one central locale: Broadway. And, by tradition, musicals have been deliberately commercial, produced with an eye to the box office and thus conceived to please their audiences and to reflect the public's changing taste over the years.

By 1930, the waltz-oriented operettas of Herbert, Friml and Romberg, with their Ruritanian settings, had given way to jazzier, more informal, often more socially conscious musicals by Jerome Kern (*Show Boat*, 1927), the Gershwins (*Lady, Be Good!*, 1924; *Strike Up the Band*, 1927; *Of Thee I Sing*, 1931; etc.), and Richard Rodgers and Lorenz Hart (*On Your Toes*, 1936; *Pal Joey*, 1940; etc.). For cynicism, however, none could touch the German Jewish emigrant Kurt Weill (1900–1950), who had achieved international celebrity with *Die Dreigroschenoper* (*The Threepenny Opera* – his and Bertolt Brecht's updated version of *The Beggar's Opera*) in Berlin in 1928. He further vented his profound political conscience in shows such as *Johnny Johnson* (1936) and *Knickerbocker Holiday* (1938), peering afterward into psychological trauma in *Lady in the Dark* (1940). Weill was always a superb melodist, though he often used his most delightful melodies for a satirical purpose, as with the "Alabama Song" in his bitter opera *Mahagonny*. A former student of the great pianist, philosopher and contrapuntist Ferruccio Busoni, Weill always wrote exceptionally sophisticated music. However, in such a magnificent number as "September Song," sung by the character Peter Stuyvesant in *Knickerbocker Holiday*, he achieved a genuinely American voice.

In 1943 Rodgers and Oscar Hammerstein II brought out their first collaboration, *Oklahoma!*, in which the sweeping, emotional waltz "Out of My Dreams" was offset by numbers such as "Ev'rything's Up-to-date in Kansas City," "Surrey with the Fringe on Top" and the show's title song, all of which had the down-home tang of rural America. At the same time, in the character of Jed, the show explored the darker side of the male libido, something unprecedented for a Broadway musical. Equally novel was the show's extended dream ballet (possibly inspired by the dream sequences in Weill's *Lady in the Dark*), probing the heroine's sexual fears through Agnes De Mille's choreography. Rodgers and Hammerstein led the field through the 1960s, exploring a variety of social issues in *Carousel* (1945), *South Pacific* (1949), *The King and*

I (1951) and *The Sound of Music* (1959). Other composers offered worthy competition, including Irving Berlin (*Annie Get Your Gun*, 1946), Cole Porter (*Kiss Me, Kate*, 1948), Frank Loesser (*Guys and Dolls*, 1950; *The Most Happy Fella*, 1956), Meredith Willson (*The Music Man*, 1957), Frederick Loewe (*Brigadoon*, 1947; *My Fair Lady*, 1956; *Camelot*, 1960) and Jerry Bock (*Fiorello!*, 1959; *She Loves Me*, 1963; *Fiddler on the Roof*, 1964). And of course the multifarious Leonard Bernstein looms over the postwar decades.

The late 1960s witnessed a move away from the traditional Broadway musical with its big production numbers for chorus, dance corps and large orchestra. On the one hand, increasing costs demanded smaller-scale shows, such as *George M!* (1968), in which Joel Grey and a small cast played multiple roles in a freely adapted biography of George M. Cohan built around Cohan's own songs. On the other hand, rock was making inroads, most notably with the Broadway production that same year of *Hair* (book and lyrics by Gerome Ragni and James Rado; score by Galt MacDermot), which gained notoriety with its fleeting moment of nudity and had audiences singing and dancing to the infectious "Age of Aquarius" and "Let the Sunshine In."

The leading Broadway composer of the late twentieth century was undoubtedly Stephen Sondheim.

Among the high points of these decades was *Cabaret* (1966), by the team of Joe Masteroff, Fred Ebb and John Kander; it was a bitter, though tuneful, reminiscence of Weimar Republic Germany that aped Kurt Weill's *The Threepenny Opera*. Another landmark was *A Chorus Line* (1975), ironic for its *lack* of chorus. Conceived, directed, and choreographed by Michael Bennett, and with music by Marvin Hamlisch, this comparative chamber musical presented a cast of principals as young hopefuls auditioning for a chorus line, and represented a heartfelt salute to the joys and sorrows of countless Broadway "gypsies."

With due respect to these worthies, however, the leading Broadway composer of the late twentieth century was undoubtedly Stephen Sondheim (b. 1930), who had first made his name as librettist of *West Side Story*. From *A Funny Thing Happened on the Way to the Forum* (1962), *Company* (1970), *Follies* (1971) and *A*

Little Night Music (1973) to *Pacific Overtures* (1976), *Sweeney Todd* (1979), *Sunday in the Park with George* (1984), *Into the Woods* (1987), *Assassins* (1991) and *Passion* (1994), Sondheim has never stopped being a true innovator of form, style and dramatic thought. His works are marked by his distinctive, often overwrought rhyme schemes and a musical idiom in which the initial arc of a soaring melody often founders upon the jagged shoals of his quirky rhythms. From *Sweeney Todd* his shows have been increasingly through-composed, with little spoken dialogue. Indeed, *Sweeney Todd*, with its dark, Grand Guignol story, its Greek chorus and its shocking finale, is as much an opera as anything by Puccini or Richard Strauss. And though written primarily for non-operatic singers, it has been produced in recent years by the New York City Opera, the Lyric Opera of Chicago, the New York Philharmonic and other major and regional companies. At the time of writing, a major Broadway revival opened to considerable acclaim, the production pared down to ten instruments, played by the ten singing actors on stage.

And thus grow the hazy lines between opera and musical theatre continually hazier.

18 Anxiety's Son: Leonard Bernstein

W.H. Auden's *The Age of Anxiety* (1947) is an appropriate starting point for a discussion of American music during the last half-century. In it the poet, who continually probed the isolation of the individual and the frailty of human relationships, examines the journey of self-discovery of four lonely people in a wartime New York bar. Grappling with their urban malaise, each searches for some spiritual quality to lend meaning to his or her hollow life. Ultimately they fail to achieve more than a flash of "negative knowledge" before returning to the loneliness of the real world. Their situation, and certainly Auden's title, captures the troubled spirit of the era following World War II, and in 1949 the poem itself inspired a symphonic interpretation by a rising young composer destined to become the most influential, indeed totemic, figure in twentieth-century American music: Leonard Bernstein (1918–1990).

The son of Russian-Jewish immigrants whose successful business enabled him to grow up in middle-class comfort, Bernstein began studying piano at the age of ten, and after graduating from Boston Latin School he entered Harvard, where his teachers included composers Edward Burlingham Hill and Walter Piston. At Harvard, Bernstein also encountered Aaron Copland, with whom he embarked upon a lasting friendship – as a mature conductor Bernstein would eventually perform and record virtually the entire Copland oeuvre. Having composed incidental music for a varsity production of Aristophanes' *The Birds*, Bernstein aimed to mold his own genuinely American musical voice, and to this end he revealed his already profound knowledge of contemporary music in his Harvard thesis, *The Absorption of Race Elements into American Music*. From Harvard, Bernstein entered the Curtis Institute, where he continued his piano studies, though he also learned orchestration with Randall Thompson and conducting with Fritz Reiner. During the summers he studied conducting at Tanglewood with Koussevitzky, who engaged Bernstein as his assistant in 1942. The following year Artur Rodzinski took on Bernstein as assistant conductor of the New York Philharmonic, where, in 1943, the twenty-five-year-old stepped up to the podium at the last minute to substitute for an ailing Bruno Walter. The concert was a national broadcast, and by the end of this debut under fire Bernstein was famous, not only for having successfully led a challenging program, but for having done so as an American.

At Harvard, Leonard Bernstein encountered Aaron Copland, with whom he embarked upon a lasting friendship – as a mature conductor Bernstein would eventually perform and record virtually the entire Copland oeuvre.

CD
track 17
www.naxosbooks.com

In 1944 Bernstein's **First Symphony**, "Jeremiah," was premiered by the Pittsburgh Symphony Orchestra and won the Music Critics' Circle Award. The score, based in part on a selection of Hebrew cantorial melodies, reflects the profound sense of Jewish heritage and learning that Bernstein received from his father, and it communicates as well the Jewish community's doubt and apprehension during World War II. Musically it is an assured piece of craftsmanship, though its language is clearly linked to the idioms of Copland and Schuman. This is especially evident in the second movement, "Profanation." The music suggests the destruction of Jerusalem, which occurred during the lifetime of the prophet Jeremiah, and to convey the brutality of the event Bernstein subjects a cantorial melody to a dance-like Coplandesque rhythmic treatment, while offering a contrasting theme that foreshadows the love music in *West Side Story*.

That April, Bernstein triumphed again when his ballet *Fancy Free*, choreographed by Jerome Robbins, was given at the Metropolitan Opera House to great acclaim. The ballet relates the experiences of three sailors on shore leave in New York, and in December 1944 there appeared another trio of sailors on shore leave, this time singing ones, in Bernstein's new show *On the Town*. With a book and lyrics by Betty Comden and Adolph Green (whom Bernstein had first met in his Harvard days while working with a cabaret group), the show added yet another feather to Bernstein's increasingly ornate cap.

Bernstein quickly evolved into a modern American counterpart of Sir Arthur Sullivan, Victorian England's pre-eminent musician. Both cut elegant and glamorous figures in society, which helped their careers immeasurably. Both were noted conductors (though by all accounts Sullivan was far less gifted in this area than Bernstein).

> *Fancy Free*, choreographed by Jerome Robbins, added yet another feather to Bernstein's increasingly ornate cap.

But, more important, Bernstein shared with Sullivan an exceptional creative genius tempered by a common touch. Like Sullivan, who wrote both operettas (with Gilbert) and oratorios (without), Bernstein composed both lighter and heavier musical works throughout his career, dipping freely into every classical and popular style to achieve his musical ends. And, like Sullivan, Bernstein was often criticized for doing so, though today such crossing of generic lines has become more common.

It was before 1958, when he accepted the music directorship of the New York Philharmonic (the first American-born conductor to be appointed), that Bernstein composed much of the concert and Broadway music for which he is best remembered: Symphony No. 2 "The Age of Anxiety" (for piano and orchestra, 1949, revised 1965), *Prelude, Fugue and Riffs*, for clarinet and jazz ensemble (1949), *Serenade* (after Plato's *Symposium*), for violin, strings, harp and percussion (1954), the symphonic suites from *Fancy Free* (1944) and from his 1954 film score to *On the Waterfront* (1955), the one-act opera

> Bernstein shared with Sir Arthur Sullivan an exceptional creative genius tempered by a common touch.

Trouble in Tahiti (1951), the musicals *Wonderful Town* (1953) and *West Side Story* (1957), and of course his comic operetta *Candide*, after Voltaire (1956, revised 1973). *Candide* provided Bernstein with an outlet for his gift for musical parody, from the scintillating overture, with its spinning Rossini-like crescendo on the "Glitter and be Gay" theme, to the Lady-with-one-buttock's Latin-flavored send-up of Yiddish theatre song ("I Am so Easily Assimilated").

Bernstein's regime at the New York Philharmonic (1958–69) remains a golden age in the memories of many subscribers as well as in the memories of numerous Philharmonic musicians. He proved a compelling – if often distractingly athletic – conductor, whose energetic readings of standard repertoire made audiences sit up and take note. He recorded prolifically, thus spreading the word not only of the basic classics, but of the symphonies of Gustav Mahler, who was still relatively unfamiliar forty years ago. Moreover, as a conductor he was also deeply committed to new music, both American and European, commissioning, performing and recording a vast number of new compositions. In addition, Bernstein was a natural teacher, and his televised series both of Young People's Concerts with the New York Philharmonic and of Norton Lectures

Leonard Bernstein conducting a recording of Mozart symphonies
at the Sofiensaal in Vienna, March 1966

at Harvard are still among the most lucid and accessible vehicles of their kind.

During and after Bernstein's New York Philharmonic regime, composition took a back seat to conducting. But still he produced several noteworthy works. His Third Symphony, "Kaddish," for speaker, chorus and orchestra (1963), dedicated to the memory of John F. Kennedy, used the Hebrew prayer for the dead in a continuing exploration of spiritual doubt. *The Chichester Psalms* (1965), commissioned by the dean of Chichester Cathedral in England, started out as an exploration of twelve-tone composition. However, Bernstein eventually rejected this and composed what he called "the most B-flat majorish tonal piece I've ever written." Indeed its harmonic simplicity and its transparent choral textures have made it one of the composer's most popular works. *Mass*, Bernstein's multimedia theatre piece with liturgical texts (written with Stephen Schwartz, author of the rock musical *Godspell*), proved one of his most controversial works upon its appearance at the Kennedy Center in 1971. Here Bernstein let out all the stops in a Vietnam-era cry of anguish and spiritual skepticism. The theme was certainly not new to him, but his distinctly populist treatment surprised and outraged many audiences at the time. (Working as an usher at the Metropolitan Opera House during the New York run of *Mass*, the present author recalls the constant flow of audience members departing angrily during the performances, especially one elderly European opera lover who slammed his way through an exit door with the cry, "Hwhaht a load ahf boorrsheet!") Bernstein raised eyebrows and tempers with his deployment of amplified guitars and keyboards, rock singers and chorus of street people, offending many listeners with the climactic moment when the baritone celebrant of the Mass desecrates the altar. However over the top the score, after the passage of three decades *Mass* is being reassessed as a work reflecting the tumult of its time. Yet even when the piece was largely being ignored, one number, "A Simple Song," remained popular because of its genuine Bernsteinian melodic appeal.

19 The Age of Anxiety: Music in the Cold War Era

The postwar decades of Bernstein's ascendancy saw Americans realizing a materialistic dream of suburban split-levels and shopping malls. But the Cold War specter of communism and the bomb, together with Western society's increased secularization, eroded the spiritual faith that had comforted earlier generations.

Ironically, though much American music reflected widespread spiritual doubt, the nation's material prosperity helped get that music written and performed. Ready money from private and public sources led to the building of new concert venues such as New York's Lincoln Center and Washington's Kennedy Center. With more money to spend, and cheaper prices, more Americans bought records, especially as the introduction of the long-playing record and the impetus to strengthen existing and new labels made more repertoire available to consumers.

Funding rose for new music. The box office began to matter less to composers than the pursuit of grants from organizations such as the Ford and Rockefeller foundations or from state-funded arts organizations. And, as grant-givers were eager to support "progressive" works, the composer's former obsession with writing "American" music gave way to the obsession with being progressive – i.e., original. Atonality was in full blossom.

Atonality means "without a tonal center." Western music from Bach to Richard Strauss revolves around tonality, which is based on the feeling of completion when an unstable harmony resolves onto a stable one. For instance, in the key of C major, a G7 chord, the dominant seventh, feels unstable. It has to go somewhere – i.e., it must resolve to the stable C major, or tonic, chord before you feel a sense of completion. In tonal music all the chords in a particular key relate audibly to the tonic chord of that key. Therefore, most tonal pieces begin and end in the same key, because ending in a different one would leave listeners feeling unstable, even if they

> With more money to spend, and cheaper prices, more Americans bought records, especially as the introduction of the long-playing record made more repertoire available to consumers.

didn't know why. Atonal music avoids both a key center and the audible relationship between chords in a particular key. Postwar atonality often involved considerable dissonance as well, especially as twelve-tone composition became the dominant language of later twentieth-century music.

At the risk of oversimplification, "twelve-tone" music (also called "dodecaphonic" and "serial") is founded on the twelve whole and half steps in any chromatic scale. Around 1907 Arnold Schoenberg had arrived at the idea of composing music around a framework of those twelve tones as a way of creating order out of what he had come to perceive as the chaos of atonality. Very briefly, in Schoenberg's dodecaphonic technique the twelve (in Greek *duodeka*) tones are arranged in a chosen series – a "tone row" – which

> Dodecaphony was adopted even by relative veterans such as Aaron Copland, who was fifty when he wrote his first serial work, the Piano Quartet.

forms the basis of the composition. The tones in the series (hence "serial") are arranged to avoid melodic intervals that allude to tonality (i.e., major thirds, major sixths, perfect fourths). To prevent any tone being more important than any other (which would suggest a tonal center or tonality), and to maintain the independence of every tone in the row, none may be repeated until all the others have been used. The row may be presented straight, in retrograde (backwards), in inversion (i.e., upside down, by changing each ascending interval into the corresponding descending interval and vice versa), and in retrograde inversion (presenting the upside-down version backwards).

Dodecaphony was adopted even by relative veterans such as Copland, who was fifty when he wrote his first serial work, the Piano Quartet (1950), which he followed with his Piano Fantasy (1952–7) and his orchestral *Connotations* (1962). Especially in the latter two works, he employed a personal approach to serial writing – instead of using a twelve-tone row, his Piano Fantasy is built around a ten-tone row, with the two remaining tones reserved for special accents.

Owing to the overwhelming popularity of his earlier ballet scores and other "Americana" works, Copland was never entirely identified with serial music by audiences; but other composers were, most importantly Hugo Weisgall, George Perle, Milton Babbitt, Leon Kirchner and Charles Wuorinen.

Czech-born Weisgall (1912–1997), a student of Roger Sessions, is best known for his operas, which reflect both his allegiance to Schoenberg and the Second Viennese School and his refined Eurocentric literary tastes: among them are *The Tenor*, after Frank Wedekind (1950); *The Stronger*, after Strindberg (1952); the witty *Six Characters in Search of an Author*, after Pirandello (1956), which secured his international reputation after its 1959 premiere at the New York City Opera; *Purgatory*, after Yeats (1959); and *Athaliah*, after Racine (1964). The success of *Six Characters* led the New York City Opera to commission and produce his *Nine Rivers from Jordan* (1968) and subsequently, in 1993, to stage his biblical *Esther*. Weisgall composed fluently in every medium; however, as the descendant of four generations of Jewish cantors he was drawn repeatedly to liturgical and biblical texts. Some of these inspired instrumental works, such as the 1985 *T'kiatot: Rituals for Rosh Hashana* (the Jewish New Year), for orchestra, which includes solo passages for the shofar, or ram's horn. Others resulted in beautifully crafted choral and vocal works, among them *Psalm of the Distant Dove*, for soprano and piano (1992), and the hauntingly beautiful **Four Choral Etudes** (1960), in which Weisgall sets three Hebrew psalm passages and a Passover hymn.

Milton Babbitt (b. 1916), having studied violin, clarinet and saxophone since childhood, was a proficient jazz musician and composer of pop music during his high-school years. The son of

Website
track 92–95
www.naxosbooks.com

Photograph by Toby Wales

Milton Babbitt, center of table, with, from left to right,
Osvaldo Golijov, Charles Wuorinen, James Levine, Robert Craft and Fred Sherry

an actuary, he was trained in mathematics as well, and his musical development was profoundly influenced both by this training and by his discovery of Schoenberg, Berg and Webern. Their work opened him to the universe of twelve-tone music at a time when dodecaphony was hardly known outside a relatively small intellectual circle and dismissed by many professional critics. Following private composition studies with Roger Sessions, Babbitt worked on his

> Milton Babbitt was trained in mathematics, and his musical development was profoundly influenced both by this training and by his discovery of Schoenberg, Berg and Webern.

graduate degree in music at New York University, and soon joined the faculty there. Later he taught mathematics at Princeton, and during World War II he worked as a government mathematician. In 1949, while teaching at Princeton, he received his first New York Critics' Circle citation for his twelve-tone *Composition for Four Instruments*. In forming his own dodecaphonic method, Babbitt started with Schoenberg's twelve tones and exponentially extended their serial possibilities to embrace twelve different note values, twelve different dynamic levels, twelve different instrumental timbres and twelve different time intervals between entries of instruments. He coined the term "combinatoriality" for his technique of combining segments of different twelve-tone rows, and he also created new terminology for the analysis of twelve-tone music – pitch class, time point – as well as five parameters of sound – pitch, duration, intensity, timbre, envelope. The breadth of his musical thinking is evident in his oeuvre, for example, *Composition for Twelve Instruments* (1948), *The Widow's Lament in Springtime*, for voice and piano, *Semi-Simple Variations*, for piano (1956), *All Set*, for jazz ensemble (1957), *Sounds and Words*, to a text of disparate syllables, for voice and piano (1958), *Four Cavalier Settings*, for voice and guitar (1991), six string quartets, two piano concertos, and the *Concerto piccolino*, for vibraphone (1999). His titles often hint at the engaging wit behind the somewhat forbidding demeanor, for instance, the cheeky *Septet, but Equal* (1992) and the Goethe–Tchaikovsky wink of *None but the Lonely Flute* (1991). Babbitt has also written important highly technical scholarly papers on his serial and rhythmic methods.

Babbitt received his first New York Critics' Circle citation for his twelve-tone *Composition for Four Instruments*.

From the late 1950s, when RCA enlisted his musical and mathematical help in developing one of the first music synthesizers, Babbitt was increasingly interested in electronic music. He organized the Columbia–Princeton electronic music center – of which he became a director, along with his fellow electronic composer Otto Luening (1900–1996) – and created an experimental electronic music program incorporating the synthesizer. In 1964 he brought out his best-known electronic composition, *Philomel*, for voice and magnetic tape, which was followed by others, including *Reflections for Piano and Synthesized Tape* (1967) and *Concerto for Violin, Small Orchestra and Synthesized Tape* (1976). His work has brought him immense honor within the international academic community and has influenced a tremendous number of composers, and he continues actively to compose. In 1958 he wrote an article for *High Fidelity* magazine explaining his "attitude towards the indisputable facts of the status and condition

Babbitt's work has brought him immense honor within the international academic community and has influenced a tremendous number of composers, and he continues actively to compose.

of the composer of … 'serious,' 'advanced,' contemporary music."
He ended this by writing, "Admittedly, if this music is not supported,
the whistling repertory of the man in the street will be little affected,
the concert-going activity of the conspicuous consumer of musical
culture will be little disturbed. But music will cease to evolve, and, in
that important sense, will cease to live." Babbitt was making a valid
point. Unfortunately, his article was published under the title (apparently not his own) "Who Cares if You Listen?," which gained him
notoriety but few friends among uninitiated listeners, and appeared
to summarize the attitude of the avant-garde at a time when gifted
conservative composers were being unjustly thrust aside.

Leon Kirchner (b. 1919), born in Brooklyn and trained in Los
Angeles, studied with Schoenberg, Sessions and Bloch and developed
an aesthetic identity with the twelve-tone language of the Second
Viennese School. With this as a foundation, he achieved a genuinely
personal voice, writing music that develops logically, and often with
a sense of emotional urgency, from a central idea. Though Kirchner
was given to ecstatic outpourings in such early works as the First
Piano Trio of 1954 (which, Copland observed, made it seem that
the music was almost "out of control"), his more mature music
tends to exploit tightly woven structures built of a few vivid motifs,
especially combinations of such intervals as seconds and thirds. To
these he lends dramatic impulse by means of expressive changes
of tempo and meter. Kirchner is most famous for his 1973 opera
Lily, for which he adapted his own libretto from Saul Bellow's
novel *Henderson the Rain King*, and which was premiered by the
New York City Opera in 1977. Nevertheless he has also composed
a rich catalogue of concert works that effectively exploit the tonal
possibilities of their respective instruments, among them a dramatic
Piano Sonata (1948), two Piano Concertos (1953, 1963), the Second
Piano Trio (1993) and the deeply poetic **Triptych**, for violin and
cello (1986–8). The post-Romantic lyricism of this score continues
to bloom in much of Kirchner's more recent work, including the
rhapsodic Music for Orchestra (1989), Music for Cello and Orchestra,
written for Yo-Yo Ma (1992), and the complex *Of Things Exactly
as They Are*, for soprano, baritone, mixed chorus and orchestra, to
texts by Robinson Jeffers, Emily Dickinson, Edna St Vincent Millay,

Website
track 96
www.naxosbooks.com

Wallace Stevens and Robert Lowell (1997).

Like Babbitt, George Perle (b. 1915) is a pillar of American serial music – his first book, *Serial Composition and Atonality* (it had been his 1956 PhD dissertation), went into a sixth edition in 1991. One of the most important American music theorists, he has composed extensively, often to prestigious commissions, in a broad spectrum of genres, including symphonic works, chamber music, concert band music and song – most notably a cycle of *Thirteen Dickenson Songs* (1978). Perle's *Serenade III* (1983), for solo piano and chamber orchestra, was choreographed by the American Ballet Theatre; his Woodwind Quintet No. 4 received a Pulitzer Prize in 1986. Perle wrote his Piano Concerto No. 1 (1990) for the pianist Richard Goode while he was the San Francisco Symphony Orchestra's resident composer, and Michael Boriskin commissioned the Piano Concerto No. 2 (1992) – Boriskin is a celebrated exponent of Perle's piano works, having performed and recorded many pieces. The New York Philharmonic commissioned *Transcendental Modulations* (1993) for its 150th anniversary. Recent years have seen no diminution of Perle's energies or inventiveness, as revealed in such works as the fourteen-movement *Brief Encounters* (String Quartet No. 9, 1998), *Critical Moments* (1996), for six players, *Critical Moments 2* (2001), in nine movements for six players, and *Triptych* (2003), for solo violin and piano. A gifted and highly influential teacher, Perle has also written important books on Berg, Schoenberg, Webern, Scriabin and Bartók.

Born in 1938, Charles Wuorinen became the youngest composer to receive a Pulitzer Prize, in 1970, for his electronic piece *Time's Ecomium*, for four- or two-channel tape of synthesized and processed synthesized sound. Not surprisingly, this entirely electronic work had been commissioned by Nonesuch Records, rather than by a performance organization or concert hall. Wuorinen's previous works in this area included *Electronic Exchanges* (1965), for orchestra and synthesized sound. Among his

---

Sidebar (left margin):

Born in 1938, Charles Wuorinen became the youngest composer to receive a Pulitzer Prize, for his electronic piece *Time's Ecomium*.

George Crumb's music has always been eclectic, incorporating references from classical icons, hymns and folk music to non-Western traditions

200 compositions are seven symphonies, four piano concertos, a Concerto for Amplified Violin and Orchestra (1972), four string quartets, and numerous works for different forces that reveal his taste for classical art and literature, among these the brief *Madrigale spirituale sopra salmo secondo* (1960); a masque, *The Politics of Harmony* (1967); *The Magic Art: An Instrumental Masque*, drawn from the works of Henry Purcell (1979); and the splendid *Dante Trilogy* for orchestra, consisting of *The Mission of Virgil* (1993), *The Great Procession* (1995) and *The River of Light* (1996).

Wuorinen's wit has lent considerable grace to much of his dodecaphonic work, for example the scintillating *Dodecadactyl* (2003), for two guitars. This is especially true of his recent two–act opera *Haroun and the Sea of Stories* (2001), based on Salman Rushdie's novel of a storyteller who loses his gift for telling stories. From it he has extracted and adapted a number of shorter works for orchestra and for piano solo.

But Wuorinen is hardly the only dodecaphonist with a sense of fun. Proof that presentation can make serial music downright infectious is the 1984 **Piano Trio** by Gunther Schuller (b. 1925). All three movements are built around a very strict tone row, but in the final one Schuller (a jazz scholar, as well as a brilliant conductor,

Website
track 97–99
www.naxosbooks.com

Photograph by Toby Wales

George Crumb

teacher and all-round musician) deploys the row as the basis of a swinging jazz trio, complete with a finger-snapping close.

As we have seen, the postwar era saw a rise in experimental music, fostered by universities and often unknown to mainstream audiences at the time – including works by such satellites of John Cage as Morton Feldman, Earle Brown and Christian Wolff. There were visionary souls among the avant-garde as well, most notably George Crumb, Morton Subotnick, Lou Harrison and Alan Hovhaness.

Crumb (b. 1929) is most widely known for his four-movement *Echoes of Time and the River* (1967), which was born of his preoccupation with time and our perception of its passing. Each movement is a "processional" and calls for the players to march about the stage in steps synchronized to the music. The music itself is remarkably colorful, scored for strings, winds and percussion, as well as tiny antique cymbals and glockenspiel plates assigned as extra instruments scattered throughout the orchestra to achieve an extra dimension.

Crumb's music has always been eclectic, incorporating references from classical icons, hymns and folk music to non-Western traditions. During the 1970s he explored novel electric timbres in scores such as *Vox balaenae* (1971), for electric flute, electric cello and amplified piano, and, with a nod to Bartók, *Makrokosmos, Volumes 1 and 2* (1972, 1973), for amplified piano. In that decade he also created his largest score – *Star-Child* (1977), for soprano, solo trombone, antiphonal children's voices, male speaking choir, bell ringers and large orchestra. Not that he requires a large ensemble to achieve all manner of unexpected sounds: passages of *Black Angels: Three Images from the Dark Land* (1970), for electric string quartet, so vividly evoke swarming mosquitoes that it takes every measure of one's self-control not to grab a bug spray. Yet other passages are exceptionally beautiful, such as "God-Music," written in electrified harmonics with a modal countermelody like a Hebrew cantorial wail, or the recurring, ghostly quotation from Schubert's "Death and the Maiden" quartet.

Crumb has also been greatly affected by the poetry of Federico García Lorca, which resulted in works such as *Ancient Voices of*

Children (1970), Madrigals, Books 1–4 (1965, 1969), *Night of the Four Moons* (1969) and *Songs, Drones and Refrains of Death* (1968). Among his latest compositions are *Eine kleine Mitternachtmusik*, for solo piano (2001), *Otherworldly Resonances*, for two pianos (2002), and a four-part song cycle, *American Songbook* (*The River of Life, A Journey Beyond Time, Unto the Hills, The Winds of Destiny*) (2001–4).

Subotnick (b. 1933), another pioneer in electronic music, first stepped into the spotlight with *Silver Apples of the Moon* (1967), which remains an icon of its time. Composing with a voltage-controlled synthesizer built by Donald Buchla, Subotnick was able to achieve in this work a variety of synthesized timbres and exotic tone colors that were unprecedented at the time, together with a contrapuntal tapestry of exciting rhythms that caught the public ear and made the recording for the Nonesuch label (which had commissioned it) a classical bestseller. Not surprisingly the score was choreographed by several dance companies, and its tremendous success led Subotnick to compose further electronic pieces, in which he experimented with increased control of settings, and with ways of preserving his settings to enable a work to be reproduced exactly in subsequent live performances. In addition to straight electronic music, Subotnick has composed works for symphony orchestra, chamber ensemble, and multimedia forces. Always at the cutting edge, his most recent compositions, including the multimedia opera *Jacob's Room* (1985–93), *And the Butterflies Begin to Sing* (1988), for chamber ensemble and computer, and *Echoes from the Silent Call of Girona* (1998), for string quartet and CD-ROM, enable the performers themselves to interact with the computer technology. Of late Subotnick has been developing a great deal of computer work, producing CD-ROMs about listening and composing.

Related to Subotnick's earlier work with the Buchla synthesizer was that of Wendy Carlos (b. 1939, and known until her transsexual procedure in 1979 as Walter Carlos), who, as a child, had built a computer that won her a Westinghouse science fair scholarship. At Columbia University, where Carlos took postgraduate studies in electronic music with pioneering electronic composers Otto Luening

> Morton Subotnick first stepped into the spotlight with *Silver Apples of the Moon,* which remains an icon of its time.

and Vladimir Ussachevsky, she met fellow student Robert Moog, then working on one of the earliest voltage-controlled synthesizers. When the Moog synthesizer was finally made commercially available,

Wendy Carlos wrote important film scores employing synthesizers – among them *A Clockwork Orange, The Shining* and *TRON.*

Carlos bought one of the first models, and in 1969 set the record and music industries on their ears with the album *Switched-on Bach*, in which celebrated Bach keyboard works were given synthesizer treatment. The album, as much a landmark of recording history as the release of the first Caruso discs in 1902, made the idea of synthesized music familiar to the man in the street and sold over a million copies. Carlos subsequently wrote important film scores employing synthesizers – among them Stanley Kubrick's *A Clockwork Orange* (1971) and *The Shining* (1980), and Disney's *TRON* (1982). Working to perfect synthesized musical sound, she employed a complete digital orchestra (the LSI Philharmonic, named for "Large Scale Integration circuits," i.e., computer chips) in works such as *Digital Moonscapes* (1984, inspired by Holst's *The Planets*) and broadened the sonic repertoire with newly devised tunings to imitate Balinese, African and Indian music for *Beauty and the Beast* (1986). In 1992, using more advanced digital technology, Carlos reworked her initial hit album as *Switched-on Bach 2000*.

Lou Harrison and Alan Hovhaness had a particular attraction toward Eastern philosophies: Harrison (1917–2003) returned from visiting the Far East in 1961 to add Japanese and Korean rhythms and modes to his experiments with percussion orchestra, which included every bangable object from drums to coffee cans. He also adopted Esperanto as the language of his vocal works and titles of his instrumental ones, for example, *Koncerto por la violono kun perkuta orkestro* (Concerto for violin and percussion, 1959).

Hovhaness (1911–2000), half Armenian, half Scottish, had been a composition student of Frederick Converse, and expressed through music his firm belief in the universality of the life-giving spirit. "I believe in melody," he said, "and to create a melody one needs to go within oneself."

Influenced by his Armenian ancestry and his studies of Indian, Japanese and other Eastern musical systems, Hovhaness developed a highly personal musical idiom, blending quasi-Oriental cantillation, long, arching melodies, repetition of themes, and unrelieved dynamic tension into awe-inspiring musical tableaux. Profoundly concerned with conservation and ecology, he incorporated actual taped whale sounds in his symphonic score *And God Created Great Whales* (1970), for humpback whale solo and orchestra. The "Angel of Light" (*Largo*) movement from his **Symphony No. 22**, "City of Light" (1971), is a vivid example of his spiritual lyricism and his plush orchestration.

Website
track 100–103
www.naxosbooks.com

Despite the lyricism of composers such as Hovhaness, mainstream audiences were suspicious of any new music – hence symphony orchestras programmed new works far less often than music by the old masters. However, from our present vantage point we can hear the power and beauty of many works that were for years unfamiliar beyond a limited circle of specialists.

Website
track 104–105
www.naxosbooks.com

Listening today, we wonder why audiences are not more familiar with this music. Take Elliott Carter's **Piano Concerto**, composed between 1964 and 1965. Born in 1908 and still active as a composer, Carter didn't embrace serialism, though his music reveals his affinity for it. This concerto expands into orchestral form his chamber-music method of deliberately avoiding a blending of voices, achieved by simultaneously presenting contrasting musical lines. By tradition, a concerto can pit the solo instrument against the orchestra in a kind of musical combat. Carter sought to minimize this gladiatorial element by introducing an additional smaller ensemble of seven instruments to "mediate." Nevertheless, his idea of simultaneous contrasting strands is in full swing here – at certain points over seventy distinct parts are present all at once, involving several different rhythmic layers and individual tempos. While this is not a "hummable" score, many individual lines are distinctly lyrical, and the overall texture is as vibrant as an action canvas by Jackson Pollock. Carter – who studied with Walter Piston at Harvard and Nadia Boulanger in Paris, and who received considerable mentoring from his friend Charles Ives – is often regarded as an architect of

Alan Hovhaness incorporated actual taped whale sounds in his symphonic score *And God Created Great Whales* for humpback whale solo and orchestra.

Elliott Carter, composing at the age of ninety-seven in his apartment
in New York, April 2005; writing Soundings *for Daniel Barenboim*
and the Chicago Symphony Orchestra

American modernism for his consummate inventiveness as an atonal
composer. His scores are often demanding, his harmony visceral, his
rhythmic sense exceptionally challenging. Apart from this concerto
he has written five towering string quartets
(1951–95), a Violin Concerto (1990, one of
his most frequently programmed scores), a
playful Clarinet Concerto (1996), and the
fifty-minute triptych *Symphonia: sum fluxae*
pretium spei ("I am the prize of flowing
hope"), a massive work composed between
1993 and 1996 which is widely considered his orchestral masterpiece.
Carter essayed his first opera *What Next?* at the invitation of the
Staatsoper Unter den Linden in Berlin, which mounted the premiere
in 1999 under Daniel Barenboim. Composed to a libretto by the
distinguished critic, Paul Griffiths, the forty-five-minute piece
concerns six characters who emerge from an automobile accident

> Elliott Carter is often
> regarded as an architect of
> American modernism for his
> consummate inventiveness as
> an atonal composer.

unhurt but shaken, and their actions offer a sardonic reflection on the human condition.

The first composer to receive the National Medal of Arts, not to mention two Pulitzer prizes, Carter is truly an American icon whose energy remains unflagging at age ninety-eight (2006). Indeed, critics have often remarked upon the profound feeling and appeal of his most recent work, which includes the *ASKO Concerto* (written for Holland's ASKO ensemble, 2000), a Cello Concerto for Yo-Yo Ma (2001), *Dialogues*, for piano and orchestra (2003), *Three Illusions*, for orchestra (in three parts: *Micomicón*, *Fons Juventatis* and *More's Utopia*) (2002–4) and *Soundings*, for piano and orchestra (2005).

Website
track 162
www.naxosbooks.com

The **Violin Concerto** (1974, revised 2001) by George Rochberg (1918–2005) boasts equally potent atonal language, though far less biting than Carter's. The good old-fashioned virtuosity of the solo part and the rhetorical beauty and the rhythmic drive of the solo and orchestral textures invite repeated listening. So do the gritty challenges of the First Symphony (1948–

> The first composer to receive the National Medal of Arts, not to mention two Pulitzer prizes, Carter is truly an American icon whose energy remains unflagging.

9) and the "hard romanticism," as Rochberg called it, of the Symphony No. 2 (1955–6), which established his national reputation at its New York premiere, by George Szell and the Cleveland Orchestra.

Robert Starer (1924–2001) was born in Vienna, and trained both there and in Jerusalem before settling in New York, where he studied with Copland, among other teachers. Combining a plaintive melodic sensibility with often rugged, biting harmony and rhythm, he composed in all genres, achieving particular acclaim for his Violin Concerto (written for Itzhak Perlman, 1979–80), his Cello Concerto (written for Janos Starker, 1988), his klezmer-flavored Clarinet Concerto ("K'li Zemer," commissioned by Giora Feidman, 1987), four ballets for Martha Graham, including *Samson Agonistes* (1961), and the operas *Pantagleize* (1967, after Michel de Ghelerode's play) and *The Last Lover* (1974), a morality play about St Pelagia the Penitent, to a libretto by his longtime partner and collaborator, the distinguished novelist Gail Godwin.

Jacob Druckman (1929–1996) explored the possibilities of both acoustic and electronic music. During the 1950s he embraced neoclassicism in works such as *Divertimento* (1950), for clarinet, horn, harp and string trio, and the *Volpone* overture (1953); then in the 1960s he experimented with electronic music and combinations of tape and live instruments and voices in his *Animus* series. He also made increasingly vigorous explorations of human violence and sexuality in unexpected ways: in *Valentine* for solo double bass (1969) the player is directed to attack the instrument fiercely and physically. During the 1970s Druckman increasingly turned to the orchestra as a primary medium, integrating fragmentary quotations from other composers as intellectual counterpoints to his own musical ideas. For example, each of the three movements of *Prism* (1980), his most frequently performed score, contains tonal passages from the Medea operas by Francesco Cavalli, Marc-Antoine Charpentier and Luigi Cherubini, to which he gives a variety of non-tonal treatments. His *Windows*, for orchestra (1972), won a Pulitzer Prize.

20 Making the Most of Minimalism

Out of atonality and serialism arose the next major development to dominate the period: minimalism. Its roots were partly in the visual arts. Critic Richard Wollheim coined the term "minimal art" in 1965 to describe the work of artists such as Frank Stella, Donald Judd and Ellsworth Kelly. But its roots went even further back, to the spare linear works of Piet Mondrian, the hermetic canvases of Marcel Duchamp, and the mathematical abstractions of Wassily Kandinsky and Sonia Delaunay. Musical minimalism manifested itself in the scores of composers La Monte Young, Terry Riley, Steve Reich and Philip Glass, and also in the often experimental interdisciplinary work of Meredith Monk.

Minimalist music is characterized by repeated melodic-rhythmic patterns, usually over simple diatonic harmonies. In its strictest application, a minimalist composition repeats a limited number of motifs, like a wallpaper pattern, sometimes with slight alterations, shifts of meter, or the rise or fall of a pitch. There is no sense of motivic development, counterpoint or formal progression. Because minimalist music was strongly linked to the contemporary art scene, and because its simple patterns and harmonies were not "ugly" to many listeners repelled by atonal dissonance, its composers caught the fancy of the New York "downtown" art crowd.

This was especially so in the case of Glass, who capitalized on his keen sense of "what's hot." However, Californian Terry Riley (b. 1935) is often credited with composing the first minimalist work, *In C* (1964), which consists of slowly shifting repetitive patterns and, more importantly, tonal harmony at a time when atonality was king. During the 1960s and 1970s such hypnotic works by Riley for soprano saxophone and keyboards as *Poppy Nogood and the Phantom Band*, *A Rainbow in Curved Air* and *The Persian Surgery Dervishes* exploited Asian-flavored improvisational techniques, layered meters and flashy instrumental colors that anticipated the "new age" music of the late 1980s, while influencing not just classical composers such as Glass, Reich and Adams, but rock groups

Terry Riley is often credited with composing the first minimalist work, *In C*.

such as The Who. Riley himself was greatly influenced by the North Indian vocalist Pandit Pran Nath, with whom he studied during a series of visits to India beginning in 1970. In the 1970s Riley also began a long and fruitful relationship with the Kronos Quartet, which resulted in such works as the Bach-like *G Song* (1981) and *Cadenza on the Night Plain* (1984), the eleven episodes of which mingle elements of classical, minimalist, jazz and North Indian traditions against a background of native-American mythology. The association also yielded Riley's monumental five-quartet cycle *Salome Dances for Peace*, a cross-cultural, neo-Bartókian musical joyride (1985–6). Apart from string quartets, Riley's catalogue includes the seven-movement *Jade Palace* for orchestra, commissioned to mark the Carnegie Hall centennial season (1990–1), the saxophone quartet *Chanting the Light of Foresight*

In the 1970s Riley began a long and fruitful relationship with the Kronos Quartet.

(1994), and his theatre piece *The Saint Adolf Ring* (1992), based on the eccentric drawings, writings and mathematical calculations of the early twentieth-century Swiss artist Adolf Woelfi. More recent, and more intimate, is the flute and guitar cycle **Cantos desiertos** (1996–8), whose complexity of musical invention is masked by its apparently tuneful simplicity.

Website
track 106–110

www.naxosbooks.com

Website
track 111–113

www.naxosbooks.com

Although Philip Glass is best known for his operas, he has also written instrumental works, one of the best being his **Violin Concerto** (1987). He composed it long after moving from a strict minimalist concept toward a broader approach that combined minimalist repetition and harmonic simplicity with more independent melodic invention for the solo part. The sheer excitement of the whirling solo and orchestral textures of the third movement, with its accents of

Philip Glass

Chinese block, timpani and brush cymbal, make it quite irresistible. Glass has continued to exploit this vein in his dark-hued, monolithic Second Symphony (1994), which suffers from the composer's typically monochrome orchestration. His lighter, tauter **Third Symphony** (1995) is scored for a chamber orchestra of nineteen strings. Of its four movements, the first, according to the composer's plan, serves as an introduction to the middle two movements, which he characterizes as the main body of the work. The third movement is in the form of a chaconne (i.e., a piece written over a repeated harmonic sequence), with a beguiling solo violin passage. The final movement recalls the frenetic material of the second movement, with its fast-moving, decisive motifs in shifting meters. Glass has found writing symphonies particularly congenial during the past decade, and 2005 saw the premiere of his Symphony No. 8.

Like Glass and Terry Riley, Steve Reich has continually been influenced by non-Western musical traditions, not to mention extra-musical ones, having received his degree in philosophy from Cornell University before embarking on advanced musical studies with composers William Bergsma and Vincent Persichetti at Juilliard and Luciano Berio and Darius Milhaud at Mills College. Afterward he successively studied African drumming at the University of Ghana, Balinese gamelan at the American Society for Eastern Arts in Seattle, and traditional Hebrew cantillation in New York and Jerusalem. A survey of his

Steve Reich's evocative and mesmerizing Different Trains (1988), for string quartet and tape, was his first essay in traditional Western ensemble writing, though the result is hardly conventional.

work reveals these manifold influences, from the taped speech pieces *It's Gonna Rain* (1965) and *Come Out* (1966) to massed instrumental works such as *Phase Patterns* (1970), for four electric organs, and *Six Pianos* (1973), for six pianos; percussion works such as *Music for Pieces of Wood* (1973), for five pairs of tuned claves; and Hebraic vocal works such as *Tehillim* (1981), for voices and orchestra, to texts from the Psalms. Reich's evocative and mesmerizing *Different Trains* (1988), for string quartet and tape, was his first essay in traditional Western ensemble writing, though the result is hardly conventional. Commissioned by the Kronos Quartet, it considers the parallel experiences of 1940s American travelers in comfortable

Photograph by Malcolm Crowthers

Steve Reich, 1995

Pullmans and Nazi Holocaust victims loaded into cattle cars bound for Auschwitz. Technically it poses a challenge to the four live musicians to synchronize their repetitive chugging figuration with the playing of three taped quartets as well as a series of sampled sounds and speech – steam whistles, air-raid sirens, conductors' announcements and voices of Holocaust survivors. Reich's most recent works include the soundtrack to the film *The Dying Gaul* (2005), by playwright and director Craig Lucas, the digital video opera *Three Tales* (2002), which he created in collaboration with the video artist Beryl Korot, and *You Are (Variations)*, for amplified instrumental ensemble and voices, with Hebrew and English texts selected from the writings of Rabbi Nachman of Breslov, philosopher Paul Wittgenstein and the Book of Psalms.

With La Monte Young (b. 1935) we encounter an avant-garde trajectory even beyond Cage's visionary expanses. Young's String Trio (1958), made up of very long rests and sustained tones, distressed his composition teacher at the University of California in Berkeley, but in retrospect presents a source of musical minimalism predating Riley's landmark *In C* by six years. In 1962 Young founded the Theatre of Eternal Music, in which he has since collaborated with artists and musicians such as Terry Riley, violinist Tony Conrad, viol player John Cale, percussionist Angus MacLise, and Marian Zazeela, a creator of sculptural forms in light. Ms. Zazeela, whom Young married, also contributed her vocal droning to the mix.

This, together with Cage's idea that "relevant action is theatrical, inclusive and intentionally purposeless," spurred Young to embark upon several long-term works in progress, notably *The Tortoise, his Dreams and Journeys* (1964–), which includes *The Tortoise Droning Selected Pitches from the Holy Numbers of the Two Black Tigers, the Green Tiger and the Hermit* (1964) and *The Tortoise Recalling the Drone of the Holy Numbers as they were Revealed in the Dreams of the Whirlwind and the Obsidian Gong, Illuminated by the Sawmill, the Green Sawtooth Ocelot, and the High-Tension Line Stepdown Transformer* (1964).

The Well-Tuned Piano is widely regarded as La Monte Young's masterpiece. Its title is a play on Bach's *Well-Tempered Clavier*.

While visiting India in 1970 to study Eastern philosophy, Young gradually postulated the idea that *any* activity, human or otherwise, is art. This soon resulted in a series of conceptual works based on chance operations, such as releasing a host of butterflies into the concert hall while starting a fire on stage. Other works consist exclusively of verbal commands, such as "Push the piano to the wall" or, more viscerally, "Urinate." From the viewpoint of deliberate shock value, we might regard the latter as a musical riposte to such iconoclastic works of visual art as Marcel Duchamp's aforementioned *Urinal* (1916) and Andre Serrano's controversial

Piss Christ (1987), actually an almost sentimental image of a *faux-ivoire* crucifix bathed in golden light, were it not for a jarring title that reveals how that lighting effect was achieved.

The Well-Tuned Piano (1964–) is widely regarded as La Monte Young's masterpiece. Its title is a play on Bach's *Well-Tempered Clavier*, which exploited the advantages of the tempered scale for writing chromatic harmony on the eighteenth-century keyboard. According to the composer Michael Harrison (b. 1958), who studied with Young and who, as pianist, is an important exponent of his music, *The Well-Tuned Piano* is written for a Bösendorfer Imperial grand piano tuned to a system Young himself invented, but which is based on what is called "just intonation."

Very briefly, the principles of intonation are based on mathematical relationships between the frequencies that determine each pitch. In equal temperament the octave from C to C is divided into twelve acoustically equal half-steps. Every step – every interval – between a note and its nearest neighbour is exactly the same. This means that each pitch has been slightly adjusted from its position within the acoustically pure "untempered" scale. But this adjustment, this tempering, allows the relationship between sharps and flats to remain constant in all keys: for instance, the black key for A flat is the same one for G sharp. This enables triads to sound "in tune" whether they are in C major (with no sharps or flats) or in complex keys such as D flat or F sharp, and it allows composers to move freely from one key to another on the keyboard without relationships sounding out of tune. In just intonation, the half-steps within an octave are not evenly divided. Instead they are derived from acoustically pure (i.e., untempered) fifths and thirds as they occur naturally in the series of overtones that make up the sound of every note. Pitches are therefore not constant from key to key. So in the key of G major, for instance, the first three notes of the scale, G–A–B, have between them audibly different intervals compared to the first three notes of the C major scale, C–D–E. Because the intervals differ from key to key, that second note in G major – A – is different from the note A that you would play in a C major scale.

Some of Young's conceptual works consist exclusively of verbal commands, such as "Push the piano to the wall."

Moreover, sharps and flats differ audibly from key to key: the note A flat is slightly different from G sharp (and D flat is different from C sharp, etc.). Thanks to these internal relationships, every key has its own "flavor," but those flavors would clash wildly to our ears when moving from key to key, especially in richly chromatic piano music like that of Brahms.

Suffice it to say that, while playing in a form of just intonation would make a hash of Brahms, or for that matter Bach or Chopin, it suited La Monte Young's purposes admirably, letting him explore the often wild harmonic possibilities inherent in unequally divided, or "untempered" scales. And following his own conviction that "a piece of music may play without stopping for thousands of years," he kept adding more explorations to his *Well-Tuned Piano*, so that by 1987 his performances of this evolving composition had reached around six and a half hours in duration. Young's own perfectionism has militated against much recording of his music. Nevertheless he remains a seminal figure in minimalism and the cross-currents between rock, blues and contemporary classical music.

Meredith Monk, born in 1942 in Lima, Peru, to American parents, has enjoyed an extraordinarily varied career as a singer, filmmaker, theatre director, choreographer, recording artist and composer. Monk, who has always been comfortable blurring the lines between performance, performance art and museum installations, styled her first significant score, *Juice* (1969), a "theatre cantata." Scored for eighty-five solo voices, eighty-five jew's harps and two violins, it was unveiled at the Guggenheim Museum in New York. Thereafter Monk adopted the term "opera" for her pieces, though this is more a throwback to the sixteenth-century Florentine Camerata's use of the word *opera* to mean "a work" than any attempt to identify herself with the traditions of Verdi or Puccini. For example, she calls her *Education of the Girlchild* (1972–3) an opera for six solo voices, electric organ and piano. In *Atlas* (1991), in three acts for voices and chamber orchestra, Monk adopts a more obvious narrative line to illustrate the spiritual as well as geographical discoveries of a woman explorer through wordless vocalism instead

Joan La Barbara has devoted her career as a composer and a pioneering vocal performer to investigating the voice as a many-sided musical instrument.

of a conventional libretto. Central to her compositional idiom are extended vocal technique and body movement, which she exploits in such singular pieces as *Dolmen Music*, *Fields/Clouds* and *Astronaut Anthem*.

Similarly, Joan La Barbara (b. 1947) has devoted her career as a composer and a pioneering vocal performer (of her own and other composers' music) to investigating the voice as a many-sided musical instrument. She has thus developed a noteworthy musical language of experimental vocal techniques far beyond the traditional realm of classical singing, including glottal clicks, circular singing (i.e., singing while inhaling and exhaling), and the sounding of two or more pitches at once ("multiphonics"), all of which have become identified with her unique idiom. Among her most recent works are *Tales and Mosaics* (1999), for voice, saxophones, p'iri (a Korean double-reed bamboo pipe) and pre-recorded sounds (of herself and her co-composer, Peter Gordon), *Dragons on the Wall* (2001), for solo voice, instrumental ensemble and pre-recorded dancers' voices, and *Snowbird's Dance*, *Into the Light*, *and Beyond* (2004), for voice, flute and string quartet.

John Adams used the mesmerizing pulsation and slow harmonic movement of minimalism in his first major works, *Phrygian Gates* (1977) and *Shaker Loops* (1978, revised 1983). But he soon broadened his creative outlook. *Harmonielehre* (1984–5) combines minimalist repetition with the emotive language of the nineteenth-century symphony, and the Violin Concerto (1993) places a seductively sinuous solo line against an orchestral backdrop of conflicting meters and dense counterpoint that evokes the work of the German Max Reger at the beginning of the twentieth century. His piano concerto *Century Rolls* (1996) salutes the complex mechanics of the old-time player piano. *The Wound-Dresser* (1988), a song cycle for baritone and orchestra, is a deeply sensitive interpretation of Walt Whitman's introspective Civil War poem, while the kinetic energy and scintillating instrumentation of his fanfare **Short Ride in a Fast Machine** (1986) quickly made it a standard orchestral showpiece.

Website
track 114
www.naxosbooks.com

Adams achieves a truly magical quality in his staged nativity oratorio *El niño* (Paris, 2000), which blends minimalist orchestral patterns, prolonged harmonies, shimmering instrumentation and the expressive setting of a variety of carefully selected texts. He received a

John Adams

Pulitzer Prize for his profoundly moving work *On the Transmigration of Souls* (2002), composed for the New York Philharmonic in memory of the victims of the 9/11 terrorist attack on the World Trade Center. The score layers taped street noises, voices speaking significant words and phrases and names of victims, choral passages, and haunting orchestral material in a counterpoint of music and speech.

In October 2003, architect Frank Gehry's Disney Concert Hall in Los Angeles was inaugurated with a performance of Adams' *The Dharma at Big Sur*. Commissioned by the Los Angeles Philharmonic and its music director Esa-Pekka Salonen, the work was inspired by Jack Kerouac's book *Big Sur*. Musically, Adams salutes two earlier California composers, Lou Harrison and Terry Riley, by employing just intonation, which allows him to exploit a variety of new sonic possibilities. With an electric violin as its featured

> John Adams received a Pulitzer Prize for his profoundly moving work *On the Transmigration of Souls*, composed in memory of the victims of the 9/11 terrorist attack on the World Trade Center.

solo instrument, explorations of Buddhist and Hindu meditative traditions, suggestions of Appalachian fiddling, and Indian sitar, jazz and Jimi Hendrix, the score culminates with a rapturous joyful noise of a finale.

Famous above all for his operas, Adams has also proven a gifted conductor and personable representative of new music. Indeed if any composer seems fit to don Aaron Copland's iconic mantle, not just as a musical creator but as an American musical statesman, it is Adams.

21 Today and into Tomorrow: Old Glory and New

Despite serialism's overwhelming pre-eminence during the last half-century, some composers refused to bow to that call, and today their music is, happily, being revived. Outstanding names among the once-embattled old guard include David Diamond, Nicolas Flagello, David Amram, the great jazz musician Dave Brubeck and the ever youthful Ned Rorem.

Diamond's *Kaddish*, for cello and orchestra (1987), written for Yo-Yo Ma, develops an entirely original set of themes rather than the familiar Jewish liturgical one to which the memorial prayer for the dead is regularly chanted; nevertheless, its expressive poise is immediately apparent to non-Jewish listeners, and its melodic beauty is undeniable.

The oratorio *The Passion of Martin Luther King* by Flagello (1928–1994) was warmly received at its premiere by the National Symphony Orchestra at the Kennedy Center in 1974, and subsequent performances at other venues confirmed its stature as a modern response to the Passion music of Bach. Flagello's tuneful short opera *The Piper of Hamelin*, commissioned by the Manhattan School of Music Preparatory Division, gives a surprising, very sympathetic twist to the familiar legend treated poetically by Robert Browning. His **Symphony No. 1** (1964–8) is wonderfully expressive, and from the exciting first movement its humanist passion and thematic inspiration never flag.

David Amram (b. 1930), who has gathered jazz and world

Website
track 115–118

www.naxosbooks.com

music to his symphonic bosom, has composed in all genres, and among his finest works are the opera *The Final Ingredient* (1966), a tale of concentration-camp prisoners managing against all odds to celebrate the Passover festival, the dramatically subtle film score for *The Manchurian Candidate* (1962), the delightful Shakespeare opera *Twelfth Night* (1965–8), with its singable blend of neo-Elizabethan modality and tart harmony, and the symphony *Songs of the Soul* (1987). At the present time of writing, Amram and author Frank McCourt are collaborating on *Missa Manhattan*, a choral and orchestral celebration of New York's varied cultural history.

Pianist Dave Brubeck (b. 1920) is best known for his seminal jazz inventions with the Dave Brubeck Quartet from 1958 to 1967, among them pieces in tempos unusual in jazz, such as *Take Five* and *Blue Rondo à la Turk*. A student of Milhaud, he has also composed a substantial corpus of large-scale choral and symphonic works that often explore ethical questions as well as the subtle relationship between traditional instrumental complements and jazz ensemble, notably *The Truth is Fallen* (1971), *La fiesta de la posada* (1975) and the powerful cantata *The Gates of Justice* (1969).

> Nicolas Flagello's oratorio *The Passion of Martin Luther King* was warmly received at its premiere by the National Symphony Orchestra at the Kennedy Center in 1974.

Ned Rorem (b. 1923), a student of Sowerby, Thomson and Copland, is probably the finest American song composer since Barber. In such works as "**Alleluia**" and "**I Am Rose**" (to Gertrude Stein's words), his music reflects his predilection for French clarity and polish filtered through a thoroughly American directness in the setting of notes to words. Possibly his vocal masterpiece is the 1997 cycle *Evidence of Things Not Seen*, comprising thirty-six songs to texts by twenty-four authors. It is divided into three sections, entitled "Beginnings," "Middles" and "Ends," which deal respectively with the optimism of youthful love, the trials of coming of age and the awfulness of war, and death, especially AIDS-related deaths suffered by the composer's friends. Ironically,

Website
track 119–120
www.naxosbooks.com

> Pianist Dave Brubeck, best known for his seminal jazz inventions, has also composed a substantial corpus of large-scale choral and symphonic works.

Photograph by Toby Wales

Ned Rorem

Rorem's fame in this area – he has composed some 400 songs – as well as his celebrity as a candid diarist and trenchant essayist on musical subjects, has somewhat overshadowed his undisputed gifts as a composer of chamber and orchestral music. Among his finest instrumental works are three symphonies (composed between 1950 and 1958), the orchestral suite *Air Music* (1974), which received a Pulitzer Prize, such chamber works as **End of Summer**, for clarinet, violin and piano (1985), and a masterful body of choral works, such as the Walt Whitman-inspired oratorio *Goodbye my Fancy* (1988). Of Rorem's operas, the only full-length one, *Miss Julie*, after August Strindberg, was premiered by the New York City Opera in 1965 and has enjoyed revivals since then.

André Previn (b. 1929) is a commanding figure in both classical and jazz fields, his concert, chamber and vocal music notable for technical finesse and unabashed lyricism. Among his most recent

Website
track 121–123
www.naxosbooks.com

From left to right, Aaron Copland, Lukas Foss and Elliott Carter

compositions are the song cycle *Sallie Chisum Remembers Billy the Kid* (1995), the passionate Violin Concerto (2001), composed as a wedding gift for his now ex-wife, the violinist Anne-Sophie Mutter, and the Double Concerto for Double Bass, Violin and Orchestra (2004).

A grand old man of American music, Lukas Foss (b. 1922), known as a pianist and a conductor as well as a composer, embraced minimalism in his Third String Quartet (1975). But his career is distinguished for its stylistic flexibility, from the most experimental improvisations, such as the interludes between the composed soprano movements of *Time Cycle* (1960), to Cage-like explorations of sound in *Thirteen Ways of Looking at a Blackbird* (1978), to electronic sounds, and finally to the evocation of early music in *Renaissance Concerto* (1985) – a piece in which the clicking of the solo flute keys adds a deliberate percussive effect.

William Kraft (b. 1923) is a prominent composer who has

also been a major timpanist and percussionist for the Los Angeles Philharmonic. Not surprisingly this student of Henry Cowell, Otto Luening and Vladimir Ussachevsky has moved easily between serial, electronic and jazz idioms, both as a performer and as a composer. His works reflect his intimate knowledge of every rhythmic instrument. Among them are a Symphony for Strings and Percussion (1960), a Concerto for Four Percussion Soloists and Orchestra (1966), *Contextures II*, for soprano, tenor, chorus and chamber ensemble (to texts by Longfellow, Wilfred Owen and others, 1985), and Music for String Quartet and Percussion (1993).

Pulitzer Prize-winner Michael Colgrass (b. 1932), who trained as a percussionist, left dodecaphonic writing in the 1960s for more traditional melody and tonality. Among his most successful works have been the orchestral suite *As Quiet As* (1966), *Déjà vu*, for four percussionists and orchestra (1977), and *Dream Dancer*, for alto saxophone and wind orchestra (2001).

David Del Tredici (b. 1937) made a similar change around the same time, increasingly exploiting a consonant, lyrical idiom in his series of works inspired by Lewis Carroll's *Alice in Wonderland*, beginning in 1971. *Final Alice* (1975) and *In Memory of a Summer Day* (1980) have been his greatest successes with audiences. He maintains his fondness for ironic whimsy in his newer works, among them the beguiling setting for coloratura soprano, baritone and orchestra of Mary Howitt's poem of seduction and resistance *The Spider and the Fly* (1998), *Paul Revere's Ride*, for orchestra and soprano (2005), and *Rip Van Winkle*, for orchestra and narrator (2005).

> Joan Tower's titles have captured listeners' imaginations by suggesting imagery without actually being descriptive.

Joan Tower (b. 1938) has always aimed to communicate with her audience while remaining true to her belief in atonality. "If somebody is … listening to a piece of mine and they don't 'get it,' then I haven't done my job," she said in a videotaped interview in 2005 with Frank J. Oteri, editor of the American Music Center's web magazine *New Music Box*. Thus, in *Petroushskates* (1980), she wittily pays tribute to Stravinsky by blending excerpts from his familiar ballet with atonal material. Similarly, her Piano Concerto No. 1 (1985) is subtitled "Homage to Beethoven"; the three *Fanfares for the Uncommon Woman*

Photograph by Toby Wales

Joan Tower

(1986–91) honor Copland; and *Très Lent*, for cello and piano (1994), salutes Messiaen. Other titles have captured listeners' imaginations by suggesting imagery without actually being descriptive, such as *Wild Purple*, for solo viola (1998), *In Memory* (String Quartet No. 2) (2002), *DNA* (Percussion Quintet, 2003), and the rapturous piano trio **Big Sky** (2000). Tower's latest orchestral work, *Made in America* (2005), is the first in an ambitious and unprecedented program commissioning new compositions for successive performances by smaller-budget orchestras in all fifty United States.

Website
track 124
www.naxosbooks.com

Gloria Coates (b. 1938) was a singer, actor, painter and composer before moving to Munich in 1969 to focus on composition. She has written symphonic works as well as vocal, choral and chamber music. In particular, the limitless chromatic freedom of the string quartet has made it an ideal medium for Coates to explore the manifold effects of intervallic and contrapuntal combinations. Canons continually fascinate her – for instance, the palindrome (mirror) canon in Quartet No. 1 (1966) and the canon at the quarter-tone in Quartet No. 6 (1999). **String Quartet No. 5** (1988) offers a microcosm of Coates' style, which itself seems to revel in minimalist simplicity. The first movement ("Through Time") is a double canon at the quarter-tone in A minor. Confining herself entirely to the

Website
track 125–127
www.naxosbooks.com

natural tones of the A minor scale, Coates calls for the strings of the first violin and the viola to be tuned a quarter-tone higher than those of the second violin and the cello, and the succeeding lines weave around one another slowly, eerily and with exceptional clarity so that the ear can discern the theme as it twists around itself, until the final A minor chord (with the third in the bass). In the second movement ("Through Space") Coates camouflages the familiar carol tune "I heard the bells on Christmas Day" in an aural fabric made up of another favorite device, string glissandos (i.e., sliding effects up and down the strings). The final movement comprises nothing but glissandos, starting slowly, and gradually building in speed and intensity toward a climax before the pace slows again to a final, prolonged and luminous chord of open strings.

During the 1980s John Harbison (b. 1938) moved gradually from Central European atonality and expressionism toward an increasingly warm and inviting personal idiom. Among the outstanding works of this period are his Violin Concerto (1980, revised 1987), four symphonies (1981–2004), *Motetti di Montale* (1980, 1998, 1990) and *Mirabai Songs* (1982, to sixteenth-century Indian religious poetry). More recent compositions include *Six American Painters* (2000) and his Requiem (2002). Harbison has also composed fine chamber works, notably the ingenious Variations for Clarinet, Violin and Piano (1982) and *Four Songs of Solitude* (1985) – both written for his wife, violinist Rose Mary Harbison – as well as four string quartets and the lovely **Twilight Music** (1985), for violin, horn and piano.

> Noteworthy among John Corigliano's more recent compositions are Symphony No. 1 and its choral sequel, *Of Rage and Remembrance,* both memorializing the victims of AIDS.

Website
track 128–131
www.naxosbooks.com

Healthily eclectic, John Corigliano (b. 1938) has ranged freely though tonal, serial, timbral, microtonal and aleatory techniques, while preserving his fundamental commitment to intelligibility for his listener. Noteworthy among his more recent compositions are Symphony No. 1 (1989) and its choral sequel, *Of Rage and Remembrance* (1991), both memorializing the victims of AIDS, the gentle guitar concerto *Troubadours* (1993), the String Quartet (a valediction composed for the disbanding Cleveland Quartet, 1996) and *The Red Violin*, for violin and orchestra (1997), based on themes from his eponymous Oscar-winning film score. (Film music forms a small part of his output, but his psychologically probing score for Ken Russell's 1979 film *Altered States* is now regarded as a classic.)

Invited to write a new work for the centenary of Boston's Symphony Hall, Corigliano "extensively recomposed" (his words) his quartet, transforming it into a string symphony; this contained a nocturne, inspired by his nocturnal experience listening to muezzin calls while visiting Fez, and an "anti-contrapuntal" fugue (his words again) in which, rather than "setting multiple themes against a common beat[, he] sets a single theme in separate voices traveling at precisely decided but slightly different *tempi*." Premiered by the Boston Symphony Orchestra in 2000, Corigliano's Symphony No. 2 won the 2001 Pulitzer Prize for music.

Massachusetts-born Frederic Rzewski (b. 1938), professor of composition at Belgium's Conservatoire Royal de Musique in Liège since 1977, experimented with electronic and improvised music as well as music requiring graphic and conventional notation. Apart from its technical versatility, Rzewski's music is often fired by vigorous political consciousness. During the 1970s such works as the fifty-minute set of piano variations *The People United Will Never Be Defeated!* explored forms treating style and language as structural elements. Works from the 1980s, among them *Antigone-Legend*, experiment with novel ways of using dodecaphonic technique. His largest-scale piece to date is the oratorio *The Triumph of Death* (1987–8), with texts adapted from the play *Die Ermittlung* ("The Investigation," 1965). More recent is his *Pocket Symphony* (2000), composed for the provocative American chamber ensemble eighth blackbird [*sic*].

Ellen Taaffe Zwilich (b. 1939) has been particularly successful at molding a personal and very memorable eclectic style. Her **Violin Concerto** (1998) exemplifies this admirably. The idiomatic solo writing bespeaks her own background as a professional violinist, while the concerto's assured architecture and craftsmanship reflect her tutelage under Elliott Carter and Roger Sessions. But more important, from the arresting opening movement to the dramatic finale, the concerto's bracing rhetoric and lyrical warmth stick in the

Website
track 132–134

www.naxosbooks.com

mind. Literally, and from the viewpoint of imagination, the work's centerpiece is the slow movement, a contemporary treatment of the opening measures of Bach's Chaconne for solo violin.

Indeed, though this Pulitzer Prize-winner sharpened her intellectual skills with Carter and Sessions, the heartfelt expressiveness of her writing reveals the influence of her earlier teacher, the late-Romantic Hungarian composer Ernő Dohnányi. This is evident in such works as the Chamber Symphony (1979), the Double Concerto for Violin and Cello (1991), the exhilarating Symphony No. 2 (1985), effectively a concerto for the cello section, and the powerfully dramatic Symphony No. 3 (1992), with its introspective slow movement as the finale. This observation holds true even for a work as completely different from these as the four-movement **Rituals**, for five percussionists and orchestra (2002), in which Zwilich has distilled her own reflections on the multicultural drumming influences represented by the percussion ensemble NEXUS, for which it was composed.

Premiered by the Boston Symphony Orchestra in 2000, Corigliano's Symphony No. 2 won the Pulitzer Prize for music.

Website
track 163
www.naxosbooks.com

Richard Wilson (b. 1941) a professor at Vassar since 1976, has quietly but efficiently built up an often sensuous body of work in all the major genres. Blessed with a fine ear for instrumental color, a genuine melodic inventiveness, and, in his vocal music, an affinity for humorous texts, he has filtered elements of Impressionism, tonality and atonality through the lens of his keen literary wit to produce such memorable compositions as his four string quartets (1969-2001), two symphonies (1984, 1986), *Three Painters* (tenor, piano, 1985), *Lord Chesterfield to his Son* (solo cello, 1987), Triple Concerto (bass clarinet, horn, marimba, 1994), Peregrinations for Viola and Orchestra (2003), and the opera *Aethelred the Unready* (1994, chamber version, 2001).

The chamber and orchestral music of Joseph Schwantner (b. 1943) reveals his individual approach to tonality and atonality, jazz, folk music and minimalism. Influenced by George Crumb and by Olivier Messiaen, Schwantner's love of mystical atmosphere and luminescent timbres produces irresistible mental imagery in such brilliantly crafted chamber scores as the two-part *Music of Amber*, for flute, clarinet, percussion, piano, violin and cello, which received

Website
track 135
www.naxosbooks.com

the Kennedy Center Friedheim Award in 1981. Works such as the Percussion Concerto (1994), the symphony *Evening Land* (1995) and his most famous composition, *New Morning for the World: Daybreak of Freedom* (1982), which uses texts from Martin Luther King's *New Morning*, have helped dispel audience distrust of new music.

So have the works of Peter Lieberson (b. 1946), Steven Stuckey (b. 1949) and Christopher Rouse (b. 1949). Lieberson, son of the record executive Goddard Lieberson (who produced numerous important recordings of modern American music and Broadway musicals for Columbia Masterworks from the 1940s through the 1970s) and the celebrated dancer Vera Zorina, studied with Milton Babbitt and Charles Wuorinen, among others, and first achieved recognition when his Variations for solo flute was performed by the Group for Contemporary Music in 1972. Studies of Tibetan Buddhism from 1976 through 1981 had a profound influence on his work, including his first Piano Concerto, composed for Peter Serkin to mark the centennial of the Boston Symphony Orchestra (1981–3). The success of this large-scale virtuoso work led to another Boston Symphony Orchestra commission: the symphony *Drala* (1986), inspired by the Tibetan concept of achieving a higher spiritual plane by transcending ordinary violence. Other scores inspired by Tibetan themes include *Ziji* ("Shining Out", 1987) and *Raising the Gaze* (1998), in which he seeks to evoke the spirit of dance through a complex web of shifting meters. Lieberson's opera, *Ashoka's Dream* (premiered at the Santa Fe Festival in 1997), treats the legend of an Indian emperor who subdues his own weaknesses before bringing peace and compassion to his subjects. Marriage to the gifted mezzo-soprano Lorraine Hunt Lieberson (who died of cancer in 2006) inspired two of the composer's most profoundly moving works: orchestral song cycles to poems by Rilke (1999–2000) and Pablo Neruda (2005).

> Joseph Schwantner's love of mystical atmosphere and luminescent timbres produces irresistible mental imagery in brilliantly crafted chamber scores.

Stuckey, a professor at Cornell University, won the 2005 Pulitzer Prize in music for his Second Concerto for Orchestra (2004). Other recent works include his percussion concerto *Spirit Voices*, the orchestral *Jeux de timbres*, and the song cycle *To Whom I Said Farewell*, for mezzo-soprano and chamber orchestra. Ironically, Stuckey's greatest commercial success has been his oft-recorded arrangement of Henry Purcell's Funeral Music for Queen Mary.

Christopher Rouse's work reflects his wide musical and non-musical interests – for example, his Spanish-flavored *Concerto de Gaudí*, for guitar (1999), commissioned by the American guitarist Sharon Isbin, was inspired by his admiration for the buildings of the great Barcelona architect Antoni Gaudí, especially the surreal Church of the Sagrada Familia. His Trombone Concerto (1991), with its central scherzo flanked by two slow movements, is a memorial to Leonard Bernstein, incorporating a quotation of the Credo theme from Bernstein's "Kaddish" Symphony. Rouse's music often exhibits an alluring tension between the steady influence of Classical and Romantic European tradition and his own penchant for the violent, driving expression of Led Zeppelin and other rock bands.

Rouse is not the only notable composer to carry rock influence into the classical arena. Paul Dresher (b. 1951) had studied classical piano before he picked up a guitar at the age of thirteen "and immediately fell in love." Rigorously schooled in composition at the University of California, Berkeley, Dresher brought that love, as well as his love for the 1960s rock scene, to his mature compositions. With his Paul Dresher Ensemble, he is continually searching for the thread that binds classical, jazz, rock and world music, not to mention perpetuating the experimental tradition of Cage, Partch and Harrison by creating new instruments to create new sounds – among them the Quadrachord, with four 160-inch strings and electric bass pickups near its two bridges. This has yielded such stimulating works as *Din of Iniquity*, for violin, bassoon, electronic keyboard, electronic guitar, electronic mallet percussion and electronic drum set (1994); the *Concerto for Violin and Electro-Acoustic Band* (1996–7), comprising the jagged and menacing *Cage Machine* and *Chorale Times Two*, a haunting episode of lyric melancholia; and *Unequal Distemperament*, for cello, violin, bassoon, electronic percussion, electronic keyboard and electric guitar (2001). Dresher has been a notably generous colleague, commissioning numerous works from

> Christopher Rouse's music often exhibits an alluring tension between Classical and Romantic European tradition and his penchant for the violent, driving expression of rock bands.

other composers for the Dresher Ensemble.

Likewise, Steve Mackey (b. 1956) channeled his early experience as a rock and jazz guitarist into concert works that combine electric guitar or rock ensemble with string quartet, voice or orchestra. Among these are *Troubadour Songs* (1991), *TILT* (1992), *Tuck and Roll* (2000), a concerto for electric guitar and orchestra, and the one-man opera *Ravenshead* (1997), which was commissioned and performed by the Paul Dresher Ensemble.

Eclecticism and the continuing effort to write "audience-friendly" music characterizes the current generation of American composers, whether they fall under the "New Romantic" banner or not. Among the leading figures, Libby Larsen (b. 1950) has proven one of the finest composers of art song and choral song. In works such as *Just Lightning*, for women's chorus, Mazatec chant and percussion (1994), a contemporary treatment of the Mushroom Ceremony of the Mazatec Indians of New Mexico, and the song sets *Beloved, Thou Hast Brought Me Many Flowers* (1994) and *Cowboy Songs* (1979), she conveys the vividness of the words with the panache of a born storyteller. Not surprisingly, her operas have been equally effective, among them *Frankenstein, or the Modern Prometheus* (1990) and *Barnum's Bird* (2000), a choral opera about P.T. Barnum and Jenny Lind. Larsen's orchestral works reveal her creative thinking and what has been described as her "liberated tonality," among them *Deep Summer Music* (1982), the *Marimba Concerto: After Hampton* (1992), and *A Brandenburg for the New Millennium* (2002), for trumpet, marimba, electric guitar, amplified harpsichord and string orchestra.

A protégé of Jacob Druckman, Anthony Davis (b. 1951) has variously been professor of music, composition and Afro-American studies at Yale, Harvard and (currently) the University of California at San Diego. He composes in a variety of concert and dramatic genres, often inspired by themes related to the African-American experience. His idiom, founded on solid academic technique, mingles jazz, blues, catchy melodies and contemporary classical elements,

> Anthony Davis composes in a variety of concert and dramatic genres, often inspired by themes related to the African-American experience.

> Eclecticism and the continuing effort to write "audience-friendly" music characterizes the current generation of American composers.

all of which impart a vivid, almost physical presence to his scores. Widely known for his operas *The Life and Times of Malcolm X* (1986), *Under the Double Moon* (1989) and *Amistad* (1997, dramatizing the historic rebellion of captives aboard the slave ship *Amistad*), he has also been acclaimed for such orchestral works as *Esu Variations* (1995) and *Tales (Tails) of the Signifying Monkey* (1998), as well as for his music for Tony Kushner's play *Angels in America*, with which he made his Broadway debut as a composer.

While a graduate student under George Rochberg, Stephen Hartke (b. 1952) was influenced by his teacher's move away from postwar serialism. He emerged during the 1980s as part of the neo-Romantic school with music that reflects his taste for lean textures of "Stravinsky-like" neoclassicism and Franco-Flemish polyphony, fired by the energy of jazz (especially bebop), Balinese gamelan music and minimalist repetition. His violin concerto *Auld swaara* (1992), piano quartet *The King of the Sun* (1988) and **Pacific Rim**, for orchestra (1988), have become part of the contemporary repertoire, while his *Suite for Summer*, for flute, oboe, clarinet, violin and cello (2004), gives promise of doing the same.

Website
track 136
www.naxosbooks.com

A composer, cellist and inventor of electronic musical instruments, Tod Machover (b. 1953) studied with Luigi Dallapiccola, Roger Sessions and Elliott Carter, and since 1985 he has been professor of music and media at Massachusetts Institute of Technology. He has composed both acoustic and electronic works, often using electronic technology to expand upon the tonal properties of acoustical instruments. Among his major acoustic works is his opera *Resurrection* (1999), based on Tolstoy's novel. During the 1990s Machover began exploiting what he calls "hyperinstrument" technology to take this idea further. For example, in *Begin Again Again …*, for hypercello (1991), a conventional cello is wired to a computer, which allows the cellist to create and combine a variety of new sonic textures through the instrument. This and two further pieces, *Song of Penance*, for voice, hyperviola and instrumental ensemble (1992), and *Forever and Ever*, for hyperviolin and chamber orchestra (1993), comprise his *Hyperstring Trilogy*. In addition to the hyperinstruments, Machover has created such electronic musical devices as a "sensor chair," conducting "data glove" and "digital baton." His *Brain Opera*

(1995–6), which he described as "an interactive experience," involves a number of these apparatuses. In part one, audience members proceed through a room, an "interactive Mind Forest," where they can play upon an array of hyperinstruments; in part two they proceed to another room, where they can listen to the music they created on the hyperinstruments combined with Machover's own music. His *Toy Symphony* (2001) combines a solo hyperviolin with interactive computer electronics, a children's choir with specialized computerized voice transformation, and orchestra. At the world premiere, in Dublin's National Concert Hall in 2002, the hyperviolin solo was performed by Joshua Bell. Among Machover's most recent works is *I Dreamt a Dream* (2004), for treble chorus, piano and electronics, and ... *but not simpler* ..., for string quartet (2005), commissioned by the innovative Ying Quartet, and which the composer calls "an homage to Elliott Carter, my mentor."

> Tobias Picker has won great acclaim for his operas.

Tobias Picker (b. 1954) has won great acclaim for his operas, among them *Emmeline* (1996) and *Thérèse Raquin* (1999–2000), which place neo-Romantic tonality and more acerbic harmony and texture at the dictates of the drama. The inventiveness and expressive quality of his instrumental music has yielded an admirable corpus of works that have entered the standard repertoire, notably the brief but exquisite tone poem *Old and Lost Rivers* (1986) and *The Encantadas*, a concerto for narrator and orchestra based on writings of Herman Melville (1983; a later version for chamber orchestra was premiered as a ballet). Picker's oeuvre also includes three symphonies, concertos for violin, piano and cello, and excellent chamber music.

Richard Danielpour (b. 1956) combines sweeping musical lines and rich orchestration in a musical language influenced by (harsher critics have said "derived from") wide-ranging sources, from Copland to musical theatre. The idiomatic quality of his writing for voice and instruments has led to numerous commissions, among them the opera *Margaret Garner* (2004, libretto by Toni Morrison from her novel *Beloved*), three symphonies, including *Celestial Night*, the violin concerto *A Fool's Paradise* (2000), three piano concertos, the concerto for string quartet *Voices of Remembrance*, song cycles such as the impressionistic *Sonnets to Orpheus* (1991, 1993), and choral music, most notably the *American Requiem* (2001).

Bridging the musical cultures of his native China and his adopted USA, Bright Sheng (b. 1955) has composed such notable operas as *The Song of Majnun* (for the Lyric Opera of Chicago, 1992) and *Madame Mao* (for the Santa Fe Opera, 2003). His instrumental works include the piano concerto *Red Silk Dance* (2000), *The Colors of Crimson* (for percussionist Evelyn Glennie, 2004) and the forthcoming *Concerto for Orchestra: Zodiac Tales*, commissioned by the Philadelphia Orchestra.

His Chinese-born colleague Tan Dun (b. 1957) is probably most familiar for his film scores *Crouching Tiger, Hidden Dragon* (2000) and *Hero* (2004). Notable among his other works have been *Water Passion after St Matthew* (2000), the operas *Marco Polo* (1995–6) and *Peony Pavilion* (1998), and *Inventions for Paper Instruments and Orchestra* (2003), composed for the opening of the Los Angeles Philharmonic's new Disney Hall.

Paul Moravec (b. 1957) is a masterfully engaging colorist, who derives inspiration from a variety of sources. For example, *The Time Gallery*, written for the adventuresome American new-music ensemble, eighth blackbird [sic], is, according to Moravec himself, "a musical meditation of the nature of time and the experience of temporal duration," which was inspired by his 1992 visit to an exhibition of time-keeping devices at the Royal Observatory at Greenwich (England). *Protean Fantasy*, for violin and piano (1992), is an imaginative and virtuosic set of variations on a haunting melodic phrase, while the flighty, kinetic energy of *Ariel Fantasy*, for violin and piano (2002), unmistakably suggests the quicksilver nature of Shakespeare's airy spirit. Indeed *Ariel* is the prototype, according to the composer, for the first movement of the five-movement *Tempest Fantasy*, which won the 2004 Pulitzer Prize for music. Moravec's other works include *Spiritdance* [sic] for orchestra (1989), *Songs of Love and War*, for chorus, trumpet and strings (1997), a cello concerto entitled *Montserrat* (1999), and *Vita Brevis*, for tenor and piano (premiered 2002).

Color Wheel (2001), a commissioned work for the opening of the Philadelphia Orchestra's new Kimmel Center, typifies the lyricism,

Paul Moravec, a masterfully engaging colorist, derives inspiration from a variety of sources.

magical color and atmosphere in the music of Aaron Jay Kernis (b. 1960). Kernis won a Pulitzer Prize for his 1997 String Quartet No. 2 "Musica instrumentalis," inspired by renaissance and baroque dances. His powerful Second Symphony (1991) laments the horrors of the Gulf War; *Goblin Market*, for narrator and ensemble (1995), captures the decadence of Christina Rossetti's erotic poem. A more recent composition, the tone poem *Newly Drawn Sky* (2005), commissioned by the Ravinia Festival, is exquisitely orchestrated, with shifting motifs and sonorities that seem to embody the evanescent light of a cloud-scudded evening.

Argentinian-born Osvaldo Golijov (b. 1960), a student of George Crumb and Oliver Knussen, has lived in the United States since 1986. In works such as *Yiddishbuk*, for string quartet (1990–2), *The Last Round*, for chamber orchestra (1996), *The St Mark Passion* (2000) and the opera *Ainadamar* ("Fountain of Tears", libretto by David

Michael Torke

Henry Hwang, based on Federico García Lorca, 2003), he blends threads of Yiddish klezmer music, Spanish Flamenco and Argentine tango with his own postmodern ideas to create provocative, quirky and gutsy music.

Widely performed, the music of the prolific Lowell Liebermann (b. 1961) filters a genuinely Romantic sensibility through contemporary technique. For example, his splendid *Picture of Dorian Gray* (1995), the first American opera performed by the Opéra de Monte Carlo, is based on a twelve-tone row used tonally rather than serially. His second opera, *Miss Lonelyhearts*, after Nathanael West's novel, received its premiere in April 2006 as part of the Juilliard centenary celebrations. *Gargoyles* (1989) embodies "Lisztian" virtuosity in postmodern language and has become a standard piano work. Another repertoire standard, the **Sonata,** for flute and guitar (1988), demands equivalent virtuosity, especially for its fiery gigue finale. Liebermann's melodic predilection for the flute and the piano has resulted in concertos for flute (1992, commissioned by Sir James Galway), flute and harp (1995, premiered by Galway), and two for piano (1983 and 1992, both premiered by Stephen Hough).

Lowell Liebermann's *Gargoyles* embodies "Lisztian" virtuosity in postmodern language and has become a standard piano work.

Michael Torke (b. 1961) achieved international familiarity when his colorful orchestral piece *Javelin* (1994) became an official theme of the 1996 Olympics. In his music, warm melodies (often called optimistic in style) ride upon the relentless driving energy of post-minimalist rhythm. His keen sense of instrumental color informs his celebrated series *Color Music* (1985–91), which includes *Ecstatic Orange*, *Yellow Pages* and *Bright Blue Music*, which started it all. In this last, the brilliant brass edge combined with the dance-like rhythmic underpinning lends the music a suggestion of Janáček meeting Villa-Lobos. Moreover, you understand why Torke's music was vigorously championed by the director of the New York City Ballet, Peter Martins, who choreographed *Ecstatic Orange* in 1987 and urged Torke to add *Green* and *Purple* as preliminary episodes

Michael Torke's music was vigorously championed by the director of the New York City Ballet.

in a three-movement ballet. Martins and the New York City Ballet subsequently commissioned *Black & White* (1988), *Slate* (1989) and *Mass* (1990). Torke's characteristic color and rhythm are also at the heart of his W.B. Yeats-inspired percussion concerto *Rapture* (2001).

Website
track 139–141
www.naxosbooks.com

Like Torke, Jennifer Higdon (b. 1962) uses instrumental forces with the aplomb of a virtuoso colorist, whether writing for orchestra, chamber ensemble or voices. Among her recent works, the poignant otherworldly *blue cathedral* [*sic*] (1999) is one of the most frequently programmed orchestral scores in the contemporary repertoire. In pieces such as *Dooryard Bloom*, for baritone and orchestra (2004), written to mark the sesquicentenary of the publication of Whitman's *Leaves of Grass*, the wind quintet *Autumn Music* (1995), and *City Scape* and Concerto for Orchestra (both 2002), her abundance of distinctive ideas and her communicative urgency reveal the teaching of her two great mentors, George Crumb and Ned Rorem.

Augusta Read Thomas (b. 1964) reflects how the old nationalist borders have virtually been swept away, at least in mainstream education: after training at Northwestern and Yale universities with, among others, Jacob Druckman, the native New Yorker completed her studies at London's Royal Academy of Music. Thomas is often drawn to large-scale canvases, upon which she can exercise her flair for bold statements and boldly colored instrumentation. For example, there are the leaping, jagged vocal lines, incandescent colors and percussive textures of *In My Sky at Twilight* (2002), a song cycle for soprano and eighteen musicians to texts representing the history of world poetry from Sappho to Merwin; the rhetorical sweep of her second trombone concerto, *Canticle Weaving* (2003); the interplay of dying keyboard notes and furious chordal orchestral attacks in her chamber piano concerto *Aurora* (2000); the fine lyrical impulse of her opera *Ligeia*; and the choral wildness of her Tennyson cantata *Ring Out, Wild Bells, to the Wild Sky* (2000).

Thomas is married to Bernard Rands (b. 1934), an English émigré who is a professor of music at Harvard and a former resident composer of the Philadelphia Orchestra, and who has achieved considerable distinction for his own music. His long catalogue of works in nearly every genre includes an important trilogy of orchestral song cycles, *Canti lunatici*, for soprano (1981), *Canti del sol*, for tenor (1983), and *Canti del eclisse*, for bass, the second of which won a Pulitzer Prize in 1984. Among his works in progress are commissions for a string quartet and a guitar concerto, as well as an opera on the life and work of Vincent Van Gogh.

Michael Hersch (b. 1971) is a composer who has certainly made up for lost time: a pianist, born in Washington, DC, and raised in Virginia, he discovered classical music at the relatively advanced age of nineteen, and after composition studies at the Moscow Conservatory in Russia and Baltimore's Peabody Conservatory he became one of the youngest composers to win a Guggenheim Fellowship, in 1997. Since then his rise to international prominence has been notable for its speed. Hersch's musical language is subtle, as he floats between tonality and atonality, and his penchant for complex pitch clusters and unexpected shifts of rhythm add to the expressive power of such works as the Symphony No. 1 and the Piano Quartet (both 1999), the Symphony No. 2 (completed in 2001 in Berlin and premiered in 2002), the Piano Concerto (2002), the Octet for strings (revised version, 2003), *Fracta*, for orchestra (2003), and his most frequently performed work, *Ashes of Memory* (2000).

Michael Hersch, a pianist, became one of the youngest composers to win a Guggenheim Fellowship.

Rhythm, color and a cheeky delight in commercial jingles and pop tunes lend variety and buoyancy to the work of Carter Pann (b. 1972). The richly varied stylistic influence of his teacher William Bolcom (b. 1938) informs many of his compositions, among them the Piano Concerto (1996–7), the devilishly baroque **Dance Partita** (1995), the *Two Portraits of Barcelona* (1994), in which he tips his hat to Christopher Rouse, and the witty *Deux Séjours* (1994), his take on Eric Satie's *Gymnopédies*.

William Bolcom himself capitalizes on his own exceptional grasp of contrasting styles – from bracing dissonance to folk and rock – in his epic choral song cycle *Songs of Innocence and of Experience* (1956–81), a complete setting of William Blake's poetic examination

Website
track 142–149
www.naxosbooks.com

of the ineffable flame that illuminates the many sides of the human spirit. Endowed with a sensitive understanding of the voice and a longstanding interest in the world's vocal literature (he and his songstress wife, Joan Morris, have long been fixtures on the concert stage), Bolcom has also directed this eclecticism towards his bountiful instrumental music, and from sultry *Recuerdos*, for two pianos (1991), to the jazz-flavored Clarinet Concerto (1988), with its effervescent waltz and tango finale, and his Concerto grosso for Saxophone Quartet and Orchestra (1999–2000), his music seems to embody the all-embracing spirit of America's musical past and present.

Website
track 150–152
www.naxosbooks.com

22 Conclusion

Thus ends our history of American classical music – at least for now. For, even as these final words are written, new music is being composed, new composers are being nurtured, new audiences are emerging. There still are many names and works to conjure with, but space permits only a litany, and, I fear, one that hardly dents the surface: Derek Bermel (*Language Instruction*, for clarinet, violin, cello and piano, 2003), Peter Boyer (*Ellis Island: The Dream of America*, for actors with orchestra, 2002), Richard Cornell (*Tidal Light*, for orchestra, 2001), Cuban-born Paquito d'Rivera (*Gran Danzon* concerto, 2002), Randall Woolf (known for his Maurice Sendak-based ballet *Where the Wild Things Are*, 1997), Stefania de Kenessey (*September Requiem*, 2002), Eric Ewazen (*Woodland Quartet*, for four horns, 2003), Elena Ruehr (*Toussaint Before the Spirits*, opera, 2003), Jefferson Friedman (*The Throne of the Third Heaven of the Nations Millennium General Assembly*, for orchestra, 2004), Daniel Bernard Roumain (*Voodoo Violin Concerto No. 1*, 2002), Michael Harrison (*Revelation*, for piano in just intonation, 1999–2005), Raphael Mostel (*The Travels of Barbar*, narrator with orchestra, 2000), Ashley Fure (*Inescapable*, for chamber ensemble, 2005), Marcus Maroney (*Hudson*, for chamber orchestra, 2005), Nico Muhly, whose influences range from English renaissance church composers to Philip Glass and Icelandic pop singer Björk (*Bright Mass with Canons*, 2005; song cycle *Elements of Style*, 2005), Russell Platt (Concerto for Clarinet, Percussion and Strings, 2003);

> New music is being composed, new composers are being nurtured, new audiences are emerging.

Evan Ziporyn (*ShadowBang* theater piece for Balinese shadow puppeteer and instruments, 2001), *War Chant* for orchestra, 2004; Douglas J. Cuomo (oratorio *Arjuna's Dilemma*, forthcoming, 2008), Turkish-American Kamran Ince (*Requiem Without Words*, 2003, Symphony No. 5 for orchestra, choir and soloists, 2005, *Gloria*, Mass movement to a Sufi text for the unaccompanied male ensemble Chanticleer, 2007), and prodigy Jay Greenberg (b. 1991) whose Fifth Symphony, begun when he was twelve, and String Quintet (both recorded in 2006), bespeak extraordinary gifts.

> At the dawn of the twenty-first century America's contemporary voice has grown increasingly international as travel and technology flood composers with every conceivable musical influence.

Others are still in universities, in conservatories, in high schools, in basement music studios and behind garage doors. Unborn yet, in terms of the public's awareness of them, these composers' powers of invention are quietly – and surely in some cases not so quietly – rising, percolating and pounding to the surface. In the wings of music's glorious stage they await their cues.

America's composers have moved in cycles: first to show the Old World that the New World could actually play the game according to the established rules; then, in the twentieth century, to sing out with a recognizably American voice. At the dawn of the twenty-first century America's contemporary voice has grown increasingly international again, as travel and technology have flooded composers with every conceivable musical influence from throughout the world. More importantly, where once American music absorbed and imitated foreign models, the pendulum now swings in the opposite direction: American music influences the rest of the world. As long as the imagination remains boundless, as long as humanity's basic need for music remains unquenched, there shall be music, *new* music, fresh, alive and invigorating. And we listeners shall rejoice.

Selected Bibliography

Aldrich, Richard, *Concert Life in New York, 1902-1923*, New York, 1941

Berlin, Edward A., *King of Ragtime: Scott Joplin and his Era*, New York, 1994

Bordman, Gerald, *American Musical Theatre: A Chronicle*, New York, 1978

> *American Operetta: From H.M.S. Pinafore to Sweeney Todd*, New York, 1981

Brooks, Henry M., *Olden-Time Music: A Compilation from Newspapers and Books*,
Boston, 1888

Clarke, Gary E., *Essays on American* Music, Westport, CT, and London, 1977

Davis, Peter G., *The American Opera Singer*, New York, 1997

Dichter, Harry, and **Shapiro**, Elliot, *Handbook of Early American Sheet Music*,
1768-1889, New York, 1977

Elson, Louis C., *The History of American* Music, New York, 1971

Ewen, David, *Popular American Composers*, New York, 1962

> *Composers for the American Musical Theatre*, New York, 1968

Finck, Henry T., "German Opera in New York," in *Chopin and Other Musical Essays*,
London, 1889

> "English and American Song Writers," in *Songs and Song Writers*,
New York, 1900

Gann, Kyle, *American Music in the Twentieth Century*, New York, 1997

Gatti-Casazza, Giulio, *Memories of the Opera*, London, 1973

Goss, Madeleine, *Modern Music Makers*, Westport, CT, 1970

Gottschalk, Louis Moreau, *Notes of a Pianist*, ed. Jeanne Behrend, New York, 1979

Hamm, Charles, *Yesterdays: Popular Song in America*, New York, 1979

Hitchcock, H. Wiley, *Music in the United States: A Historical Introduction*,
fourth edition, Englewood Cliffs, NJ, 1999

Holden, Amanda, ed., *The Viking Opera Guide*, London, 1993

Howard, John Tasker, and **Bellows**, George Kent, *A Short History of Music in*
America, New York, 1967

Jackson, Richard, ed., *Popular Songs of Nineteenth-Century America*, New York, 1976

Koegler, Horst, *The Concise Oxford Dictionary of Ballet*, second edition, London and
New York, 1982

Krehbiel, H. E., *The Philharmonic Society of New York ... A Memorial Published on*
the Occasion of the Fiftieth Anniversary of the Founding of the Philharmonic Society,
April 1892, London and New York, 1892

Lanier, Sidney, *Poems*, edited by his wife, New York, 1884

Le Huray, Peter, *Music and the Reformation in England, 1549-1660*, New York, 1967

Martin, George, *The Damrosch Dynasty: America's First Family of Music*, Boston,1983

Mattfeld, Julius, *A Handbook of American Operatic Premieres 1731-1962*, Detroit, 1963

Oja, Carol J., *Making Music Modern: New York in the 1920s*, New York, 2000

Palmer, A.W., *A Dictionary of Modern History 1789-1945*, London, 1978

Peyser, Joan, *The Memory of All That: The Life of George Gershwin*, New York, 1993

Randel, Don Michael, ed., *The Harvard Dictionary of Music*, fourth edition, Cambridge, MA, 2003

Raynor, Henry, *Music and Society since 1815*, New York, 1978

    A Social History of Music: From the Middle Ages to Beethoven, New York, 1978

Root, Deane L., *American Popular Stage Music, 1860-1880*, Ann Arbor, MI, 1981

Rosenberg, Donald, *The Cleveland Orchestra Story: "Second to None,"* Cleveland, 2000

Sadie, Stanley, ed., *History of Opera*, New York and London, 1989

    The New Grove Dictionary of Music and Musicians, second edition, London and New York, 2001

Scherer, Barrymore Laurence, *Bravo! A Guide to Opera for the Perplexed*, New York, 1996

Schlereth, Thomas J., *Victorian America: Transformations in Everyday Life, 1876-1915*, New York, 1992

Schonberg, Harold, *The Great Pianists*, New York, 1963

Schwartz, Elliot, and **Childs**, Barney, eds, *Contemporary Composers on Contemporary Music*, New York, 1978

Shanet, Howard, *Philharmonic: A History of New York's Orchestra*, New York, 1975

Sonneck, Oscar, *A Bibliography of Early Secular American Music (18th Century)*, rev. W.T. Upton, New York, 1964

Tawa, Nicholas E., *A Most Wondrous Babble: American Art Composers, their Music, and the American Scene, 1950-1985*, New York and Westport, CT, 1987

    From Psalm to Symphony: A History of Music in New England, Boston, 2001

Temperley, Nicholas, "First Forty: The Earliest American Compositions," in *American Music*, Spring 1997

Thomson, Virgil, *American Music since 1910*, New York, Chicago and San Francisco, 1970

Wendant, Elwyn A., and **Young**, Robert H., *The Anthem in England and America*, New York, 1970

Whittier, John Greenleaf, *The Complete Poetical Works of JGW*, Boston and New York, 1894

Yellin, Victor Fell, *Chadwick, Yankee Composer*, Washington, DC, 1990

Index

About the Author

Barrymore Laurence Scherer, a native New Yorker, is a music critic for *The Wall Street Journal* and a contributing editor of *Art & Auction* magazine, where he specializes in nineteenth-century art and decorative arts. On radio, he has been a commentator for NPR's *Performance Today*. Named a Speaker in the Humanities by the New York Council for the Humanities, he has taught on "Oscar Wilde and the Belle Epoque" at Sarah Lawrence College, and as an independent scholar he has lectured extensively on opera, classical music, and the Victorian age for Lincoln Center Great Performers, the Cooper-Hewitt National Design Museum, the Metropolitan Opera and the New York Philharmonic as well as at venues around the country. In addition, as a scriptwriter and actor he writes and does voiceover work. Mr. Scherer is also author of the critically acclaimed book *Bravo! A Guide to Opera for the Perplexed* (1996). With his wife and their dog he lives amidst a gratifying number of kindred spirits in Westchester, New York.